EBURY PRESS

PASSION ECONOMY AND THE SIDE-HUSTLE REVOLUTION

Utkarsh Amitabh is the chief executive officer of Network Capital and chief marketing officer of 5ire.org, a blockchain unicorn valued at $1.5 billion. 5ire.org acquired a stake in his company Network Capital (networkcapital.tv), one of the world's largest mentorship platforms that empowers 1.6 million school students and 1,50,000-plus young professionals to build meaningful careers. He is a writer at *Harvard Business Review*, Chevening fellow at the University of Oxford and a World Economic Forum Global Shaper who represented the community at their annual meeting in Davos. An engineer by training, Utkarsh read philosophy at Pembroke College, Oxford, and earned his MBA from INSEAD Business School, where he was recognized as the Andy Burgess Scholar for Social Entrepreneurship. He is also the torchbearer of Ashoka University's Young India Fellowship. Utkarsh worked at Microsoft for seven years across the US, Europe and India, leading business development for big-bet projects. He is a TED speaker, Raisina fellow and recipient of the INK Fellowship. He is also a trained actor and played 'Major Metcalf' in one of the world's longest-running plays. He loves to travel and has been to more than eighty countries.

T0307570

PRAISE FOR THE BOOK

'Mentorship and community building are important focus areas of the book. Utkarsh offers mental models for creators and passion economy participants to build a tribe of mentors and, leveraging the power of communities, propel others to do the same. Scaling mentorship is about scaling trust, empathy and kindness. Utkarsh has done that effectively with Network Capital and explains that with clarity and conviction in *Passion Economy and the Side-Hustle Revolution*'—Sanjiv Saraf, founder, Rekhta.org

'Utkarsh captures the essence of the passion economy with fascinating stories from across the world. He deftly engages with the "impossible triangle" of policy, platform and passion, which influences our professional endeavours and defines our place and purpose in these exciting times. Utkarsh's book mirrors his own experiments with all aspects of life'—Samir Saran, president, Observer Research Foundation

'In the Network Capital masterclasses and podcasts, Utkarsh asked me thought-provoking questions about the future of work and emerging trends in employment. I found his clarity of thinking remarkable and am glad that he wrote a book to unpack how the world of work will look like in the post-pandemic world. As the founder of a global mentorship platform, he is uniquely positioned to discuss what people want with their work lives and why. His book suggests that the ability to reinvent oneself will be the most critical skill in the times to come. Even though the majority of case studies are about millennials, Utkarsh effectively makes the point that we are entering an era of multi-generational leadership where people across age groups will need to collaborate and support each other in their reinvention. The last few years permanently changed our relationship with work. Things aren't likely to go back to the way they were. Perhaps that is a good thing. This way we get to redefine the norms, reduce the biases and co-create a new normal for work that is equitable and impactful. By writing a book on the passion economy, Utkarsh has initiated an important conversation not only about work but also our guiding philosophy of the society of tomorrow'—Shashi Tharoor, member of Parliament and award-winning author

'Jobs in 2030 will require us to reinvent ourselves. Utkarsh's book demystifies the future of work. He explains how we can prepare ourselves and offers concrete ideas for people and organizations hungry to build what he calls a "category of one"'—Tarun Khanna, professor, Harvard Business School

'Utkarsh's book makes a strong case for building a portfolio of careers in the twenty-first century. As someone who started his career in finance, built a private equity fund and then transitioned to shaping the education landscape, I found the frameworks in the book highly relevant and actionable. He has done a great job of capturing stories of changemakers from around the world who are building new kinds of careers drawing upon their intrinsic curiosity. We are witnessing a subtle shift from the gig economy to the passion economy. Utkarsh's book offers a comprehensive analysis of why this is happening and what can we do about it to create meaningful opportunities for ourselves and our communities—Ashish Dhawan, founder of Central Square Foundation and Ashoka University

'As we moved from the industrial economy of the last two centuries where the workforce were mere cogs in a wheel, the shared economy of today gave birth to the concept of mass customization. The perfect coming together of pursuit of purpose, deep tech and design principles provides a new opportunity to pursue what's right for each of us and yet build companies that create more wealth than ever before. By writing a book on the passion economy, Utkarsh has initiated an important conversation of not just improving on the past but redesigning our guiding philosophy of the society of tomorrow'—Lakshmi Pratury, founder and CEO, INK

'Utkarsh's book provides a comprehensive road map about the future of work. He connects the dots across industries and geographies with deeply researched case studies about the passion economy. It is a gripping read that makes you think about your future self with a sense of adventure and possibility—T.N. Hari, CHRO, Bigbasket

'I found *Passion Economy and the Side-Hustle Revolution* to be a comprehensive analysis of how the world of work will look like in the twenty-first century. It offers tools and mental models for millennials, Gen Z and baby boomers to reinvent themselves. This inter-generational shift in our attitude towards work is a difficult subject to capture. Utkarsh has done a great job of capturing the nuances and presenting them with interesting examples from around the world'—Pramath Raj Sinha, founder, Harappa Education and Ashoka University

PASSION ECONOMY
AND THE
SIDE-HUSTLE REVOLUTION

UTKARSH AMITABH

EBURY
PRESS

An imprint of Penguin Random House

EBURY PRESS

USA | Canada | UK | Ireland | Australia
New Zealand | India | South Africa | China

Ebury Press is part of the Penguin Random House group of companies
whose addresses can be found at global.penguinrandomhouse.com

Published by Penguin Random House India Pvt. Ltd
4th Floor, Capital Tower 1, MG Road,
Gurugram 122 002, Haryana, India

Penguin
Random House
India

First published by SAGE Publications in 2022
Published in Ebury Press by Penguin Random House India 2023

Copyright © Utkarsh Amitabh 2022

ISBN 9780143461357

www.penguin.co.in

This book is dedicated to anyone who has ever felt lost or confused about career choices. I heard the phrase 'I don't know what I want to do with my life' so many times that I decided to start a full-fledged cohort-based course to unpack its nuances. I remember coming up with the name of the course sitting next to my grandmother. I lost her before this book got published. Will miss brainstorming with her.

Confusion isn't a bad thing. With effort, deliberate practice and reflection, it can push us into exploring new adventures and possibilities. Anyone who has felt constructively confused has the potential to play a major role in shaping the passion economy. The creativity unleashed through this journey has massive economic potential and cultural impact. That's why I salute anyone who has ever felt directionless but persisted in making sense of the chaos. Giving up and settling for the suboptimal might have felt comforting in the short term, but the lingering feeling of 'what if' can haunt us for years. Hopefully, reading this book will help discover your superpower and create tangible economic value for the society along the way.

CONTENTS

FOREWORD

The Fourth Industrial Revolution represents a fundamental change in the way we live, work and relate to one another. It is even challenging ideas about what it means to be human. The new revolution can be considered as a new chapter in human development, as it's enabled by technological advances commensurate with those of the First, Second and Third Industrial Revolutions, which are merging the physical, digital and biological worlds in ways that create both promise and peril.

Utkarsh's book talks about the power of communities to shape the future of work. He makes it clear that the future of work not only entails the creation of new jobs but also figuring out how to augment human intelligence with new tools of technology.

Utkarsh discusses the unbundling of work from employment and the emergence of passion economy as the new normal. Through relatable examples and deeply researched case studies, he demonstrates interesting ideas such as building a portfolio of careers, leveraging technology platforms and creator tools to create new kinds of jobs and shaping a more synergistic relationship among policymakers, platforms and passion economy participants.

Passion Economy and the Side-Hustle Revolution has been written after conducting detailed research and ethnographic interviews with Shapers, Young Global Leaders and other Forum constituents. Utkarsh explores themes such as emotional intelligence, adaptability quotient and mental health in the context of the modern workplace. He has added concrete examples from his experience of being a Global Shaper, running Network Capital and working with technology companies and non-profits.

An important point of focus for the book is radical collaboration. Every day, I witness different stakeholders collaborate across age groups, regions, religions and boundaries, and it makes it clear to me that such a collaborative approach is essential for addressing complex challenges of the 21st century. We must move from a world which priorities materialism to a human-centred world with intergenerational perspectives. Utkarsh's focus on peer-to-peer learning and sharing is a good example of how we can build robust collaboration principles at work which can be scaled to other domains as well.

The year 2022 is the second year when World Economic Forum's Annual Meeting in Davos took place virtually. While there were many debates and discussions around the challenging state of global affairs, our focus was on establishing stakeholder capitalism as a way of addressing the world's greatest challenges, from societal divisions created by income inequality and political polarization to the climate crisis we face today. It was energizing to learn that businesses are embracing stakeholder capitalism, which means not only maximizing profits but also using their capabilities and resources in cooperation with governments and civil society to address the key issues of this decade. They must actively contribute to a more cohesive and sustainable world.

Utkarsh's work explains why the world demands a new kind of 'advanced' business leader who makes conscious attempts to find meaningful work, create opportunities for others and solve problems beyond the bottom line. That's the spirit of being a Global Shaper, and I am glad that Utkarsh has put forward crisp mental models and operating principles for people committed to leading from the front.

Klaus Schwab
Founder and Executive Chairman, World Economic Forum

ACKNOWLEDGEMENTS

Since the beginning of this pandemic, I quit my job, made my passion project into a community-funded venture, moved countries, got married, bought a new house and embarked upon redesigning my life from scratch. It was exhilarating, challenging, exhausting and confusing. Navigating such critical decisions was not something I did alone. I had a tribe of mentors who helped me at every step of the way. I am ever so grateful for their love and support.

Building Network Capital was never just about business. In my own way, I wanted to shape a new world on the Internet where kindness and connection would be the norm, not the exception. With a click of a button, I wanted to enable people to find all the support they need to build a career they truly care about. While we built the technology and figured out a viable business model, I found deep connection, care and empathy from our community members. They made tough times seem meaningful, and I always had this conviction that we are in this mission together. I cherish every handshake, every call and every discussion along the way.

Like most families, mine had to deal with multiple health-related emergencies. This was excruciatingly painful for everyone, but the way my family came together to figure things out made me realize what depth of commitment looks like. It strengthens with chaos. It is anti-fragile. Seeing them in action reaffirmed my faith in building intimate communities for people who may not be born with the privilege of a close-knit family.

In this challenging period, my pen became my mentor. I was able to capture my adventures and misadventures with some objectivity and some wonder, and share them in the form of newsletters and essays to Network Capital subscribers on a daily basis. Communicating with them helped me crystalize my thoughts about the passion economy and the new world of work we are co-creating with every passing day.

It is impossible to name everyone, so I am going to stick to experiences that shaped me. The people who made it happen know who they are, and this book is largely a result of their love. This book would not have happened without my *Harvard Business Review*, World Economic Forum and *Mint* essays. I would not have had the opportunity to write for such illustrious publications without the Network Capital community members who connected me to the editors. I am grateful to the community members, my editors and the publications that trusted my voice. I take their faith seriously, and it propels me to try and become a better writer every single day.

I have been blessed to be part of several iconic institutions and communities. This book captures some of my experiences and that of my peers and mentors. Without their insights and generosity of spirit, I would not have been able to capture the complexity of work life.

For the last five years, writing emerged as my tool for reflection and synthesis. It helped me cut through the clutter and stumble into clarity. This was far from being a solitary pursuit. My grandparents read everything I wrote and provided feedback, which helped make the book relevant to people of all age groups. They shared detailed comments with vintage ink pens and eventually embraced digital mediums. Now they get to know where I am published before anyone else and share it fondly on their social media feeds. I lost my grandma just before the book got published. She read several chapters and played a pivotal role in shaping the structure. I will miss her.

I come from a family where the pursuit of knowledge is the most important life goal. Home has always been thousands of books spread around, waiting to be explored with a fresh set of eyes. Growing up in such an environment helped. I didn't need to wander around for inspiration. I picked up a strong work ethic from my parents and little brother. To give you an example, I don't remember a day where I woke up and didn't find my mother with a book in her hand, writing furiously on its margins.

Over the course of writing this book, I got a chance to travel 20 countries and innumerable cities: from capturing stories of an 'unemployable' philosophy professor trying to build an online school in Lebanon when the country was woefully short of petrol, electricity and the Internet to a gamer in the Philippines who is trying to solve unemployment in his country through videogames. Many chapters in this book are a direct result of my travels. The pandemic made things challenging, but with some luck, some hustle, lots of visa appointments and lots of caution, I made it through.

What are stories without people and what are people without communities? A big shout-out to the people and communities who have translated this book from being a medley of happenstances to a compendium of stories sprinkled with practical insights and mental models! I deserve no credit for these stories. If I did something well, it was to find these gems, especially that one French-Lebanese computer scientist who I met after a long, meandering afternoon on the Great Wall of China. She said, 'You should write.' I followed her advice.

P.S. The last sentence of this section is the same as that of my first book. That charming computer scientist is now my wife.

INTRODUCTION

When are people most likely to quit their job?

It turns out that it's about a year after they start. Some people might attribute this to the myth that we have to spend at least one year in a role before moving on to something better (at least if we want to look like responsible human beings to future employers). But if you dive a bit deeper into the data, you will find a more fascinating pattern.

Job hunting actually spikes on work anniversaries, along with milestone birthdays, major life events and, oddly, high school and college reunions. Researchers believe that this happens because what we consider 'the end of an era' or 'a momentous life event' inspires us to re-evaluate our present situation and consider a fresh start.

I admit that I'm interested in this research for more than academic reasons. I quit my job at Microsoft on my sixth anniversary, and it just so happened that I did it right in the middle of a global pandemic.

Summer 2020 flipped my life upside down. I was supposed to head to the University of Oxford as a Chevening Fellow and marry my girlfriend, a data scientist based in London, at a quaint location with our friends from around the world. I was to return to India after the fellowship and continue working on my passion project (Network Capital, a peer-to-peer mentoring community) on weekends while I supported my life with the day job at Microsoft.

But as you can guess, that's not how things unfolded.

On 7 June, the day of my wedding that wasn't happening, I was sitting in my study in New Delhi, reminiscing on what could have been and thinking about what would come next. I loved what I did at Microsoft and derived great meaning from building Network Capital, but I also needed to figure out a way to be close to my girlfriend who was an ocean away. There were global lockdowns and travel restrictions. The international borders were sealed. People transitioned to working from home overnight. I knew that many things, including my relationship, would never be the same again, at least if I didn't make some kind of change.

I once heard that emergencies fast-forward history—personal, political and societal. As historian Yuval Noah Harari explains, decisions which in normal times could take years of deliberation are passed in a matter of hours during a crisis.

This was the sentiment I felt, sitting in my study, thinking about what I needed to do to piece my relationship back together. Here were my options:

1. Move to London to be with my girlfriend while continuing my job (remotely) at Microsoft.

2. Transfer to Microsoft's London office and continue building Network Capital as a passion project.

3. Focus all my efforts on Network Capital and build a remote-first company which I could lead from anywhere.

After much deliberation, I chose to take on my passion project full-time. It wasn't an easy decision, but I want to share with you how I came to it. Although every situation is unique, I know that anyone with a side hustle they love, or anyone thinking about starting one, may be forced to deliberate similar questions at some point.

If you're stuck in a job, should you stay simply because you're lucky to have one or take a risk on your passion project? If you're just entering the workforce, should you spend time competing for a role or focus on building a business of your own?

There are many factors you need to weigh before making these decisions. Here's what I asked myself before making mine.

1. Is my passion project solving a problem?

If you have a business idea in mind but you aren't sure that it's addressing a real problem, you might end up spending your time and energy building the wrong thing. Great businesses are built on deep insights. Consider if you truly understand the unmet needs of the customers or community you are serving and if you have enough data to validate your idea.

Ask yourself:

- Does the customer really see this as a problem?
- Would it make their life better?
- Would they be willing to pay for it?

I had identified a clear gap in the education and learning space for millennials, but before going all out on my side hustle, I needed to test my hypothesis. There are many ways to do this, including focus group discussions, one-on-one interviews with your customers or market research (to name a few). For Network Capital, I launched an 'I don't know what I want to do with my life' Fellowship for millennials, which enabled me to learn more about the pressures and anxieties young people face and ultimately build a better product.

As you collect evidence and data with your own experiments, connect them back to your original idea to see if you're going in the right direction or if you need to go back to the drawing board.

2. Does my product actually work?

Even after you validate your hypothesis, you need to test your minimum viable product (MVP). Simply put, an MVP is a functional prototype with just enough features to convey your idea in its simplest form. The goal is to build something that your customer can actually use so that they can give you critical feedback on what's working and what's not.

Network Capital's MVP was a Facebook group. We allowed users to ask for customized subscription plans for the few services we had to offer. Having that MVP was precious to the development of our full suite of services when the website did finally launch.

In essence, you want to use this stage of product development to (a) build a community interested in what you have to offer and (b) figure out a business model which serves their needs based on their feedback. Doing this will empower you in two ways: First, it will help eliminate the gap between your product development and revenue generation. Through your MVP, you may have opportunities to make a decent revenue before officially launching. Second, you can use any revenue you do make to help yourself build the next version of your product or service.

3. Have I reached at least 1,000 customers? Can I?

As Kevin Kelley, co-founder of *WIRED*, advises in his essay '1,000 True Fans',

> 1,000 true fans is an alternative path to success other than stardom. Instead of trying to reach the narrow and unlikely peaks of platinum bestseller hits, blockbusters, and celebrity status, you can aim for direct connection with a thousand true fans. On your way, no matter how many fans you actually succeed in gaining, you'll be surrounded not by faddish infatuation, but by genuine and true appreciation. It's a much saner destiny to hope for. And you are much more likely to actually arrive there.[1]

In other words, your goal doesn't necessarily need to be to build the next Google or Facebook. And even if that is your goal, you still need to figure out how to get those first 1,000 people to pay for what you are building if you want to succeed. It may sound easy, but getting people to pay for a product requires substantial grit, especially if you don't have investors on board.

You should start your journey to 1,000 customers by obsessively focusing on the community experience. If people feel connected with how you are delivering on your said mission, they are more likely to place their faith in you. Network Capital got its first 1,000 subscribers much sooner than I thought, and I can only

1 https://kk.org/thetechnium/1000-true-fans/

attribute that to the community we had built and nurtured on Facebook before launching. A large chunk of that community-building entailed doing things which didn't have the potential to scale, such as the founders reaching out to potential subscribers to make a personal connection.

In the early days of Airbnb, the co-founders did something similar. They personally responded to customer care queries, showed them around the city, photographed house listings and even put together a customized breakfast for guests comprised of cereals themed on the presidential candidates at the time, Barack Obama and John McCain (Obama O's and Captain McCain's). In other words, they made a genuine attempt to develop a personal connection. They didn't need to do all this, but their efforts to build a true community of travellers helped scale trust. Precisely because of that, Airbnb got off the ground, acquired the momentum, built the right systems and processes, and became the multi-billion-dollar behemoth we know today.

4. Do I really have the skills and resources required to manage a business right now?

   Organizational psychologist and author Adam Grant once wrote, 'Quitting your full-time job to start a company is like proposing marriage on the first date.... The most durable businesses are typically started by people who play it safe.' As a twenty-five-year-old with a $200,000 education loan, I couldn't have just quit my job on a whim. I wanted the work experience, skills, network, and financial stability before venturing out on my own. Risk-taking is often glamorized by touting isolated examples of moonshot successes, but the best entrepreneurs are those who are able to figure out the optimum risk–reward ratio that works for them.

   When Phil Knight started Nike, he spent five years as a certified public accountant, putting in six days a week at PwC. *Shark Tank*'s Daymond John eased into the entrepreneurial life by constantly tinkering after his day job as a waiter at Red Lobster. Herb Keller, the co-founder of Southwest Airlines, kept practising as an attorney for almost five years as he got the business off to a start.

Getting some work experience can help arm you with the basic management skills you need to get a business off the ground, but as an entrepreneur, you need to understand what you're inherently good at and like to do and what you need help with. You don't need to possess all the skills required to run a business, but you need to be able to find people with skills that complement your own to help you realize your dream.

In the same way, I draw a lot of strength from the fact that there is a wide spectrum of peer mentors, city leaders and team members who are aligned in helping my company reach its full potential.

So those are the questions I asked myself before deciding to leave a stable job to pursue my passion project. Were my personal reasons a contributing factor? Absolutely. Did the coronavirus pandemic fast-forward my decision-making? 100 per cent. Was I nervous? You bet! But I am also excited to embark upon a new phase of my life with a decision that feels timely and right.

How about you? I hope my experience helps you feel armed to follow your curiosity and, one day, transform your passion project into your profession.

365 DAYS

Exactly one year after quitting Microsoft to build Network Capital full time, I found myself working in a gorgeous village in the mountains of Lebanon. One advantage of being an entrepreneur is that you can work on what you want from where you want. As luck would have it, the country plunged into deep economic and social crisis, and I was left stranded with no electricity, petrol and the Internet for days. I had to use my mobile hotspot to send the final draft of this book *Passion Economy and the Side Hustle Revolution* to my publisher. It took 2 hours and 45 minutes to upload. Just as

I was about to press send, I got an unexpected call from an unknown number.

It turned out to be from Facebook. I was told that Network Capital was one of the 130 communities selected for funding and strategic support as part of the Facebook Community Accelerator. There are over 620 million of groups on Facebook and 1.8 billion people use Facebook groups globally. Being recognized as one of the 130 most impactful communities gave me confidence to build and scale a new kind of company, one that is owned, managed and funded by its members.

This is a book about transforming your passion project or side hustle into a full-time job, redesigning your career and building something meaningful with your wild and precious life. The passion economy is transforming our relationship with work. What we choose to work on, who we partner with and how we spend our time are going through a tectonic shift. Technology platforms are enabling this new outlook towards work, but the passion economy cannot be explained by technology alone. To get a full picture, we need to dive into policy, politics, philosophy, pop culture and the pandemic. I call them the 5 Ps of the passion economy.

In the subsequent chapters, I will walk you through the frameworks I used to make my career transition and leverage the passion economy to build my category of one. I loved my job at Microsoft, but by reflecting on the kind of life I wanted to design, I took the call to jump into my passion project—Network Capital—with eyes wide open. I knew it would be an adventure with lots of ups and downs, but the prospect of discovery energized me to try.

Network Capital started out as a hobby and turned into a passion project and eventually a community-powered technology platform which raised funding from Facebook. You may wonder why I still think of Network Capital as a company operating in the passion economy space. Are we a funded tech start-up or is our primary identity something different? People ask me this question wherever I go.

At a fundamental level, I still see passion, curiosity and storytelling as central pillars of Network Capital. Even if one day we become a massive multinational, I will consider it a failure if Network Capital becomes a soulless corporation which prioritizes profit over purpose. My vision is to scale trust with the power of stories and meaningful human connections. Retaining the community orientation is pivotal to translate the vision into action. I think of myself as a passion economy builder who works at the intersection of education technology, careers and the big elusive phrase 'meaning of life'.

LinkedIn co-founder Reid Hoffman once said, 'If you don't find risk, risk will find you.' Risk is all around us. Whether you are a hacker tinkering away in your garage or a senior corporate executive, you will need to develop an intimate relationship with risk. I knew I had to.

I had to understand the passion economy, contextualize it to my life and conduct experiments to figure out whether I could build a meaningful career in it. With the help of mental models and case studies, I will explain my thought process. You don't need to agree with all my points. I just hope you consider it as one of the many ways to go about following your dream.

In this book, you will find myriad examples of people who built multi-million-dollar newsletters; acquired hundreds of millions of followers on platforms like YouTube, Instagram and TikTok; created innovative investment vehicles; and even helped alleviate national poverty with the help of videogames. I refer to such people as creators and passion economy builders in the book.

Reading their stories will hopefully inspire you, but please resist the urge of mimicking them or following their path without due consideration. Your ultimate goal should be to build your category of one.

Passion economy and side hustles are not some fringe elements in work life. Every person on the planet is passionately curious about something. Unfortunately, we are taught the wrong lesson— finish your studies, get a stable job, find a suitable partner, save up for retirement and then think about passion. The creator economy is the 'fastest-growing type of small business', according to a report last year by SignalFire, a venture capital firm.

Legendary investor Warren Buffett was once talking to a thirty-year-old MBA from a great school with a great resume. He asked him what he wanted to do with this life, and he replied that he wanted to go into a particular field but thought that he should work for the consulting firm McKinsey for a few years first to add to his resume. Buffett found this person's career strategy akin to saving sex for your old age. He remarked, 'You want to have a passion for what you are doing. You don't want to wait until 80 to have sex.'

This is not a book on motivation or happiness. This is a strategy book which invites you to rethink the way you define your work life in the 21st century. If it leaves you with a sense of wonder, I would consider myself successful.

I don't want you to quit your job or stay on for insurance. It needs to be your decision. I just want to give you the tools to tinker and experiment. The passion economy and the side-hustle revolution are here to stay, and I hope you play a meaningful role in it.

The book is divided into six sections:

1. Passion Economy Fundamentals
2. Passion Economy Career Principles
3. Alternate Careers, Passion Economy Platforms and the New World of Work
4. Mental Models and Principles for Making Passion Economy Work for You
5. Passion Economy Challenges
6. Conclusion

SECTION 1

PASSION ECONOMY FUNDAMENTALS

CHAPTER 1

WHAT IS PASSION ECONOMY?

'Passion economy' refers to the emerging economic and cultural trends where people are building new kinds of careers working on things they are intrinsically curious about. The phrase was coined by Adam Davidson, a reporter at NPR, and Li Jin, a former investor at Andreessen Horowitz who quit her job to create her own venture capital (VC) fund. Unbeknown to each other, both Adam and Li were studying how people were reshaping the world of work with the help of new technology platforms. There was a clear schism between the gig economy popularized by the 'Uber for X' model and the creative economy. Let's explore why.

The gig economy resulted in massive productivity gains and huge consumer surplus. Cabs, food delivery and grocery shopping—practically all aspects of day-to-day life—aided by the efficiency of technology platforms and VC money became accessible to a large chunk of the global population. Millions of new jobs were created, innovative business models revitalized entire industries and the GDP of the Internet exploded. While there were many practical benefits which accrued, new challenges came to fore. It wasn't tech utopia by any means.

The gig economy jobs standardized creativity and offered limited security and hourly rates which were often less than the minimum wages. These jobs were important but did not rank high in terms of personal fulfilment, meaning and career advancement. There was an overwhelming sense of drudgery among gig workers. Most of them work longer hours than investment bankers and top software engineers but barely make enough from the toil.

The tech platforms, on the other hand, made billions of dollars from their process and business model innovations. The distribution of wealth created a tension among participants, policymakers and platforms. Later in the book, I will explain that tension, offer some suggestions to mitigate it and paint a picture of the new normal of work.

THE CREATIVITY–PRODUCTIVITY SCHISM

For the longest time, creativity and productivity were at odds. Those who wanted to pursue creative fields found it hard to make ends meet. That is changing. Gig workers are looking for more meaningful ways to make a living. The era of passion economy and side hustles is here.

New platforms are emerging for creators to monetize their craft and do what they love. The Internet is shaping culture and transforming the way we work. Even white-collar professionals are quitting their day jobs to venture into the passion economy. Gen Z creators, influencers and investors are making different career choices than their parents. There is a subtle shift in what they learn, how they learn and how they earn. They do not see creativity and productivity as two different things. Both are part of the new creator stack that is emerging in the third era of the Internet which is often called Web 3.0, a distributed, decentralized Internet we will explore later in the book.

For now, let us attempt to figure out why it is easy to misunderstand the passion economy.

CHAPTER 2

DON'T FOLLOW YOUR
PASSION, FUEL IT

Venturing into the passion economy can be frustrating if we get seduced by catchphrases like 'follow your passion'. Use of the phrase 'follow your passion' has increased ninefold in English books since 1990. While I agree with the larger sentiment, I question its practical utility. What makes me a tad bit sceptical is the underlying assumption that following one's passion will make work an unmitigated pleasure.

There are three things one should keep in mind when it comes to passion.

First, it can change over a period of time. Second, we constantly underestimate the change we will go through. Third, accepting change gets harder every year. That is why venturing into the passion economy with a fixed mindset and an immutable idea of passion can seriously backfire.

Stanford Professor Carol Dweck once asked her students, 'How many of you are waiting to find your passion?' It turned out that many of them were in fact waiting for the metaphorical apple to fall on their head. Isaac Newton sitting under the apple tree and Archimedes lounging in his bathing tub are memorable stories because they align with our romantic idea about inspiration and genius. Comparing our real-life existence with apocryphal stories (yes, the apple never really fell on Newton's head) is a sure shot way to burn out before starting.

Carol Dweck and Greg Walton published a paper in *Psychological Science* where they argue that passions aren't found, they are nurtured and developed over time with the help of micro-experiments, grit and resilience. When I started Network Capital, I cared about building communities, but that wasn't the only thing I was passionate about. Through the thousands of hours of experimentation and work, I found my calling. The big takeaway for me was that hard work, tinkering and experimentation preceded the discovery of passion.

If we quit every time, we find a stumbling block and blame it on lack of passion; we are in for a rough ride.

Why is passion economy more than following your passion? The first version of Network Capital was a 1:1 mentoring service. Mentors and mentees would get matched based on complementary skills and contextual relevance. I had built a sleek minimum viable product (MVP) and expected the system to work efficiently. Things started out well, but as we scaled, scheduling calls and ensuring everybody showed up on time became tricky. Despite multiple reminders, there were times when either the mentor or the mentee would not show up. Getting the system to work was not a pleasure by any stretch. That said, it gave me meaning and made me realize the importance of perseverance in making passion projects work.

Replacing passion with curiosity worked well for me. Instead of asking myself existential questions every few days and getting bothered by all that wasn't working, I started approaching the challenge like a detective. Curiosity is one of the most important tools for the passion economy. Genuine interest in the problems we are solving ensures that we have the motivation to bring our best on days that don't go well.

CHAPTER 3

LET YOUR CURIOSITY GUIDE YOU

Ikigai (生き甲斐, pronounced ikigai) is a Japanese concept which means 'a reason for being'. It is seen as the convergence of four primary elements:

- What you love
- What you are good at
- What the world needs
- What you can get paid for

Author Daniel Pink offers a three-pronged approach which can help us navigate the passion/motivation challenge. With the help of scientific research in the labs of MIT and practical advice gleaned from being someone who got into a prestigious law school (Yale) but didn't practise law for a day, Pink suggests that unless we have the combination of autonomy, mastery and purpose, we will continue to be unmotivated. And if we are not motivated, our passion will either misguide us or fade away. Both can be disastrous.

With this in mind, let us dive deep into Pink's framework.

COMPLEMENTING YOUR CURIOSITY WITH AUTONOMY, MASTERY AND PURPOSE

The first factor is autonomy. It is our innate desire to be self-directed, but the extent of autonomy depends upon the kind of person we are. Some of us thrive in anarchy, and some need direction to function. Thinking about where we stand on the spectrum is critical. There is a reason why some terrific entrepreneurs are terrible employees and vice versa.

The second is mastery.

Passion is a by-product of focused work – achieving mastery with deliberate practice. Real estate investor and Shark Tank's 'Shark' Barbara Corcoran is often heard saying that she didn't follow her passion. She stumbled on it as she was working relentlessly to solve a problem she cared about. As per research done by the likes of Oxford University's William MacAskill and author Cal Newport, engaging work helps us develop passion, not the other way around.

The third and last factor is purpose. We all want our work to contribute to something larger than us. Voltaire was right when he said that work spares us from three evils—boredom, vice and need—but he didn't live in the age of artificial intelligence (AI). In the digital era, if work doesn't add meaning to our lives, it will cease to exist.

CHAPTER 4

SOCIETY AND PASSION ECONOMY

Every day during the pandemic, I spent three–four hours speaking to students and young professionals about their career aspirations. It turned out to be one of the most meaningful things I did. Speaking to them helped me figure out the underexplored nuances of what I was trying to build at Network Capital. The larger thesis was clear to me: Millennials and Gen Zs needed a platform to experiment with career aspirations and figure out ways to find work which offered them autonomy, mastery and purpose. That said, I needed to figure out practical ways to translate this hypothesis into a tangible offering.

The more I spoke to my community members at Network Capital, the more I realized that there was widespread confusion about how to choose careers. The phrase 'I don't know what I want to do with my life' kept coming up. To add to this confusion was guilt. People felt guilty about the lack of clarity. It occurred to me that there were three reasons creating this general malaise about future career choices.

First was societal pressure. From a young age, most children are nudged into thinking about their careers in a certain way. In India, a running joke is that people first do engineering and then figure out what to do with their lives. My first degree was in mechanical engineering, and it helped me develop my critical thinking skills, but I understand the challenges of choosing something without having a clear understanding of what that entails for one's life ahead.

One of the reasons engineering is a popular choice is that it offers prospects of employment after graduation. Today, India is considered a hub for top engineering talent. World-class technology start-ups have come out of India. There is a clear market demand for quality engineering talent, but choosing careers solely on that basis can backfire.

9

Most societies value conformity, and if the popular choice seems to offer stability, growth and prestige, why not go for it? I think that people should be free to study things like engineering if they are drawn to it or pick something else if they find their curiosities pointing in a different direction. In the 21st century, having a degree is less important than being good at whatever you choose. Less than 1 per cent of Indian engineers know how to code. It doesn't mean that they are not smart. Perhaps they never got the right set of teachers and mentors. Perhaps they were pushed into pursuing something they weren't interested in.

Second reason is a combination of standardized aspirations and status games. Intentionally or unintentionally, most societies have developed a fixed, relatable idea of success in the world of work. We are often told to be like someone or become the next XYZ. There is nothing wrong in seeking inspiration from others, but trying to replicate someone else's career trajectory can be risky. Even if you get there, you might realize that you never cared for it. Unfortunately, there is a fairly codified hierarchy of careers. People are made to believe that if they are off-script, they are big disappointments.

Eugene Wei, a former product leader at Amazon, Hulu, Flipboard and Oculus, wrote an essay 'Status as a Service', which starts off with two key points.

- People are status-seeking monkeys.
- People seek out the most efficient path to maximizing social capital.

Wei's essay is about social capital and online behaviour, but it can also be used to explain why status matters in the real world. He goes on to say,

> Social capital is, in many ways, a leading indicator of financial capital, and so its nature bears greater scrutiny. Not only is it good investment or business practice, but analyzing social

capital dynamics can help to explain all sorts of behavior that would otherwise seem irrational.[1]

Following predictable career paths which offer security, stability and prestige has been the shared societal dream of the global middle class. If we agree with Wei's premise that we are status-seeking monkeys who optimize for social capital, it is understandable why aspirations are getting standardized. When you try something new, the path to acquiring higher status is unclear. The path to getting validation from others is even more tricky.

Imagine the future of the world where people choose what they want to do with their lives solely on the basis of status value. It won't be a particularly innovative world. Life would become even more of a theatre than it already is.

1 https://www.eugenewei.com/blog/2019/2/19/status-as-a-service

CHAPTER 5

WHAT WOULD WORK LOOK LIKE 50/10 YEARS FROM NOW?

To answer this question, one has to go back to 1930 when British economist John Maynard Keynes wrote 'Economic Possibilities for Our Grandchildren'.[1] In his essay, Keynes argues that the fears about economic stagnation were overblown, and the world was actually going through unparalleled technological advancement and capital accumulation. Because the rate of change was so high, it could be uncomfortable. He talked about how 100 years from then, people would have more time for leisure, and hours spent on work would be reduced drastically, thereby redefining our relationship with employment. Many of Keynes's assertions seem to be coming true, while others are still being figured out/discovered.

THE 2021 EDITION OF 'ECONOMIC POSSIBILITIES FOR Y(OUR) GRANDCHILDREN'

What does the future of our relationship with work look like. John Maynard Keynes was a colourful man revered as an economist, investor and hedge fund pioneer. He was bisexual and married Russian ballerina Lydia Lopokova at the age of 42. His former lover Duncan Grant was the best man at their wedding. Among other things, he is famous for his words from deathbed: 'My only regret is that I have not drunk more champagne in my life.'

1 http://www.econ.yale.edu/smith/econ116a/keynes1.pdf

Keynes forecasted that the 'standard of life' in Europe and the United States would be so improved that no one would need to worry about making ends meet. 'Our grandchildren', Keynes reckoned, would work about 3 hours a day (15 hour work weeks), and even this reduced schedule would represent more labour than was actually necessary.

This essay was written and revised right around the time of the Great Depression, perhaps the worst economic downturn in the history of the industrialized world. Keynes was not ignorant of what was going on. He quickly recognized the gravity of the situation and wrote, 'The slump which will take its place in history amongst the most acute ever experienced—over the long run, this would prove to be just a minor hiccup in the grand scheme of things.'

WAS KEYNES DELUSIONAL?

According to Keynes, the technological innovations in the 19th century—'electricity, petrol, steel, rubber, cotton, the chemical industries, automatic machinery and the methods of mass production'—were bound to make growth inevitable. The growth would create abundance, which would be welcome of course but would pose a different challenge.

'For the first time since his creation man will be faced with his real, his permanent problem—how to use his freedom from pressing economic cares, how to occupy the leisure, which science and compound interest will have won.

Yet there is no country and no people, I think, who can look forward to the age of leisure and of abundance without a dread.'

This is the punchline: 'For we have been trained too long to strive and not to enjoy.'

Doesn't this sound familiar? Strive, prepare, work and postpone what you want to do with your life for one insurance policy after another. This had led to a nagging sense of frustration. Delayed gratification as a career strategy is being questioned by everyone, especially millennials and Gen Zs.

The need to find autonomy, mastery and purpose at work is gaining traction all around, and passion economy is becoming a major cultural influence. There is a lot more acceptance of alternate career choices today than even a few years back. At least part of the reason is wider economic security among the middle class. Technology has played a role in increasing overall productivity.

Keynes was right when he wrote,

> We are suffering, not from the rheumatics of old age, but from the growing-pains of over-rapid changes, from the painfulness of readjustment between one economic period and another. The increase of technical efficiency has been taking place faster than we can deal with the problem of labour absorption; the improvement in the standard of life has been a little too quick.

ECONOMIC POSSIBILITIES FOR YOUR GRANDCHILDREN

One can't help but wonder what would the economic possibilities for our grandchildren look like. What if, like Keynes, we look beyond the short term and take wings into the future?

If our grandchildren were to have all the economic security in the world, perhaps some version of basic income, lots of leisure and just 15 hours to work, what would they choose to do?

Will platforms like Twitter, TikTok, Instagram, etc., still be alive in 100 years? Will people spend all their time performing online, striving for flickering fame by climbing the social hierarchy? Will they channel their economic security into creating social and economic wealth for those in need? Will the struggle for meaning become more pronounced? Will work revolutionize play or the other way around? What would culture really mean?

Ask yourself that if you don't have to prove a point to anyone, what would you do with your wild and precious life? You will not continue playing status games. Now project that 100 years from now, will your grandchildren be interested in status? Would you want them to be?

If status signalling loses its appeal, people are likely to experiment more to fulfil their curiosities. Today, people have built decent careers creating videos, writing newsletters and producing digital products, but they all come with a performative zeal attached. It is this elusive war of likes and swipes in the currency of hyperscale.

For our grandchildren, the meaning of scale will be redefined. They will be more interested in depth of impact than with metrics. It will change the way social networks function, and alter the alchemy of relationships – both personal and professional.

The world will become more local in addition to being connected globally. The centre for economic opportunity will also be the neighbourhood, which in turn will not necessarily be dictated by our place of birth. Our grandchildren might be more interested in creating countries than in building apps that tantalize. They might be more keen on spending their time writing the constitution of the country they built than on trying to get any job that pays the bills.

They are unlikely to waste the economic security they will be bestowed with. It isn't a guaranteed outcome but a likely one. The 22nd century challenge will be far more social and meaning-oriented than economic. In fact, their economic possibilities will emerge from crafting meaningful social and communal experiences. Think of your neighbourhood convenience store. Instead of just stacking up groceries, it might be the hub of dazzling experiences driven by technology but founded in human experiences.

Experimenting to figure out your passion and having the tools to pursue your passions without guilt would be the norm rather than the exception.

Future follows fiction. That is why we should all spend a large chunk of time reading and writing fiction for tomorrow. The sad truth is that most of us are so busy just getting through the present that we never really sit and think about the most critical questions about the future, including but not limited to what would our grandchildren do with their wild and precious lives.

Keynes wrote an economic essay, but in a way it was fiction. Based on a wide range of assumptions and some truths, he drafted his future vision. You should do the same. Don't try to make sense of the future only by going through sound bites and memes. It is time to create some distance between the world we live in and the world we want to shape for our grandchildren. The future economic and social possibilities are not preordained. How we think of our story today and how we write them will pave the way for an uncertain, unpredictable but hopefully exciting future.

In this essay, I shared one way forward. Now I want you to create your story. Think about how you want to create new economic vistas for your grandchildren. What excites you the most about this exercise? Now that we have taken the long view into the future, let us try and analyze the world of work a decade from now.

Eighty-five per cent of jobs of 2030 do not exist yet. It is impossible to predict specifics, but it is evident that passion economy will be a crucial role in shaping the ambition of the new world of work. Before we begin exploring the answers, let's highlight the key questions.

1. What would education look like? What would schools, colleges and higher education institutions look like?

2. What would success mean? Would being an acclaimed YouTuber become as important as being an astronaut?

3. Would multigenerational offices become the norm?

4. Would the Internet truly be decentralized?

5. Would people become more important than the platforms? How would that power structure evolve?

6. Would young people want to work in the government? What would the role of policymakers be like?

7. Would communities be the new countries? Would community builders become the ultimate power brokers?

Now let's try and visualize work in 2030 step by step.

Unbundling of education will create new economic opportunities for entrepreneurs and meaningful learning opportunities for learners. Today, despite all technological advances, there is a huge talent–opportunity mismatch. That needs to change. While there is no way to guarantee equality of learning outcomes, new educational institutions must strive to create equality of opportunities. They could consider making learning need-blind, that is, providing scholarships at scale via endowment funds and income share agreements (ISAs).

I see education being reimagined from ground up. The confluence of the 3 Es—education, employment and entertainment—will create a fifth wave of much-needed disruption in the space. Imagine students learning in an immersive metaverse, applying their knowledge to real-world problems, leveraging platforms like Minecraft and Roblox, and finding internships/employment based on what they learned.

In Gaza, for example, students use Minecraft to build virtual models of how they want their neighbourhoods[2] to look. As I write this book, the political situation in Gaza is terrifying, but during slightly better times, local organizations turned those virtual models into reality—despite all constraints. A few parks, beaches and streets were built this way.

The Gaza Minecraft story is both tragic and hope-inducing. Even though it is a warzone today, locals have figured out a way to visualize and create a world they want to live in. Such is the power of imagination, and technology gives it wings. In the years to come, this education–entertainment–employment trinity will become more mainstreamed.

The case of Axie Infinity from the Philippines is yet another example of learning something new while having fun, in addition to solving the unemployment crisis in the region. This isn't futuristic fantasy but something that is happening right now. Who would have thought that unemployment could be addressed through blockchain-powered videogames?

The changing landscape of education is bound to transform ambition.

Based on a survey published by *The Sun* in 2017,[3] 'YouTuber' is the career today's kids aspire to above all others. Being an online creator is two times as popular as being a film star and three times as popular as an astronaut. There might be differences in countries based on cultural and economic factors, but this massive inversion of career preferences is going to be a defining characteristic of 2030.

The first question you may have is whether being a YouTuber is better for the world than being an astronaut. Is it really a good thing that more kids want to grow up online creating videos than trying to conquer the frontier of space?

Well, kids should answer this for themselves, shouldn't they? We should empower them to conduct micro-experiments and figure out what they want to do. Why should we overlay our value system on them?

To do anything meaningful in any field, one has to transcend playing status games even if they are deeply ingrained in our psyche. Status games are finite; the game of life is infinite. We will discuss this later in the book, but for now you should remember that status optimization has been a driver of career choices for most of modern history. If we are not careful, they will end up doing the same in the passion economy space.

3 https://www.tubefilter.com/2017/05/24/most-desired-career-young-people-youtube/

CHAPTER 6

STUPID STATUS GAMES
AND CAREERS TO AVOID

Just keep the German word *schadenfreude* in mind as you go through this chapter. It roughly translates to pleasure derived by someone from another person's misfortune.

There is a sports subscription website called The Athletic, which reportedly lost $100 million over two years. They were recently acquired by *The New York Times* but before that there was a long period when many deals fell through.[1]

During that rough phase for the company, many commentators seemed to be celebrating the downfall of the company. Perhaps the company was mismanaged, perhaps some strategies backfired, perhaps the pandemic took a toll on the way it was run. Maybe all of the above, maybe none of the above.

What was hard to figure out is why were some people so delighted. Do we live in the times of *schadenfreude*?

STATUS AS A SERVICE

To answer this question, let us refresh the 'Status as a Service' mental model.

- People are status-seeking monkeys.
- People seek out the most efficient path to maximizing social capital.

Wei's essay helps us analyse why the online behaviour is perhaps more/as much status signalling than *schadenfreude*. According to

1 https://www.axios.com/new-york-times-nytimes-acquisition-athletic-7f1dabf4-9315-4975-93f9-68e13c642a43.html

Wei, we are optimizing for status in efficient ways. What's the most efficient way to signal virtue/status these days? It is provocation Provocation scales without advertising. If used smartly, it can be used as a digital marketing strategy. When one famous person attacks another famous person, they are essentially signalling moral superiority. While their exchange is often toothless, it leads to some online entertainment and interesting (but meaningless) status games that no one wins.

The truth is that when you play stupid status games, you win silly prizes that no one cares about. Getting more likes on your post or stirring up a controversy for attention are not long-term ways to succeed. You can signal status for gaining Internet fame for 15 seconds, but what will move things forward in a meaningful way? Passion economy builders are better off optimizing for consistency than for effect.

Here, we are not talking about committed activists trying to make a positive change in the world, for example, the unravelling of Theranos scam which began with a 2015 article in *The Wall Street Journal* which revealed how the 'revolutionary technology' promoted by the start-up was a total sham. The reporter John Carreyrou exposed how the investors and consumers were being fooled. Truth seekers and activists like John deserve our respect, attention and consideration.

In this chapter, however, we are referencing digital messiahs trying to build long-lasting careers on clickbait. There are people today who are almost waiting for chaos to emerge so that they can milk it by adding fuel to fire.

Let's assume you are a politician who hasn't really delivered or don't have much to show. What's the most efficient way to be considered effective? Distract, distort, arrest and stir up a conspiracy. Do some virtue signalling and try to cover up your failures by taking others down. Doing tangible work and creating a measurable difference take time. It is hard. Gaining status by bringing others down is easy. Sometimes it just takes a tweet or a post.

The efficiency of takedowns is intense, but it is proven to be a remarkably ineffective strategy in the medium to long run. If your whole career is dependent on finding faults with others and magnifying them on social media, you are likely to be unemployed pretty soon. For some reason, if you escape that outcome, do you think you will have iota of meaning in your life? Are you likely to be on the path of financial well-being? Which expertise should people pay you for?

The smartest way forward for all of us is to avoid playing stupid status games. If you feel compelled to play any game at all, let it be one that you are intrinsically curious about, one that augments business, society and your own self. Don't waste your time bringing others down for the heck of it, signalling virtue or trying to monetize *schadenfreude*.

Because ideas of what success entails remain fixed, people feel scared to experiment. Even if they want to, there are very few opportunities to tinker and test career choices. Without experimentation, you basically roll a dice and hope things fall into place. I have always been sceptical of hope serving as one's career strategy, but such is the way things are. In this environment, a handful manage to do well, but a large chunk of people end up with deep regrets and disappointments. They obviously did not excel in what the society considered appropriate; they also missed out on the chance to figure things out for themselves. I believe that every person on the planet has a superpower. That superpower is not the same for everyone. Instead of trying to make someone else's superpower your own, what if you built on your own strengths?

For each of the challenges referenced above, passion economy is going to offer a new perspective. The central premise of the passion economy is that everyone can monetize their curiosities, passions and talents with the right guidance. That is why I started Network Capital's 'I don't know what I want to do with my life' Fellowship.

Our founding principle was simple: create a safe space for career experimentation and advancement because most people don't really know what they want to do with their lives. Through the fellowship, I wanted to remove the stigma attached to career confusion. One of the first things we do is to orient our fellows and their parents about the passion economy. Parents are important stakeholders because in most countries they have a strong say in how students and young professionals make career choices. By having them onboard with us on this journey, we help open their minds to this new era of work where the alchemy of career design is changing rapidly. Trying to make sense of the new world with an old lens exacerbates confusion and leads to choices that might haunt everyone involved for the rest of their lives.

An interesting by-product of this fellowship has been multigenerational participation. We had a sixteen-year-old student from San Francisco who joined the fellowship along with his grandfather, a retired army veteran planning to create a new venture in plastics. There isn't an age at which one figures out what to do with one's life. The process of discovery and reinvention needs to be an ongoing pursuit. That is why the ability to reinvent oneself is the most important 21st-century skill. We focus obsessively on it during all our fellowships, especially the ones focused on career discovery.

In the 'I don't know what I want to do with my life' Fellowship, we attempt to destigmatize confusion. Confusion occurs because our prior experiences—academic, professional and social—leave us unprepared to deal with new situations which are bound to come up every so often.

While confusion can be crippling in the short term, it is a vital tool for personal growth. It can help discover what we really want to do and make sense of the world around.

The University of Notre Dame Associate Professor Dr Sidney D'Mello suggests[2] that confusion augments learning if it is properly induced, effectively regulated and ultimately resolved. He found that students who dealt with uncertainty triggered by the contradictions scored higher on a difficult post-test and could more successfully identify flaws in new case studies.

It turns out that there is a three-pronged framework to leverage confusion and make it work for us.

2 https://news.nd.edu/news/confusion-can-be-beneficial-for-learning-study/

First, be productively confused instead of hopelessly confused. In a classroom, productive confusion occurs when the source of the confusion is closely linked to the content of the learning session. This happens when the learning ecosystem provides concrete help when students are struggling. At work, it means that our confusions can be resolved with the help of peers and overall office support system.

Second, manage negative emotions when they occur. Dealing with ambiguity can take a toll on our well-being if we start taking things personally. This is of course easier said than done. It is worth keeping in mind that the occasional bad day is a natural by-product of dealing with complexity. We need to separate the problem at hand and our warped perspective due to the emotional roller coaster we have just gone through. We can't let it get to us.

Third, be willing to risk failure. While dealing with unfamiliar situations is likely to make us resilient and strengthen our decision-making faculties, it isn't a guaranteed outcome. We need to be open to embracing the occasional failure. It is a fair price to pay for the accelerated learning it offers.

For the longest time I used to resent myself for being confused about my personal and professional life. I would compare my life to the glittering lives of peers on social media and wonder how they were all so sorted. It was only after years of thinking that I realized that envy and confusion were great equalizers: We all experience and deal with them in different shapes and forms.

My life changed for the better the day I accepted that my confusion was perhaps a step towards learning and self-discovery. I took heart from the fact that great scientists and philosophers dedicated their lives to negotiating with the spectre of confusion. Yale University Professor of Biomedical Engineering Martin Schwartz once said that if we don't feel stupid and confused, it means that we are not really trying.

As someone who has never been shy of trying, I realized that without confusion, it was impossible to stumble into truth. In a way, being chronically confused made the pursuit to clarity worth it for me. Knowing that others were in the same boat and attempting to help fellow community members figure out a path to clarity turned out to be an immensely fulfilling experience. In a way it shaped my career and turned out to be a superpower. The larger point of these insights on confusion is that experimentation with the mindset of a scientist can be transformational in shaping a meaningful career. As passion economy becomes more mainstreamed, thoughtful experimentation will be the need of the hour. The problems to focus on, the people to partner with and the platforms to choose aren't standardized for everyone. Try, iterate and find your fit. The spectrum of possibilities is wide, the opportunities are everywhere. It is time to look for new vistas even if the society seems reticent to give its stamp of approval. Remember that their scepticism might just be stemming from lack of exposure. You don't need anyone's validation and even if you crave for that, know that it will happen over time. Inaction because you lack validation will likely haunt you over the long term.

CHAPTER 7

PASSION ECONOMY PLATFORMS

Lenny Rachitsky, a former product manager at Airbnb, quit his job to write a newsletter about the emerging trends in the technology industry. Later in the book, we will dive into the economics of newsletters, but what you need to know at this stage is that Lenny's income from his writing this newsletter crossed his salary at Airbnb in Silicon Valley.

To complement his writing income and to add more diversity to his portfolio, he recently added a job board using a platform called Pallet, which was set up by Jake Berry, a Stanford wrestler turned tech CEO, who we hosted on Network Capital. Today, top companies pay Lenny to put their jobs on his job board. He curates customized jobs which are appealing to his core reader base—twenty-five-to-forty-five-year-old technology enthusiasts. In few months since its launch, Lenny's job board is making thousands of dollars in recurring revenue for Lenny. There is something remarkable about a successful Silicon Valley executive quitting his job to write newsletters. It is not only about the financial upside he created but also about the new normal about work in the passion economy era.

Stories of professionals are indicative of a larger trend called the 'enterprization of consumer'. Unlike the gig economy which flattens the individuality of workers, the passion economy empowers anyone to monetize their unique skills or stories. It could be a product manager like Lenny or someone like Dave Dahl, an ex-convict turned organic bread maker who sold his company for $275 million after spending 15 years in jail, based on the quality of his product and the power of storytelling.

While the passion economy can be immensely rewarding for creators, it won't be all fun and games. Unlike regular employment, creators will need to figure out human resources (HR), accounting and legal issues themselves. Paul Jarvis, the author of *Company of One:Why Staying Small Is the Next Big Thing for Business*, shares that today creators spend more than 50 per cent of their time doing extraneous stuff. That is a colossal waste of income and potential. I see a huge opportunity for new platforms to address these challenges and create new opportunities.

We will discuss the debate on platforms later in the book. For now, let us explore how new platforms are fuelling the passion economy and empowering creators to craft new kinds of careers. Newsletter writer, podcaster, YouTuber, TikTok curator and Instagram influencer are just a small slice of alternate careers on the map today. Let's categorize the available platforms:

1. Platforms which help create digital products, services and media like Substack for newsletter writers, TikTok and YouTube for video creation, and Anchor FM for audio

2. Platforms which help find audience like Twitter, Facebook and Spotify

3. Platforms which enable audience to become part of communities like Discord and Circle

4. Platforms which help communities become companies by offering monetization tools like Stripe and Gumroad

5. Platforms which bridge the online–offline gap like Luma and Eventbrite

6. Platforms which help manage businesses like Shopify, Kajabi and Karat

I have listed a small number of platforms because new platforms will be emerging at breakneck pace in the times to come. According to SignalFire investor Yuanling Yuan,[1] there are 50 million creators around the world, of which 2 million are able to make a full-time living out of it. They need simple and efficient tools to meet their specific needs. Platforms in these six categories are likely to play a major role in enabling a broader passion economy movement.

1 https://signalfire.com/blog/creator-economy/

Today, most creators stitch together a solution which gets the job done, but it is challenging to manage and makes for a clunky experience for the customers. For example, a teacher might use YouTube for creating some videos, leverage platforms like Teachable to enrol students for their course, build an audience for their course using TikTok and a newsletter hosted on Substack, collect fee via Stripe, and organize offline roadshows using Eventbrite or Luma. All these platforms offer quick and easy solutions, but integrating them into one, easy-to-understand offering is not a trivial challenge.

Even Network Capital used multiple platforms to get the MVP going, but after a certain scale, we had to build our own platform. We still use other platforms. For example, our newsletter has over 100,000 readers, but it is hosted on Substack. Even though we have linked it to our website, occasionally our new community members get confused navigating through multiple service providers. Despite that, the overall benefit of using a third-party software for managing newsletters is substantial. Even though we pay a small part of our revenue to the newsletter provider, it makes sense for now.

The sheer market size is enough of a pull for new platforms to emerge. Ghost, another newsletter-hosting platform, does not charge platform fee. Revue, a newsletter platform acquired by Twitter, charges a lower platform fee than Substack in addition to integrating with its social network.

Network Capital also uses Facebook and WhatsApp to manage community, Stripe for payments, and Zoom and Microsoft Teams for live cohort-based courses (CBCs). There are alternative platforms for every single use case, and that is good news. You never want to be overreliant on any one platform. Why? In the off-chance, the platform shuts down or bans you or stops functioning in the country you live, you could lose years of hard work. This happened in India during the pandemic when due to border tension with China, the government banned all Chinese apps. India went from having more than 200 million monthly active TikTok users to zero on 29 June 2020. New apps with similar functionalities came up, but the creators who had put in tens of thousands of hours in building their online persona had to start from scratch. The larger lesson here is that creators should leverage platforms to the full but keep their eyes open. A third-party platform is always a rented territory. You can have excellent relationship with your landlord, but ultimately it is not your home. The China–India technology controversy is beyond the scope of this book. I referred to it only to explain the invisible forces creators must be aware of, as they march into the passion economy. Keeping eyes wide open is generally a good strategy. Paraphrasing a quote from Malcolm Gladwell's book *Talking to Strangers*, trust with caution and humility.

Let me explain this further with the help of a real example from Network Capital.

One morning I woke up to an email from Facebook which changed the trajectory of what I was building. At that time, Network Capital was among the handful of large Facebook groups with an inbuilt subscription feature. We had quite a few subscribers at that time, and things were going well but everything was about to pivot.

Some changes at Facebook's end made it unviable for us to continue the subscription feature, so we had to take a difficult, nerve-racking and challenging call to build our own platform in a matter of days.

We still have a large Facebook group for peer-to-peer (P2P) collaboration, but our primary platform is Network Capital TV.

The challenge of building our own platform was threefold.

1. **Technical:** How to create a familiar but more nuanced social network which was primarily focused on peer learning and consuming long-form video/audio content?

2. **Operational:** Most Indian credit/debit cards don't work for subscriptions and recurring payments. Even today, setting up recurring payments for a company in India is a mammoth task.

3. **Communication:** Behaviour change is excruciatingly hard. Our existing users were familiar with the Facebook ecosystem. Moving them all to a new platform needed us to start all over again. We had to explain why we were doing it, what the suite

of new services would be and what the new Network Capital experience would feel like.

FIGURING OUT NEXT STEPS

Our product and government affairs head Varya worked with her team 24 × 7 (literally) to give us the fighting chance of living for another day. We had to take things one hour at a time. After hundreds of iterations, we hacked our way into Network Capital TV.

All our masterclasses were edited, uploaded and categorized. Our platform looked good. We thought that people would be able to search for what they were looking for and navigate their way forward.

We were 'wrong'. With the pandemic taking dangerous turns, there was an onslaught of webinars, newsletters and podcasts. 'Death by Webinars' became one of the most popular memes of 2020.

Looking at our data, we realized that despite the high quality of content on our platform, the consumption was much lower than what it used to be. It occurred to us that our content alone would not be enough to get new users onboard.

UNDERSTANDING YOUR 'WHY'

I did have an intuitive understanding of why people use Network Capital, but it was time to document and present it in a seamless, interesting way. It took many unsuccessful and often embarrassing iterations before we found our catchy 3 Cs.

1. **Content:** Daily masterclasses + Podcasts + Newsletters
2. **Community:** Strong peer network, subgroups and serendipitous experiences
3. **Career intelligence:** Daily office hours + Expert reviews

THE DESIGN CHALLENGE

What made Network Capital challenging to design is what made it interesting: Network Capital meant different things to different people. For some, it was a platform for career advice and mentoring, for some it was a forum for upskilling, for others it was a way to network with interesting people and for some, subscribing to Network Capital was just a way of supporting our mission.

Figuring out our reason for being meant reflecting on our purpose. In practical terms, it meant figuring out learning outcomes for our subscribers, essentially what people can expect to learn once they come on board and how we might quantify the impact of our interventions.

POWER OF COMPOUNDING

We are big believers in the power of compounding, so we told ourselves, 'Let's do whatever we can to make our subscribers 1 per cent smarter every day.' Compounding may be the eighth wonder of the world, but its effects are slow and steady.

We had to complement the slow power of compounding with accelerated outcomes. Daily office hours worked well.

**I would have spent 1,000+ hours speaking to our subscribers 1:1 in the last 365 days. We also launched office hours for our community members who needed mentorship but could not afford to pay for the Network Capital subscription. My vision has always been to make Network Capital need-blind. One year since our pivot, we are now inching towards it in small ways. For example, our subscribers have started gifting subscriptions to others in need, and some instructors have been making fellowships free for people who can't afford it.

1:1 CONVERSATIONS → CUSTOMER INSIGHTS

Conversations that are 1:1 take time but leave you with deep customer insights. It was through some such discussions that we decided to make the Network Capital learning experience cohort-based. That's when we launched our short, focused cohort-based courses (CBCs). Few months later, I also decided to invest in Maven, a platform which enables CBCs.

Our CBCs complemented our 3 Cs. We started getting a lot more traction and finally found the missing link plaguing many ed-tech start-ups in the pandemic: community-powered learning for specific career/skilling goals.

DISCOVERING THE COMMUNITY–MARKET FIT

One of the first CBCs we launched was 'I don't know what I want to do with my life' Fellowship. Our cohort included 100 curious people across age groups, countries, convictions and orientations. Witnessing them learn with and from each other gave us confidence to add new fellowships every month.

Broadly speaking, we now have three kinds of CBCs/fellowships:

Foundational Learning

1. 'I don't know what I want to do with my life' Fellowship: A deep generalist approach to career exploration
2. CEO Fellowship: Building your category of one

Skill-based Fellowships Based on Micro Adventures

1. Product Management Fellowship
2. Investing Fellowship
3. Policy Fellowship
4. D2C Fellowship
5. Sports Administration Fellowship

Lifelong Learning Fellowships

1. Writing Fellowship
2. Public Speaking Fellowship

3. Community Building Fellowship
4. Personal Branding Fellowship

With the launch of each of our fellowships, we wanted our sub-scribers to experiment, tinker and take calculated risks, knowing they are not alone. The whole premise of community-based learning is that it takes the pressure off. Passion isn't found sitting under a tree waiting for the metaphoric apple to fall. It is nurtured through deliberate experimentation.

We aren't perfect today, and we will 'never' be. Perfection is not what we strive for. Our goal is progress: slow, steady and compounding.

MANAGING TIME, ENERGY AND ATTENTION

Each fellowship takes hundreds of hours to put together. Since we don't do paid advertising or sales, we spend all our time, energy and attention on growing our community and figuring out ways to serve in our own unique way. We call it contribution capital.

Through a combination of serendipity, peer recommendations and community-enabled connections, we are able to get inspiring faculty for our students, including but not limited to Nobel Laureates, Fortune 500 CEOs/ CXOs, award-winning authors, top investors and change makers from around the world.

THE CHALLENGE OF MAKING FELLOWSHIPS/CBCS WORK

Pulling off each fellowship seems impossible when we start, but somehow things figure themselves out. A good strategy and solid execution are only parts of the puzzle. There is a generous dose of luck and even more of community love which makes the Network Capital experience come alive.

THE HARD STUFF

So much happened between 2020 and 2022. One of the hardest things was to keep our heads down, focus on the fundamentals of business and add specific value to those in need. We are a community, not a typical business. We will never measure our success simply in terms of revenues and costs.

Job losses, bankruptcy, deaths, desperation and exasperation were widespread. It was our duty to step up. We did all we could to do our bit, but a lot more needs to be done.

This section is not about figuring which platform works better but about giving you the mental models to find your platform–market fit. Some of you might be tempted to build your own platforms, and that is great. For others, you can be encouraged by this growing trend of platforms sprouting up to enable you to do the work you truly care about.

CHAPTER 8

TO BUILD A PLATFORM OR TO USE ONE?

Bill Gates has an interesting way of defining platforms.[1] He suggests that you are not a platform until people make more money from your platform than you do. Executives from companies like Shopify, Spotify and Stripe often use this 'Gates test' to figure out the health of their platforms. Almost every creator and every passion economy enthusiast uses some combination of these platforms. Some of them make millions of dollars doing so, but a large chunk of them barely make enough to make ends meet. Let's look at a creator's earnings. According to Digital Music News, approximately 7,500 artists—0.09 per cent of about eight million on-platform creators—earn $100,000 per year or more on Spotify.

Basically millions of likes and views do not translate to millions of dollars, not even close. As of today, despite all the enthusiasm around passion economy, creator earnings are skewed towards the megastars. Just like the world of VC, the passion economy is following the power law where a small number of people enjoy disproportionate chunk of fame, money, influence and power.

So far, we have identified two clear winners: a handful of platforms and small coterie of megastars. What happens to others? Things are still getting defined, but it is important that those venturing into the passion economy have a clear sense of whether they want to build their own platform or leverage existing platforms to create interesting content/products. Being aware of the power law in the passion economy will be a useful first step.

1 https://stratechery.com/2018/the-bill-gates-line/#:~:text=A%20platform%20is%20when%20the,Then%20it's%20a%20platform.%E2%80%9D

Awareness does not mean acceptance. Just because most creators don't make enough money doesn't mean that things will always remain the same. Investors like Ji Lin have made a compelling case for a creator middle class in order to make the earnings more fairly distributed across the spectrum.

In this book, I will often reference *WIRED* co-founder Keven Kelley's 1000 True Fans framework which suggests that creators don't need millions of fans to scale; just 1,000 who truly believe in the mission would create a ripple effect along with financial stability that most of us value. Through real-life examples, I will demonstrate how 1,000 true fans can make you wealthy on your terms, but before we go there, we still need to answer one question: to build a new platform or use an existing one?

Should you write a newsletter or build a platform like Revue or Substack on which millions can write newsletters? Should you create your own podcast or build a platform like Spotify to empower other audio creators? In a 2019 interview,[2] Spotify CEO Daniel Ek said that he wanted to see Spotify emerge as a platform which helps one million artists earn a living doing what they love. Since then, things have worked out well for Spotify and also for a few creators like Joe Rogan who made millions via an acquisition (there is a case study on him in subsequent chapters).

There is no doubt that platforms like Spotify—with a great product, discovery mechanisms and community support—have enormous influence on the Internet culture. They also pocket a large chunk of earnings. Anyone creating on Spotify is using rented real estate to use a real estate analogy. In the years to come, we will see important debates among platform owners, participants and policymakers. The power balance and revenue split is likely to undergo important changes which are impossible to predict with accuracy today.

All this said, the decision to build a platform or create on it should not be driven by external factors like power and profits. You need to identify what you are driven by and what you want to produce.

---

2 https://www.theverge.com/2021/2/23/22295315/spotify-ceo-interview-podcast-daniel-ek-music-stream-on

Daniel Ek, the founder of Spotify, comes from a family of musicians. He trained to become one himself but chose to go down the entrepreneurial path and build a platform. He is still deeply interested in music, but he found his ultimate creative satisfaction in building Spotify. My mother is a poet and a writer. She loves writing; building a platform is not something she has considered. Can she? Of course. Will she? It depends. Maybe she finds an important challenge faced by writers and decides to solve it with the power of technology. Maybe she will continue to focus on writing, as she has since she was a child.

Building a platform and being a creator require different skills. There is no hierarchy of skills, achievement or impact. There are market factors, power equations and financial considerations, but most creators do what they love for the pursuit, not for the upside.

I am both a creator and a platform builder. I choose to do both because of my interest. I started off as a creator, built a community and when the community reached critical mass, I decided to build a platform. You can choose to go down a similar path or build your own platform or stick to creation. There is value in each of these options. Just be aware that not everything you try will work, and that is a good thing. The key is to keep tinkering till you find the sweet spot between creative satisfaction and financial viability.

Platforms without participants (creators) will be barren lands. Creators without platforms will find it challenging to create and distribute their work. It is a symbiotic relationship; at least, it can become one. Not every creator needs to build a platform, and not every platform builder needs to create stuff.

Artists don't need to be poor, and platform owners don't need to pocket all the financial upside. Figuring out the optimum balance will be one of the most interesting aspects of the passion economy.

DESIGN OPTIONALITY INTO YOUR PLATFORM CHOICE

On October 4, 2021, hours before Facebook was planning to announce funding and strategic support to Network Capital,

Facebook and all its sister platforms had a massive outage. For almost 10 hours, Facebook, Instagram and WhatsApp were inaccessible. My team and I had planned a wide range of celebrations around the world. It was supposed to be the giant leap my start-up needed to further accelerate into new vistas. We had locked in several large business partnerships ahead of the announcements. Our subscriptions were growing exponentially, and things were looking up. These are days every start-up/community builder looks forward to, but things changed rather rapidly.

The outage wasn't the only surprise that awaited us. Days before the outage, a whistle-blower who worked at Facebook leaked internal documents which led to a huge backlash against the company. These were both massive events with global impact but to a smaller scale, I had witnessed surprises from Facebook's side, for example, when they decided to halt subscription services. That is why, to some extent, I was prepared to handle what lay ahead.

To be clear, Facebook has been a fantastic partner to Network Capital thus far and their product, engineering and community teams have collaborated on a wide range of impactful projects. I do not mean to discount their support or judge the entirety of our relationship based on few disruptive events. That said, anyone building a passion project or a community on top of a platform must design for optionality in such circumstances.

Although today we have our own standalone platform Networkcapital.tv, our 100,000+ strong global community also uses a carefully curated Facebook group. The moment we realized that this wasn't a minor outage, our content team used our tech platform and newsletter to reach out to our community members, assuring them that we were monitoring the situation on an hourly basis and would get back to them.

Having multiple platforms to reach out to our community members turned out to be critical in navigating this tricky time. It is not advisable to put all your eggs in one basket when you are building something. This is especially important for companies operating in the passion economy space, because they typically use multiple platforms to make the entire workflow function. Not all platforms are equally relevant for creators and builders.

Usually, they rely on one platform for production and multiple others for distribution. A newsletter writer typically uses Ghost, Substack or Revue and then shares the link of their content on social and professional networks. What happens if the main platform they use has a major outage or bans them due to a tech failure or disagreement about editorial freedom? Such scenarios don't happen every day, but one should be prepared for times when things go wrong.

Portability, optionality and community trust are three important pillars for building something anti-fragile, systems which strengthen with chaos.

1. **Portability:** You should build a portable system, one that can be moved from one platform to another. Say you run a community on an existing platform (say LinkedIn or WhatsApp). A portable system would be one where you could replicate the key features without causing a major disruption in user experience.

2. **Optionality:** Here, you need to understand the cost of migration. Suppose the cost of migration is disproportionately high; you have zero optionality. You are stuck and have limited leverage. That means you will never have the upper hand in negotiations and will have to live with terms dictated to you.

3. **Customer trust:** This is the most important of the three pillars. Without customer trust, portability and optionality are meaningless. Your customers must believe in your mission and your capability to fulfil your mission. Fundamentally, customer trust stems from consistency, and consistency is doing more than you said you would. A simple framework I use is keep the Do/Say ratio > 1.

Passion economy builders are monetizing their creativity and uniqueness quotient, but they need the support of platforms to create impact and make a living. The good news is that since you are leveraging something intrinsically yours, you will be able to create suitable ways to scale yourself with time, but why not be prepared for the off-chance things go awry? Building this bit of insurance early on is a much-needed step, as passion economy scales and becomes more mainstreamed.

CHAPTER 9

CHIEF COMMUNITY OFFICER: THE SECRET JOB NOBODY KNEW ABOUT

Why would chief community officer (CCO) will be among the most coveted positions in companies, both large and small?

LinkedIn recently announced that it is hiring a community head based in New York.[1] Facebook already has a global community lead,[2] whose team worked closely with Network Capital to build out a subscription-based product. That was the first of its kind in the region and helped us test out what a subscription-powered, advertisement-free community really looks like.

Twitter has rolled out a subscription feature[3] which will allow power users to monetize their followers via recurring payments and tipping. Circle, a community membership platform for creators, recently raised a $4 million seed round led by Notation Capital.[4] It recently crossed $1 million annual recurring revenue (ARR) and currently hosts 2,000 communities. There are many platforms with similar functionalities such as Mighty Networks and Discord which are focused largely on enabling community builders to shape platforms with the right culture.

Clubhouse is already a unicorn with its inbuilt audio-powered community building and is soon to see another competitor in the form of Fireside which is funded by Mark Cuban. Not to be left behind, Facebook and Twitter are also tinkering along to build

---

1 https://techcrunch.com/2021/03/30/linkedin-adds-creator-mode-video-profiles-and-in-partnership-with-microsoft-new-career-training-tools/
2 https://www.facebook.com/community/programs/
3 https://www.livemint.com/technology/apps/twitter-launches-subscription-based-feature-super-follows-11630541129728.html
4 https://techcrunch.com/2021/02/16/the-creator-movement-is-entering-primetime-and-so-is-circle-with-a-fresh-4m/

their version of Clubhouse. And of course, there are Indian and Chinese clones of these apps strutting along to explore product–market fit.

EMPOWERING SMALLER COMMUNITIES

What is common among all these platforms is that they are empowering smaller communities to flourish, thereby propelling the creator economy/passion economy. By creating the right context for creators, these platforms (at least some of them) are likely to get the stickiness they crave for. More stickiness means more data, which in turn leads to myriad monetization opportunities: subscriptions, advertisements, social commerce, etc.

The key insight is that communities are going to be the most important assets of companies, and these communities need to be built, nurtured, managed and scaled. Technology is not enough, far from it.

Community-first platforms need culture to scale. That is the first reason why CCO will be a mission-critical position. You need a person to define, shape and set culture at three levels:

1. Within the company by coordinating with HR
2. Across communities within the company (think of LinkedIn groups for LinkedIn employees)
3. Across communities built on your company's platform (think of LinkedIn groups or Facebook groups built by creators)

To illustrate the third point, meet Lola who created a masterclass for us. She is among the world's most successful community builders often referenced by Facebook CEO Mark Zuckerberg in his public talks.

Lola is originally from Nigeria and moved to the United States, started a small Facebook group to support other women, built up the community with a clear sense of purpose and within few years got to become among the top community builders in the world.

Facebook worked extensively with her to build out specific features, invest capital and HR, and build her brand even more. Ever wonder who figured out she needed support?

It was the community team—a large one—headed by an incredibly driven person. That person reported directly to the CEO, studied at the best of schools and made a handsome salary doing so.

That said, the person being referenced was still not the 'CCO'. We think that in the times to come, you will see the CCO at the same level as the COO, CTO and CFO.

WHY NOW?

Companies are soon realizing that if they want to play an active role in shaping communities, they can't sit back and let things happen. They need to be proactive, not reactive.

The power of influencers to spread anything turns out to be one of the most enduring and misleading myths in social science. Most companies have confused influencers with community builders.

If you design your community strategy keeping influencers in mind, your success will be short-lived. Your immediate counter could be Clubhouse hosting Elon Musks of the world, but you should keep in mind that stardom is a very small reason why Clubhouse worked in the early days. You were there because your friends were there. And of course the fear of missing out (FOMO) was real. We aren't discounting the well-built product, just sharing that most companies don't really get communities.

We won't be surprised if Clubhouse appoints a CCO soon. The randomness on places like Clubhouse is increasing. Many rooms are subpar, and many clubs are composed of people who want to do what they did on social media—spout venom—without thinking of their communities. Should Clubhouse ban such groups and such rooms? Is there a way to do that without seeming dictatorial? How might Clubhouse monetize the thousands of conversations going along at the same time? Now that the news is out that a Chinese company is providing security/cloud services to Clubhouse, how might it impact poets and activists and entrepreneurs who have built huge communities of supporters there?

These are all questions that will define the future of the company. These are also questions where the CEO, board members and COO will weigh in, but the most robust way of dealing with community challenges and figuring out new opportunities is to appoint a team led by a person tasked with one goal: make communities great again.

Great is of course a vague word, but it broadly comes down to enabling dialogues united by a shared mission. The challenge ahead of the CCO is to connect the mission of the community builder with the mission of their company. For example, Lola's mission for her group is very different from the mission of Facebook.

The future CCO will attempt to find synergies between the missions in a way that adds both business and social value. She/he will have a team of engineers, data scientists, anthropologists, ethnographers and artists constantly trying to find this sweet spot.

Working in such a team will be an absolute delight, because you will be solving real issues in real time. Every day will be a new adventure. Seventy to eight-five per cent of all jobs of 2030 don't exist yet.[5] CCO is one such job. People are familiar with it, but nobody is doing it smartly. You have the opportunity to create your own job: become the CCO of your own company or lead communities for an enterprise.

No one has defined this job yet, which means that you have the opportunity to build your category of one.

SECTION 2

**PASSION ECONOMY
CAREER PRINCIPLES**

CHAPTER 10

EVERYONE'S JOB IS WORLD-BUILDING, EVEN IF THEY DON'T REALIZE IT

'Everyone's job is world-building, even if they don't realize it.' The 21st century will reward great writers, philosophers and systems thinkers like Alex Danco who came up with a fascinating theory on world-building relevant to all young professionals, creators and creatives. He said, 'Everyone's job is world-building (selling is not enough), even if they don't realize it.'

Danco got a bachelor's degree in physiology and a master's degree in neuroscience. Thereafter, he started a wearable company which didn't amount to much and managed operations of an online bus company. Then he moved to California and spent a few years at Social Capital. Today, he works at Shopify, one of the most exciting e-commerce companies, in the capacity of a 'systems and crypto' person. That sounds like a cool job. Two important things to note here are as follows.

1. Nothing quite prepares you to be a 'systems and crypto' person. This is specific knowledge, one that cannot be taught but can be learned. Danco's formal education and work experience did not prepare him for the Shopify role. He created this role, augmented his luck surface area by connecting with the right set of people and figured out a way to build his category of one within the company and across the industry at large.

2. Danco is more famous for his newsletter than his role at Shopify. Thousands of sharp people subscribe to his analyses on business, philosophy and tech. 'World-building' is his most well-known concept, and we will unpack that in this chapter.

WHAT IS WORLD-BUILDING?

Attention is scarce, digital resources are plenty, and selling is not enough. We all need to build worlds which are interesting, useful, relevant and engaging to be relevant. Let's explore this deeper.

It is often said that everyone's job is in sales, even if they don't know it. Danco says that we shouldn't throw that piece of advice out but update it to stay in this world of abundance on the Internet; everyone's job is world-building.

> Your job is actually to create a world that is so interesting and so compelling and has a reason for people to go walk in and explore this world that they can go spend time in it, without you even having to be there. There is an understanding of why they want to explore it. They have an understanding of why they want to be there and what's in it for them. And what's there to learn.
>
> It's not enough to tell one good story; you have to create an entire world that people can step into, familiarize themselves with, and spend time getting to know. Initially you'll have to walk them around and show them what's in your world, but your goal is to familiarize them with your world sufficiently, and motivate them to participate, to the point that they can spend time in your world and build stuff in it without you having to be there all the time.

World-building has been such an adventure on Network Capital. Thanks to all our community members for co-creating this new world of learning. If we were in the business of selling subscriptions, we would burn out and our community members would develop a sense of detachment that arises when we realize that we are constantly being sold to.

Instead, we went about creating a whole new world starting with a community, then adding aspirational content and finally complementing it with real-time career intelligence in the form

Passion Economy and the Side-Hustle Revolution

of cohort-based fellowships and office hours. Individually, master-classes, newsletters, subgroups, fellowships, etc., can be thought of as products, but the difficult aspect hasn't been product management, it has been building the larger narrative around how different products fit into the Network Capital world.

Creating a compelling narrative, one that is familiar, surprising and inclusive, requires deep understanding of what citizens (consumers) really want from this world. It is an interesting problem to solve, requiring intimate understanding of technology, sociology, psychology, philosophy and popular culture. That's what makes work energizing for us. The world we are building is still imperfect, and there is a lot more to do.

Danco says that our success in world-building depends entirely on how successfully other people can repeat narratives, both to themselves and to others.

Know what you are selling. In a world of abundance, what is it that you are selling? Think about it. Do you think Pepsi is selling sugared water or a lifestyle or stoking Pavlovian associations with good times? When you watch Indra Nooyi's Network Capital masterclass, you will know the answer, but till then, please remember that if Pepsi was only in the business of selling sugared water, it would be bankrupt by now.

Pepsi also had to do world-building,[1] that is, paint a narrative, invite customers to be part of their world, make it interesting and offer something much beyond the grasp of utilitarian traps. Even for a multi-billion-dollar company, figuring out what they are selling is difficult.

Even for a much smaller company like ours, identifying what we are selling turned out to be challenging. Different people subscribed to Network Capital for different reasons: some wanted to learn from the best, some wanted to support the mission, some joined in to express solidarity with the founder, some wanted to network, some wanted to feel a deeper connect with the Indian/South Asian community, some wanted to prepare for the long term, some wanted to experiment with their careers and some wanted to build their category of one.

Tactically, especially in the short run, it would have been smarter for Network Capital to focus on just one thing, let's say MBA admissions or tech interview preparation, but we consciously chose to stay away from adopting one specific identity. We wanted to build a full stack career experimentation and advancement platform where ambitious millennials could discover what they cared about, connect with mentors, take relevant fellowships, consume interesting content and build their category of one.

Because our mission and scope were much beyond getting people into colleges, our world-building needed to be a lot more nuanced, interesting, engaging and captivating. It goes without saying that the more complex the world you have to build, the more effort and time it takes.

Danco says,[2]

> The more complex or valuable is whatever you're trying to sell, the more important it is for you to build a world around that idea, where other people can walk in, explore, and hang out—without you having to be there with them the whole time.

WORLD-BUILDING AND FIGURING OUT THE 'WHY'

The most important job for any builder/creator is to understand why customers/community members want to explore the world they have built. Customers need to know why they are there, what's the role they have to play and what value they might derive. For Network Capital, we had to figure out what it is really that our subscribers wanted to learn. Are subscribers paying for content, community or access or all of the above?

Danco gives the example of Microsoft, whose earlier mission was 'a computer on every desktop, in every home, running Windows'.

2 https://alexdanco.com/2021/04/10/world-building/

That's not a product that they were selling. That was a world that they were selling that they invited 'you'—software developers, IT consultants, and consumers of every possible shape and size—to come in and explore and try to understand what this world meant for you.

Even when Satya Nadella became the CEO of Microsoft, the mission was invitation to a world, not to a product. Check it out: 'Empower every person and every organization on the planet to achieve more.'

COMPLEXITY, COMPOUNDING AND WORLD-BUILDING

'Easy worlds are boring and people leave; worlds need to have challenges in them and jungle gyms for people to climb on and go explore.'

Remember Bilibili, the Chinese behemoth most people in the West haven't even heard of? It is a great example of world-building. It isn't easy to navigate. It has inbuilt challenges. Only a certain kind of person will bother navigating through such complexity, but once they do, there won't be any going back.

If you want to be part of Bilibili, you need to clear a competitive entrance examination which is sprinkled with pop culture questions on *Game of Thrones*, *Star Wars* and gaming trivia.

What this entrance exam does is build a community which feels connected with the company from the start and is culturally aligned. There is also a sense of pride that comes from a sense of belonging, much like one might feel for one's alma mater or a secret club one is a part of.

High barrier to entry is usually great for designing community/company cultures. It enables community members to engage at a deeper level, which translates to high engagement, less noise and smarter conversations.

Bilibili's strategy is interesting because unlike an elite club/institution where the number of participants is low, Internet-propelled niches like games and subcultures are intriguing to millions. Community members just need to demonstrate that they are true fans, not passive lurkers.

For communities, engagement is the hardest problem to solve for. Remember the definition of network effects? It is simple: If the system becomes better with addition of new members, you have network effects going. Else, you don't.

Let's come to compounding.

World-building cannot be done alone. You will need a community, a network of champions, a tribe of mentors and thousands of true fans, all working with you to build something that matters.

Especially if you want to bring out systemic change, sequential or disjoined effort won't do much. Danco emphasized the importance of parallel effort where several different things happen concomitantly. That's how things change, movements get built and people inch closer to building their category of one.

Immerse yourself in world-building. Whether you are a data scientist trying to figure out the metaverse or a community builder trying to make the world a more equitable place or an activist fighting for climate change, you won't get far if all you are trying to do is to sell/evangelize your ideas. It is easy to be seduced by the illusion of hard work, but do remember that if you aren't world-building, you are basically wasting your time. People might buy what you are selling once, but you will struggle to capture their interest or attention for long.

I think that world-building should be taught in every school, every college and every corporate. It isn't just a philosophy for founders and creators, it applies precisely to everyone.

Ask yourself three questions today:

1. What's the world you wish to shape?
2. How will you build a narrative around that world?
3. How will you enable others to evangelize that narrative?

CHAPTER 11

BUILD A CATEGORY OF ONE

'Competition is for losers,' says Peter Thiel, an investor and co-founder of PayPal. He adds, with a twist on Leo Tolstoy's masterpiece *Anna Karenina*, that every failed company is alike in that it fails to escape competition. Thiel's analysis is as true for businesses as it is for careers.

While we revere competition as the ultimate performance benchmark, it deludes us into believing that opportunities are finite and we can only get ahead if we follow standardized paths, perform well on standardized tests and ask standardized questions. In other words, competition nudges us into playing the wrong game.

New York University Professor Emeritus of Religion and History James Carse wrote a book in 1986 called *Finite and Infinite Games*. He explained that finite games are defined by known players, fixed rules and an agreed-upon objective. Infinite games, on the other hand, are the ones where the rules are constantly evolving, and the objective is not to win in the short term but to keep playing.

The game of work and life is infinite. There is no such thing as winning in friendship, marriage, business and practically anything that matters. To share an example, we can't 'win' a meeting. We must strive to create mutually beneficial outcomes for all stakeholders. That is how we train ourselves to play long-term games with long-term people, an integral element of success in the 21st century.

Author and motivational speaker Simon Sinek explains[1] that the challenge with a large number of business leaders is that they pay lip service to infinite games while continually optimizing for short-term outcomes. They talk about being number one, being the best and beating their competition—hallmarks of finite games—instead of asking themselves more difficult questions about the future. They aggressively promote status quo. This mode of thinking trickles down to different teams in their organizations and corrupts the decision-making frameworks of young professionals.

When we play with a finite mindset in the infinite game of work life, three things happen.

First is the decline of trust and reduction in cooperation. Cooperation only works when the time frame is long enough.

Second is short-term thinking. The biggest disadvantage of short-term thinking is that we tend to prioritize urgent over the important. Those of us who consistently do so end up either burning out or becoming average.

Third is the illusion of purpose. Without a clearly defined reason for being, we are not only unmotivated but also unprepared.

With this context, one might wonder if finite games serve any purpose. It turns out that finite and infinite games are not competing ideas. The infinite game is a context within which finite games play out. For example, meeting your sales target is an important finite game within the larger infinite game of serving your customers uniquely over a long period of time.

One of the most efficient ways for young professionals to escape competition and play infinite games is to build a category of one. VC firm Andreessen Horowitz published[2] an industry report on the future of work. One of its major takeaways is that the gig economy or the 'Uber for X' model is partially making way for the passion economy, where micro-entrepreneurs monetize their individuality and creativity. Even on networkcapital.tv, we have built a passion economy platform where anyone can create content and monetize their skills.

The basic laws of demand and supply tell us that it is challenging to defend what is abundantly available. That is why

2 https://future.a16z.com/passion-economy/

it makes sense to think outside the box, be a contrarian and build a category of one where your uniqueness quotient is your value proposition.

So how do you create a category of one?

It begins with following your curiosity (not necessarily passion) and training yourself to learn across disciplines. By combining two distinct strands of thought, you create a highly differentiated skill set which helps you escape the trappings of competition. World-famous chef Massimo Bottura created a category of one by fusing his culinary expertise with great design and memorable experience curation. There are many Italian chefs, but there is only one Massimo Bottura.

One doesn't become a category leader overnight. It takes years of consistent focus and community building, especially if one is building a category of one. *WIRED* Editor Kevin Kelley came up with the concept of 1000 True Fans, where he states that by simply finding 1,000 people who value our uniqueness, one can not only carve out a meaningful career and but also exponentially augment our earnings.

The 21st century will be sprinkled with multiple disruptions in work and life. Reinventing ourselves will be the most valuable skill, but reinvention doesn't necessarily mean recreation. Those who chase every hot new trend and compete for every outcome will be exhausted. Those who build a category of one and adapt will make a tangible impact and have fun doing so.

CHAPTER 12

QUITTING YOUR JOB FOR A BIG CAREER TRANSITION? HERE'S WHAT YOU NEED TO THINK ABOUT

When Amazon founder Jeff Bezos was deciding when to quit his well-paying hedge fund job, he went to his boss and told him that he was thinking of selling books online. He had already been talking to him about the power of the Internet, but for the first time, he was seriously considering quitting to become an entrepreneur. His boss was startled to hear that someone would actually leave a coveted investing job to work on something with so many unknowns. After all, aren't good investors experts in evaluating risk?

His boss decided to take him out for a two-hour walk in Central Park in New York City. He wanted to understand what was going on in Bezos's mind. During the walk, Bezos managed to convince him that selling books online had great potential, and e-commerce could be really big. His boss agreed that it was a good idea but said that it would be a better idea for somebody who didn't already have a good job. Bezos was given 48 hours to make a final decision.

To figure out the next steps in his career, Bezos came up with the regret minimization framework, a simple mental model to minimize the number of regrets in the long run. He asked himself what he would regret more when he was eighty years old: trying to build something he had strong conviction in and failing or failing to give it a try? He realized that not trying would haunt him every day.

When he thought about his career transition, keeping the regret minimization framework in mind, quitting turned out to be

Passion Economy and the Side-Hustle Revolution

an incredibly easy decision. He left the hedge fund in the middle of the year and walked away from his massive annual bonus.

Whether or not you are pursuing a passion or side hustle, confused about quitting your job for a new one, or just looking for a change, know that it's not a straightforward decision. It requires careful planning and thinking. I can say that with some conviction because I've had to make this tricky decision myself. Last year, in the middle of the pandemic, I quit my job at Microsoft to work full time on my passion project.

I loved my work, but the more I reflected on my core values, the kind of life I wanted to build and the way I wanted to use my skills, the more it became clear to me that entrepreneurship was the way forward. But making that decision turned out to be more complex than I had thought.

I had nurtured my passion project as a side hustle for four years: Network Capital, a global P2P networking community of 100,000+ ambitious and curious millennials. There were a lot of questions running through my head during this time. Why should I quit to make this my full-time job? Is this what I really want? When should I quit? Poet Mary Oliver's words kept ringing in my head: 'What is it you plan to do with your one wild and precious life?'

Most importantly, I wondered if I would regret not giving it a shot.

CAREER TRANSITIONS ARE MESSY

Transitions aren't just about doing something different. A career transition is a lifestyle redesign which often entails rethinking how you want to feel at the end of the day, how you want to spend your time and how this relates to your longer-term goals. When you feel this need for change, it isn't necessarily related to a fancier title or more money, but your inner voice whispering that you could do more, be more, experience more and achieve more.

If you're thinking about quitting your job to make a meaningful career transition, first think about the why, the what and the when.

'Why' (Do You Want to Change)?

Start by asking why you want to quit your current job. Is it the culture of the organization, the people you work with or something else bogging you down? Like me, you might also discover that you love your job, but you want to build something new or experiment with a different sector. It is critical to be radically honest with yourself and think things through.

I decided to conduct an experiment to figure out my career transition. For the past four years, I had been working on building Network Capital on nights and over weekends. I took two weeks off from work to focus solely on building Network Capital. That is when I realized that I could make so much more progress on my side hustle with focused effort.

That focused effort not only energized me but also propelled a whole bunch of new product road maps. In fact, I came up with the idea of launching cohort-based fellowships during that time. That was my 'why', and it made me realize that I enjoyed dedicating most of my waking hours to my side hustle, even though I loved my day job.

Pro tip: Before leaving your job, try to find ways to experience what your next position might feel like. Does it feel better than what you are doing now? Is it worth committing to this change? If you are able, take some time off work—even just a week—to focus on your passion project.

If you don't have a passion project, and are just looking for something new, use your free time (weekends or after hours) to experiment with the industries or roles you are interested in. This might mean volunteering, job shadowing or even conducting informational interviews with people who have careers you admire.

Keep the end in mind. It is challenging to plan for the long term, but it helps to have a mental image of the kind of life you want to build.

Work and life are not separate entities. Work is part of life. Try to visualize where you want to live, the kind of person you want to partner with (or if you even want a partner) and how you want to spend your time on a daily basis.

I knew I wanted geographical flexibility because I wanted to help young people navigate their careers, not only in India but also around the world. I wanted autonomy over a strict daily schedule. I wanted to master how students and early career professionals learn and unlearn. I wanted to create a job which gave my future self a deeper sense of purpose.

While I could have indirectly made an impact in the career navigation space at Microsoft, I knew I wanted a more direct connection with the people I was trying to serve. Committing to Network Capital full time would give me that opportunity.

Pro tip: Write your future autobiography. Before leaving Microsoft, I actually sat down and wrote a sort of autobiography. I reflected on what the most defining events along the way would be. I was intentional about describing (in great detail) what I wanted to be remembered for and the way I spent my time. Eventually, how you spend your time is who you become. Conducting this thought experiment gave me more clarity on what mattered most to me and why. This doesn't need to be 100 pages long, but it does need to give you an idea of what you want your journey to be like.

'What (Do You Want to Do)?

Assess yourself. While some may know already that they want to work in another industry or go back to school to learn something new, many don't know what their next step should be. But it is impossible to know where you are going if you don't know where you are. The simplest way to conduct this self-assessment is to ask yourself the following questions:

- What's my end goal?
- If I keep doing what I am doing today, will I get closer to my ultimate goal?
- Will my eighty-year-old self have more or less regrets because of my current choices?

After that, write down the steps you will need to take to make your future self proud and the problems that you might encounter in doing that. The 'I don't know what I want to with my life' Fellowship at Network Capital has been doing this exercise with our members. What we've learned is that an important part of learning where you are is in understanding the challenges that are keeping you there.

Look at the list of things you need to do to get closer to your goal. Find, know or strike out challenges you have no control over. This happens to be one of the core tenets of stoic philosophy: focusing on things you can control and ignoring those you can't.

For me, one issue that I couldn't control—at least in the short term—was that of income predictability. Would I make an equal amount of money at Network Capital as I did at Microsoft? Would I need to change my lifestyle? On average, corporate compensation is significantly higher (at least in the early days) than the income one can expect in early-stage ventures. Complaining about it or worrying about it obsessively would have been a waste of time. If quitting got me closer to my goal, and I chose to pursue that goal, how would I work around this problem?

I had to come up with a plan.

Inspired by *WIRED* co-founder Kevin Kelley's concept of 1000 True Fans, I gave myself the target of getting Network Capital 1,000 monthly paying subscribers over a period of 12 months. Kelley advises,

> 1,000 true fans is an alternative path to success other than stardom. Instead of trying to reach the narrow and unlikely peaks of platinum bestseller hits, blockbusters, and celebrity status, you can aim for direct connection with a thousand true fans. On your way, no matter how many fans you actually succeed in gaining, you'll be surrounded not by faddish infatuation, but by genuine and true appreciation. It's a much saner destiny to hope for. And you are much more likely to actually arrive there.

Pro tip: Approach your self-assessment with awareness, curiosity and a willingness to experiment. Author and entrepreneur Marie Forleo says, 'Everything is figureoutable.' When it comes to career transitions, there isn't a formula per se. Experimenting, tinkering and figuring things out is the way forward.

'When' Will the Change Happen?

Expect multiple rejections. Unfortunately, most career transitions and hiring processes rely heavily on past experience. For example, suppose you are a technology sales manager who wants to break into trading or hedge funds. Most recruiters will nudge you towards a role very similar to your current job, even if you have the skills necessary to transition to a different sector.

Even at Microsoft, when I was looking to transition from corporate strategy to business development, it turned out to be much more challenging than I had thought. After approaching peers on dozens of teams, I realized that very few wanted to take a bet on someone with a different experience. Finally, one hiring manager gave me a project to work on. I performed well on that project and got the opportunity to interview for his team. After eight months of trying relentlessly, I finally made the internal transfer happen.

Pro tip: Thankfully you don't need everyone to take a bet on you. Just one will do. Finding that person/hiring manager/recruiter will take time. Expect multiple rejections before you do. It is just the way things work. If your resolve and preparation are strong enough, you will get someone to take that chance.

Be realistic. Some transitions are unlikely in the short term. Don't set yourself up for failure by setting unrealistic goals in unrealistic time frames. We overestimate what we can do in 1 year and underestimate what we can do in 10 years. You can change your industry, your function and your geographical location, but all three are unlikely to change immediately. Gradual change is often much more sustainable.

Please don't take my suggestion of being realistic to be at odds with dreaming big. Both can coexist with the proper time frame. Dream big and act small by trying to take micro-steps in the right direction.

My first micro-step was setting up a MVP for Network Capital in the form of a Facebook group and observing two things: customer behaviour and my own interest level in figuring out the messy challenge of career exploration for millennials. Without this micro-step, Network Capital would have remained an idea in my head.

Pro tip: Micro-actions compound over a period of time to deliver exponential results. Take the first step and be consistent about it. Urgency in actions and patience with results will serve you well.

Have a backup plan. Create an alternative you can live with if things aren't going as envisioned or planned. It might be somewhere in between your ultimate aspiration and your current state. This can bridge the skill and network gap you might be facing during career transitions. More importantly, it will set you up on the journey you wish to embark upon.

Today, my backup plan isn't going back to corporate. I have, however, thought through various scenarios for Network Capital. Perhaps it will become a hyperscalable big tech company, perhaps it will evolve into a more niche offering. I am comfortable with both outcomes, as I now realize that I am more in love with the problem of career navigation than the solution. Hopefully, I will help solve it. If not, I can help others figure it out.

Pro tip: Set a timeframe. Suppose you want to transition from law to social impact consulting, and making that switch is proving to be difficult, perhaps because of lack of relevant experience. Here, your backup plan could be time-bound. You could give yourself one year to make the switch from law to social impact consulting by acquiring the right set of skills, building a tribe of mentors and networking with industry professionals. If it still doesn't work out, you can rethink your goal or look at accomplishing it in the longer term if it still interests you.

Career transitions are like Shrek. They're complex, and there is usually a lot more to them than we see on the surface. For me, transitioning from the corporate lifestyle to that of a scrappy entrepreneur has been both challenging and rewarding.

I still remember my last day at Microsoft, the day I went back to the office to submit my badge, laptop and corporate expense card. I was giving up a big part of my identity. As I took a walk across the empty floor bidding adieu to all the wonderful memories and learning experiences, I knew that my time there had prepared me well for the journey ahead.

If you aren't thinking about a career transition today, some day you will. As and when that day comes, my hope is that you approach it with curiosity, conviction and commitment. Career transitions are messy, but they can also turn out to be catalysts in shaping a future self you will be proud of. There is no way of guaranteeing success, but not trying might just leave you with regrets.

CHAPTER 13

RETHINKING YOUR CAREER

Students who are most certain about career paths at the age of twenty are often the ones with deep regrets at the age of thirty. They have not done enough rethinking, says author Adam Grant. Do you relate to this?

'I don't know what I want to do with my life' Fellowship traces its origin to our childhood when we were all asked 'What do you want to be when you grow up'? Some of us had a sense, most of us didn't.

I had multiple curiosities as a child, but no one path seemed to be the all-consuming direction. I felt this invisible pressure to excel despite having liberal parents, did well in a wide range of things and came to the realization that being good at something doesn't mean that you love it and want to build a career in it.

So what did I do? I used my teens and early twenties to do two things: experiment intensely and get interesting education and learning experiences under my belt. Sometimes people wait till their thirties/forties to think through what they want to do with their lives, and that is what leads to deep existential regrets.

'BLIRTATIOUSNESS' AND ESCALATION OF COMMITMENT

Do you remember the time when you expressed doubt about your current career path to a friend? Perhaps you were doing well at consulting but had this itch to start a non-profit and go back to school and get a PhD?

Since you were talking to a friend, you blurted out the idea you were flirting with.

'I really want to start a school of life for millennials' perhaps?

Passion Economy and the Side-Hustle Revolution

Adam Grant explains this combination of blurting + flirting as blirtatiousness, an actual psychology concept.

As interesting as blirtatiousness sounds, we tend to not take its cues seriously. Why? Because of escalation of commitment

Escalation of commitment is a behaviour pattern in which an individual or group facing increasingly negative outcomes from a decision continues the behaviour instead of altering course. We maintain behaviour which is irrational but aligns with our previous decisions and actions in both professional and personal lives.

As we have discussed earlier, we often prioritize consistency over accuracy. This is a well-established mental model, and there are hundreds of cautionary tales to warn us, but there is often a chasm among thought, ideation and action.

Escalation of commitment often happens when it comes to careers. We tend to keep following through just because we are 'on track'. Keep in mind that while escalation of commitment is dangerous, the opposite is also true. If we keep switching without giving our choices adequate time to manifest, we end up snacking on careers.

Building a portfolio of careers is different from snacking. Portfolio is experiment-based and iterative, whereas snacking is moving on without collecting enough data, that is, making inferences based on insufficient information.

Basically, we need to steer clear of both escalating commitments and running away from them the moment things get difficult.

WHY ESCALATION OF COMMITMENT HAPPENS IN CAREERS

It turns out that from an early age, our aspirations are shaped by our context. We develop half-baked ideas about the right places to live, the right schools to go to, the suitable boy/girl to marry and the respectable time to have kids. We are mimetic creatures. We mimic the aspirations of people we look up to all the time. For a recap, read René Girard's mimetic theory.

GOING INTO FORECLOSURE

When we commit to a plan and it isn't going as expected, we tend to 'not' rethink it. Instead, we double down and do what we shouldn't—prioritize consistency over accuracy. Of course, sunk costs are a factor, but the real reason is psychological rather than economic.

We are rationalizing creatures, constantly searching for self-justifications for our prior beliefs to soothe our egos.

THE DOWNSIDE OF GRIT

Grant's Penn colleague Angela Duckworth popularized the term 'grit', combination of passion and perseverance, which plays an important role in achieving meaningful long-term goals.

The same grit, however, has a dark side when it comes to rethinking. Gritty people tend to overplay their hands at roulette and are more willing to stay the course in tasks which are failing, and success is impossible.

There is a fine line between heroic persistence and foolish stubbornness. Heroic persistence sometimes gets us into challenging examinations and sought-after companies, but the entire effort is foolhardy if you didn't care about the goal. For how long will you keep signalling the world that you are cool?

SO WHAT SHOULD WE TELL KIDS?

For starters, they are better off thinking about careers and future selves as a set of actions, rather than identities to claim. When we see work as input rather than identity, they become more open to exploring different possibilities.

When second and third graders learned about 'doing science' rather than 'being scientists,' they were more excited about pursuing science.

Growing up isn't a destination. It has no end point. You never 'arrive', and we should tell kids that in no uncertain terms.

CAREER VS SOULMATE

Grant says that choosing a career isn't like finding a soulmate. It is possible that your ideal job hasn't been invented yet.

We change, economy changes and life happens. Identity foreclosure can stop us from evolving. We get seduced by status signalling, approval seeking or comfort of status quo. Some of the points I'd like to make here before stepping to the next chapter are as follows:

1. It is better to lose a year of progress than to waste the next 20.

2. Identity foreclosure is a band-aid: It covers up an identity crisis but fails to cure it.

3. You will change, what you want will change. Fixed self is an illusion.

4. Entertain the possibility of multiple career plans and keep experimenting. The goal is not to confirm a right plan and be a suitable boy/girl but to expand your professional possibilities.

5. Schedule time once a month to rethink your careers. Start by asking what you did enjoy about the work you did and what seemed like a chore.

6. Always remember John Stuart Mill:

> Those only are happy who have their minds fixed on some other object other than their own happiness; on happiness of others, on improvement of mankind, even on some art or pursuit, followed not as a means, but as itself an ideal end. Aiming thus at something else, they find happiness by the way.

CHAPTER 14

THE AMP FRAMEWORK

We launched the CEO Fellowship not because we think that everyone should get that title at some point but because of our unflinching belief that every person on the planet must have the tools to create their category of one.

The science on this is clear: Until we have the combination of autonomy, mastery and purpose, we will continue to be unmotivated. If we are unmotivated or chasing someone else's dreams, we cannot be free to live, experiment and be on our terms.

THREE POINTERS

Autonomy is the defining element of being motivated over the long run. It is our innate desire to be self-directed, but the extent of autonomy depends upon the kind of person we are. Some of us thrive in anarchy, and some need direction to function. Thinking about where we stand on the spectrum is critical. There is a reason why some terrific entrepreneurs are terrible employees and vice versa.

The second is mastery. We often make the mistake of confusing passion with purpose. While purpose is focused on a larger meaning and impact on business/society, passion turns out to be a whim.

Passion is a by-product of focused work. Real estate investor and Shark Tank's 'Shark' Barbara Corcoran is often heard saying that she didn't follow her passion. She stumbled on it as she was working relentlessly to solve a problem she cared about. As per research done by the likes of Oxford University's William MacAskill and author Cal Newport, engaging work helps us develop passion, not the other way around.

The third and last factor is purpose. We all want our work to contribute to something larger than us. Voltaire was right when he said that work spares us from three evils—boredom, vice and need—but he didn't live in the age of technology. In the digital era, if work doesn't add meaning to our lives, it will cease to exist.

THE MARKET GAP

The career intelligence market is broken. It is filled with misleading advice which seems like a twisted form of pattern matching. Your most successful relative did X, so you should aspire to that. The most famous CEO of a certain nationality did Y, so you should follow suit.

Pattern matching is indicative and should not become prescriptive. Basically, if pattern matching leads to copying, it fails to take into account the operating context of the person we admire.

It is impossible to build a category of one by emulation without improvisation. No one is stating that you should not learn from those who succeed, but by blindly following their path, we are setting ourselves for inevitable disappointment. We may not succeed in playing someone else's game and even if we succeed, we will never know if we were following our dreams and curiosities or someone else's.

THE SKILL GAP

Coding, analytical skills and the whole spectrum of hard skills are important. You cannot rise early in your career without them, but after a certain point, the game belongs to the rainmaker—the person who generates business, relationships and value.

In the current market, there is disproportionate emphasis on hard skills and too little attention to things which actually shape leadership. The prevalent norm is to acquire hard skills, degrees and skill indicators and then casually figure other things out.

The challenge is that leadership, especially one that delivers, takes deliberate practice. The word 'deliberate' is worth pondering over. Practice is insufficient. In fact, practice without feedback often backfires. We need a carefully curated system of building our leadership muscles. It isn't fundamentally different from working out under the guidance of a coach.

CHAPTER 15

ALTERNATE CAREERS, WEB 3.0 AND THE HISTORY OF THE INTERNET

WEB 1.0

The first era of the Web was about how we process and consume information. Yahoo!, Netscape, Craigslist and AOL were Web 1.0 companies. Google 'won' this era by democratizing information and building a solid advertisement-driven business model on top of it.

WEB 2.0

The second era of the Internet gave birth to platforms which enable interaction, giving us Facebook, Instagram, Twitter, Reddit, LinkedIn, etc. Information, goods, and services were brought under the same umbrella. People started taking cabs, trips, dates and work partnerships with strangers. On Uber, you could hail a cab or make some side income driving after work. On Instagram, posting content and watching leaving your friends in a state of awe became a thing. And finally, influencer became a noun instead of a verb.

P2P exchange of information was the defining characteristic of Web 2.0. It also propelled the GDP of the Internet, but most of the economic benefits went to large centralized platforms who set the rules and controlled data flow. This created a complicated relationship among the platforms, participants and policymakers.

The policymakers wanted to regulate the Internet but weren't sure how to go about it. The participants were happy with the economic benefits but disgruntled with the unequal distribution.

The platforms felt that they were attacked from all corners despite their contribution to the GDP of the Internet.

The fundamental challenge of the Web 2.0 era was concentration of power, influence, data and capital.

ENTER WEB 3.0

A new type of digital product has started gaining traction around the world, one that is co-owned, co-created and co-run. This constitutes the third era of the Internet and is defined by decentralization, declining trust in institutions and a new way of looking at value creation and value capture.

We are already seeing some of it in action in the media world. Take a look at Mirror. This is the way it describes itself[1]:

> Joining Mirror does not only make you a community member. It makes you a co-owner of the platform. As a result, our platform is a sum of our contributors. While we're eager to grow Mirror to a monumental scale, we'll first be granting access on an individual basis to ensure a quality foundation.

On Mirror, writers can raise capital to do research and draw a monthly salary for expenses in advance from readers to write the book/article/novel they want to read. And these readers/investors get a bigger stake in the pie. Essentially, it makes the relationship more well defined. The outcome is tangible, the terms are well understood and the scope of failure is reduced.

Organizations, digital products, media and social networks like Mirror would play a crucial role as the Internet evolves in its third phase.

---

1 https://mirror.xyz/

CASE STUDY TO BETTER UNDERSTAND WEB 3.0

Taylor Swift and the Elusive Ownership Scandal

Swift moved to Nashville in 2004 as a fourteen-year-old to chase her dream of becoming a country pop star. Soon after, she signed a record deal with Big Machine, a large music label. Its boss Scott Borchetta took a huge gamble on the then unproven singer, a gamble which paid almost $300 million. He paid a big cash advance in exchange for having ownership of the master recordings to her first six albums 'in perpetuity'—in other words, 'forever'.

This was a fairly common practice in the days before music streaming and social media changed the industry. Artists latched on to such deals because at that time, recording, distribution and marketing cost a ton of money. Usually artists could not afford it. Folks like Scott Borchetta behaved like VCs. They just needed a few of their gambles to pay off. Swift was Borchetta's career-defining bet.

Two other artists, Prince and George Michael, are examples of those who have taken on their record companies in the courts to varying degrees of success.

You may remember the very famous image of Prince with 'slave' written on his cheek. The tabloids had a field day with that, and there was almost zero sympathy for the artist. Now with social media, you get the undiluted un-spun message from the artists; they don't need the mass media to get their message and their frustrations across.

Today, things are radically different. All Swift fans get to hear directly from her. Who do you think they will believe? The artist they adore or the shrewd millionaire profiting of the creative output of a beloved singer?

Web 3.0 is about winning back that ownership. It is about how we interact with value and the direct connection between creators and consumers, obfuscating the gatekeepers.

Web 1.0, 2.0 and 3.0 are critical concepts to keep in mind as we think of the passion economy. Older millennials have interacted with all three phases of the Internet, but the Gen Zs are born into the third, revolutionary phase online. The rules are not preordained. They are being written as products evolve. The Gen Zs are creators, investors, consumers and policymakers of the Web 3.0 platforms. An exciting new era is about to see the light of day.

NETWORK CAPITAL AND WEB 3.0

Network Capital will be co-created, co-owned and co-run by our community members in the long run. I plan to use the funding and strategic support from Facebook to advance systems and structures which will get Network Capital ready for Web 3.0 world. While the exact road map is still being figured out, given below are some ideas for building equitable and inclusive communities. It is not an exhaustive list. I have picked three ideas on which I have collected significant amount of data over the years.

Community Design to Create a Level Playing Field

Creating a level playing field in any community involves creating a safe space for everyone. Out of our 100,000+ community members, more than 50 per cent are women. This didn't just happen on its own. We designed communication—both internal and external— in a way that women found a safe space online to learn with and from peers from other sectors, countries, industries and career aspirations. Through our weekly newsletters, podcasts, masterclasses and CBCs, we constantly reiterated the importance of gender parity to the future of Network Capital. With time, the message started to stick and people started thinking of our community as a gender-neutral platform to network and learn. The larger insight here is that community design needs to be intentional from the beginning; it can't be an afterthought.

Business Model Adaptation

Network Capital is a subscription-based community. One way to ensure that affordability does not deter economically disempowered students and young professionals to join is variable pricing. Through the funds from Facebook and our endowment fund, we have now made Network Capital need-blind. If someone can't afford our subscription fee but has the hunger to learn, we provide up to 100 per cent scholarship.

In our school and cohort-based fellowships, there are hundreds of students and young professionals who are attending classes free of cost. We plan to scale this access programme further and believe that it will be an important step towards bridging the talent–opportunity mismatch.

Scale Purposefully: Forget Cultural Fit, Seek Cultural Contribution

The question of scale needs to be addressed by every community. Even the most efficiently run communities tend to optimize for cultural fit, that is, seek individuals who are like others in the network. That is a mistake. Culture must evolve and adapt with time, space and demographic shifts.

Once Network Capital created its school, thousands of teenagers joined the community. Their engagement norms were different from existing community members; they used technology differently and wanted different outcomes. Designing digital products and experiences tailored to them was one of the most important things we did in 2021. Integrating teenagers within the Network Capital ecosystem helped strengthen our culture by making it more inclusive.

Web 3.0 will be a unique opportunity to redefine the role of communities in the economic life. With the right structural interventions and platforms, participants and policymakers can make co-owned, co-run and co-created communities the norm. Such communities will be relatively more equitable and egalitarian.

Their members will have real skin in the game, that is, equity and ability to influence key decisions. Web 3.0 communities might just make both Karl Marx and Adam Smith excited about the future.

This book was written in the middle of the global pandemic. I relocated to a different country, made my side hustle my full-time job and experienced the life of a digital nomad. Lenin once said, 'There are decades when nothing happens, and there are weeks when decades happen.' I think that all of us now have an intimate understanding of what he meant.

From Lenin, now let us head to Adam Smith and Karl Marx to figure out the future of work.

WEB 3.0 AND THE PRIMER TO METAVERSE

What is metaverse?

Science fiction has played a pivotal role in the evolution of technology. The term 'metaverse' was coined by writer Neal Stephenson in his book *Snow Crash* way back in 1992. He described a virtual world experienced by users equipped with augmented reality (AR) glasses. His idea was taken a step further in *Ready Player One* by Ernest Cline. Cline conceptualized a fully formed immersive digital world which exists way beyond the world of atoms we inhabit. When these ideas were first advanced, a small segment of techies gravitated towards it. Others ignored it as things seemed far-fetched. At a time when the Internet was barely known, very few people had the foresight to visualize immersive experiences.

Three decades out, almost all major tech companies are trying to shape this elusive techno-utopian vision.

On 28 October 2021, Mark Zuckerberg published a founder's letter explaining the evolution and rebranding of Facebook and all sister applications into something called Meta. To understand what it means, you need to go back and read about the history of the Internet, especially Web 3.0. Given below is a quick refresher. These are relatively new concepts so I thought of mentioning them a few times in the book.

The first era of the web, or Web 1.0, was about how we process and consume information. Yahoo, Netscape, Craigslist, AOL were Web 1.0 companies. Google 'won' this era by democratising information and building a solid advertisement-driven business model on top of it. The second era of the internet, Web 2.0, gave birth to platforms that enable interaction, giving us Facebook, Instagram, Twitter, Reddit, LinkedIn, etc. Information, goods, and services were brought under the same umbrella. People started taking cabs, going on trips and dates, and building work partnerships with strangers. Enter Web 3.0. A new type of digital product has started gaining traction around the world, one that is co-owned, co-created, and co-run. This constitutes the third era of the Internet and is defined by decentralisation, declining trust in institutions and a new way of looking at value creation and value capture.

Metaverse sits at the intersection of Web 3.0, AR and the blockchain. In the Web 1.0 and 2.0 era, we could only enjoy the wonders of the Internet through a browser or app. Metaverse creates a more immersive experience which Zuckerberg describes as the next evolution of social technology: 'Metaverse is an embodied internet that you're inside of rather than just looking at. We call this the metaverse, and it will touch every product we build.'

Zuckerberg adds,

The defining quality of the metaverse will be a feeling of presence—like you are right there with another person or in another place. Feeling truly present with another person is the ultimate dream of social technology. That is why we are focused on building this.

While Meta, Microsoft, Apple, etc., are gunning to play the leading role in the evolution of the metaverse, it is clear that no one company should have a monopoly in this space. This is perhaps the most important sentence in Zuckerberg's letter:'The metaverse will be built by creators and developers making new experiences and digital items that are interoperable and unlock a massively larger creative economy than the one constrained by today's platforms and their policies.'

As someone who is writing a book on the passion economy and the creator revolution, I was energized with the explicit mention of the term in the Facebook founder's letter. I see teachers creating immersive classroom experiences in the metaverse, gamers building participatory experiences for players, and tinkerers and builders conducting rapid prototypes of their designs. Education, entertainment, commerce, manufacturing, practically every industry will have to chart out a new strategy in order to be relevant in this world.

I found *Vanity Fair*'s Nick Bolton's example the most vivid in terms of the stream of possibilities he advances.

In a world where the metaverse exists, rather than hosting a weekly meeting on Zoom with all of your coworkers, you could imagine meeting in a physical representation of your office, where each person looks like a digital version of themselves, seated at a digital coffee table drinking digital artisanal coffee and snacking on digital donuts. If that sounds a bit boring, you could meet somewhere else, perhaps in the past, like in 1776 New York City, or in the future, on a spaceship, or at the zoo, on another planet—if it made sense for the meeting, of course. You could choose not to be yourself, but rather some form of digital avatar you picked up at the local online NFT swap meet, or at a virtual Balenciaga store. You could dress like a bunny rabbit to go to the meeting. A dragon. A dead dragon. And that's just one measly little meeting. Imagine what the rest of the metaverse might look like.

You could play first-person shooter video games in the metaverse, that look like they're in real life. You could take a British history class taught by a digital representation of

King George III, or learn about the theory of relativity from Albert Einstein himself. You could attend a TED Talk, or give one, or go to church. You could hook up your exercise bike to race against Maurice Garin in the Tour de France. Or your running machine to race against Usain Bolt at the Olympics (and lose). You could go to the zoo. You could be an animal at the zoo. Visit the Louvre. Le Mans. The International Space Station. You could go for a walk on Mars. Neptune. Float in space. Play 'red light, green light' with your friends in Squid Game. You could go shopping, trying on outfits that once you pay for, are actually mailed to your house. You could go to a theme park and ride the world's biggest roller coaster and maybe even throw up in real life.

THREE THINGS TO KEEP IN MIND

You need to dive deep into the metaverse: No matter what you do, you will have to contextualize your role to the changes in your industry. Now would be a good time to start. Try and imagine what your role would look like in the next five years. You may not be accurate, but attempting to project your future will empower you to ask the right questions. The good news is that both poets and quants will have a role to play. You just need to figure out what the optimum for your skills, interests and curiosities would be. Get a head start and let your imagination fly.

The future isn't preordained: Even giant companies are trying to figure things out. No one really knows how things will pan out, but tinkering around to explore your career–product–market fit would be useful.

It won't be easy: Sure the techno-utopian future sounds alluring, but getting there needs concerted effort and collaboration among techies, policymakers, creators, artists and philosophers. Typically, such collaboration takes alignment of different incentives and objectives. Negotiating this divergence will define the new normal of the 21st century.

CONCLUDING THOUGHTS

In a Davos panel discussion I had once organized, Microsoft CEO Satya Nadella concluded by saying that if we change the way we see the world, we change the world we see. Today, with the metaverse revolution in play, it is time to reimagine and review our world of work with a fresh perspective.

'Gradually, then suddenly'. These lines from Ernest Hemingway's novel *The Sun Also Rises* will likely be the way things pan out. Network Capital is there to help you navigate this transition, step by step, ferociously.

Twitter, Web 3.0 and the New CEO

How is the future of media changing?

There is significant excitement about Indian origin CEO Parag Agrawal taking over the reins of Twitter from the co-founder of the platform, Jack Dorsey. Parag joined the company as an engineer, rose to become the CTO and is known to be one of the most trusted confidantes of Dorsey. They both share deep conviction about the power of cryptocurrency, and that partly explains this surprising and unexpected decision by the CEO of a company which did very well in the pandemic, added a range of exciting products, acquired a bunch of companies and cloned Clubhouse's audio feature with breakneck speed. Why did Jack Dorsey resign and what does this mean for the future of media?

Let's explore it, starting with various theories circulating around the tech world.

1. **Elliott Management:** In 2020, Elliott Management, an activist-investor hedge fund, acquired a 4 per cent stake in Twitter, gained a board seat, and began a public campaign to push Dorsey out as CEO. According to them, Dorsey treated Twitter

like a side hustle (he is also the CEO of fintech company Square which is valued significantly higher than Twitter). Once Elliott Management got the board seat, they set aggressive growth targets for Dorsey to meet. They wanted 20 per cent growth rate in 2020 and greater market share and increased revenue growth. One criticism Twitter has always faced is that it is an excessively under-monetized product. Despite its utility and popularity, its revenues are paltry compared to competitors. Dorsey had to demonstrate progress of all parameters set by Elliott Management and their partner in plans to oust Dorsey, private equity firm Silver Lake (***Silver Lake was a big ally to Michael Dell in his plans to take the company public and back to being privately held, and changing course again). While Dorsey's resignation letter suggests that the decision to quit was his, it is possible that investors with board seats had a role to play. You don't need to worry much about the speculation stories, just keep in mind that CEOs of public companies need to keep a wide range of stakeholders satisfied—customers, analysts, board members and market—in addition to thinking about the future of the industry.

2. **Changing personal priorities:** Leading two publicly traded companies is challenging. It is possible that Dorsey got tired of trying to placate all the stakeholders and decided to focus singularly on Square. Critics of Dorsey suggest that the key reason for Twitter being under-monetized was lack of focus. Twitter tried to be too many things to too many people, resulting in confusion among product teams, customers and partners.

In 2020, Dorsey alluded to the fact that he wanted to spend most of his time in Africa, going forward. Again, investors and employees were baffled by his statement. Ultimately, he decided to not act on it, but it was indicative of someone in the mid of redesigning his life. It is a tad unfair to obsessively analyse a leader's personal choices as long as they are delivering, but you often have to trade your personal space for communal responsibilities.

3. **Web 3.0 and a more decentralized Twitter:** I wrote about the history of the Internet and the future of inclusive communities for the Observer Research Foundation. Web 3.0 refers to the emergence of a new type of digital product which is co-owned, co-created and co-run by community members. This constitutes the third era of the Internet and is defined by decentralization, declining trust in institutions and a new way of looking at value creation and value capture.

In 2019, Jack Dorsey shared six key points which give us a glimpse of how Twitter was thinking about reinventing itself in the Web 3.0 era.

a. Twitter is funding a small independent team of up to five open source architects, engineers and designers to develop an open and decentralized standard for social media. The goal is for Twitter to ultimately be a client of this standard.

b. Twitter was so open early on that many saw its potential to be a decentralized Internet standard, like SMTP (email protocol). For a variety of reasons, all reasonable at the time, we took a different path and increasingly centralized Twitter. But a lot has changed over the years.

c. First, we're facing entirely new challenges and centralized solutions are struggling to meet. For instance, centralized enforcement of global policy to address abuse and misleading information is unlikely to scale over the long term without placing far too much burden on people.

d. Second, the value of social media is shifting away from content hosting and removal, and towards recommendation algorithms directing one's attention. Unfortunately, these algorithms are typically proprietary, and one can't choose or build alternatives, Yet.

e. Third, existing social media incentives frequently lead to attention being focused on content and conversation which sparks controversy and outrage, rather than conversation which informs and promotes health.

f. Finally, new technologies have emerged to make a decentralized approach more viable. Blockchain points to a series of decentralized solutions for open and durable hosting, governance and even monetization. Much work has to be done, but the fundamentals are there.

Since 2019, Twitter has been working behind the scene to launch a new kind of blockchain-powered social network, fully recognizing that it may not be profitable in the short term.

Agrawal, like his predecessor Dorsey, is a big believer in crypto. His shared world view, deep technical skills and awareness of key policy issues about social network design would surely have added to strengthening his candidature for the top job.

Putting It All Together

Parag Agrawal is obviously a sharp guy who has done incredibly well for himself, but leading a public company is a different ball game all together. So far, he has largely worked alone or in small teams providing counsel to Dorsey. Now he will need to reinvent how he works, how he presents himself to the market and how he keeps investors, customers and partners happy. Dorsey will not be on the board of Twitter much longer, so in a way he will have a fresh start but time will tell whether he is able to 'hit refresh' like Satya Nadella did when he took over Microsoft.

What does this mean for the future of media and social networks?

In a sense, Twitter is the media. Stories often break on Twitter before being latched onto by other news outlets. With the evolution of trust from being institutional to P2P, power of telling stories rests with individuals. Twitter played a pivotal role in helping such individuals build one-person media empires. A case in point is Ben Thompson.

By becoming one of the best distribution channels, Twitter propelled the Web 2.0 era, captured some of the economic value but left a large chunk of it on the table. With the launch of its subscription-based offering, newsletter services, audio chats, etc., Twitter built a range of tools to monetize and better serve its users.

With the momentum in place, a new full-time leader (after long) and moving towards building a decentralized social network, it is positioned well for the third wave of the Internet. Media is about to see a new phase of innovation and realignment as well.

One direction Twitter can take is to build more creator tools and take a small chunk of creator earnings. As of today, when you tweet something, it is on Twitter's territory. Its algorithm becomes stronger, and it makes advertising dollars by pointing you to things you may buy.

In the Web 3.0 era, you could use Twitter to create content; invite collaborators, supporters and patrons; create an income; and distribute content ownership and profit. In a way, Twitter's leverage will reduce, as it won't be the omnipotent platform it used to be, but by carving out space for greater transparency, clearer regulation and shared ownership, it could make way for a better Internet which is driven by values rather than clickbait content.

Advertising will still be important in the times to come, but the bulk of media revenues will come from subscriptions, co-ownership, investing and merchandising. Successful media companies in the 21st century will need to partake of rigorous world-building where the norms will be decided not based on what an individual or an organization thinks but on transparent rules of engagement.

CHAPTER 16

MARX, ADAM SMITH AND PART-TIME RETIREMENTS

It will be possible 'to hunt in the morning, fish in the afternoon, rear cattle in the evening, criticize after dinner ... without ever becoming hunter, fisherman, herdsman, or critic.'

Seems like a passion economy manifesto, right?

Believe it or not, this quote comes from Karl Marx, who famously said that communism is the solution to the riddle of history and knows itself as this solution.

Marx's views on work are starkly opposite of Adam Smith's, the father of modern capitalism who made a compelling case for hyperspecialization as the tool for economic progress. Marx worried that such specialization will make work devoid of meaning, as people would not be able to connect their micro inputs with macro outputs.

Some of that rings a bell even today. Most, if not all, of us have had some jobs where we were super busy doing something that didn't matter. Marx's explanation would have been that we got so specialized in doing something so narrow that we lost sight of the bigger picture.

WHY CONSERVATIVES GET KARL MARX VERY, VERY WRONG

In the quote above, Marx seems to be describing two critical components of work in the largely capitalist 21st century:

1. Portfolio of careers
2. Passion economy

MARX AND MILLENNIALS

Instead of chasing one standardized career path, millennials and Gen Zs are likely to tinker, experiment, think and rethink career choices multiple times during their work life.

A software engineer who quits their job at Google to write poetry in the mornings, run an Indie cafe in the afternoon, learn Japanese in the evening and serve as a tech consultant at night would no longer be the exception. Such career pivots will become the norm, and side hustles will be democratized.

Freelancing will no longer be expected to be free. In fact, it will emerge as the career of choice, especially for women. In her latest *The Atlantic* piece, 'The Professional Women Who Are Leaning Out', Olga Khazan argues that some women have been so worn down by the competing stressors of the pandemic that they welcome the shift to fewer paid working hours.

> The majority of Dutch women work part-time, and nearly 45 per cent of Swiss women do. By American standards, these women lead lives of enviable slowness. In a 2010 article for *Slate*, Jessica Olien, a writer living in the Netherlands, described neighbors who spent the workweek 'playing sports, planting gardens, doing art projects, hanging out with their children, volunteering, and meeting their family friends.' As one study on this topic cheerily concluded, 'Our results suggest that part-time jobs are what most Dutch women want.'[1]

There is a catch though.

'But Dutch women pay a price for this freedom: They are less likely than American women to be managers. And all over the world, part-time work tends to convey less prestige and lower pay.'

---

1 https://www.theatlantic.com/politics/archive/2021/05/why-dont-more-american-moms-work-part-time/618741/

This may be the case today, but in the future, the demand for flexible, output-driven work is bound to rise—not only among women but also among men.

CHANGING RELATIONSHIP WITH WORK

In their book *The 100-year Life: Living and Working in an Age of Longevity*, Lynda Gratton and Andrew Scott make three key points:

- First, people have a real shot at living up to or more than 100 years.
- Second, the longevity of companies will shrink.
- Third, the whole concept of retirement and savings will change. The traditional three-stage life—full-time education leading to full-time work leading to full-time retirement—will give way to something a great deal more fluid, flexible and multi-staged.

Pandemics and emergencies accelerate history. There is no going back to the way things were. Work has changed. It was going to anyway. The year gone by accelerated everything.

With the trauma of the pandemic fresh in our minds, we are likely to recalibrate what matters to us most and why? Why do we work? Is work really about accomplishing goals one after the other?

These questions are personal, and each of us need to figure out our own answers. Let's explore the facts at hand. On average, we will have 60+ years to work. Can we really do 60 years at 10–12 hours/day? Some of us might, but most won't.

The old notion of earning enough by forty to forty-five years of age and retiring seems anachronistic. Do we really want to spend 50 years of our life doing nothing of value? No one needs that much chilling.

Perhaps we want to spend our lives pursuing our passions. Passion economy now enables people to make a decent living doing what they love, but burnout is so very common among creators.

Passions change, economies change and passion economy will change as well. To make sense of all this change, mini-retirements will be precious.

Moral of the story is that we will need multiple breaks—let's call them mini-retirements or incubation periods—to rethink, recharge and repivot. In a 60+ year work life, taking even a decade off seems plausible. It might be a smart strategic bet if we want to maintain our smarts, our focus and our drive to be the best version of our curious selves.

PUTTING IT ALL TOGETHER

Back in the day, Marx, a champion of communism, made a case for passion economy, the economic engine of the 21st-century capitalism. He was an advocate of people working to find meaning and fulfil a deeper purpose than just keeping the economic engine churning.

Some critics of Marx argue that he didn't really provide a viable alternative for economic growth, so his views are utopian at best. Today, however, Marx's vision for work can be coupled with technology tools such as Stripe, Zoom, YouTube, Facebook, Circle and Teachable to offer tangible economic prospects.

The 'leaning out' Olga describes in her article is essentially a demand for flexibility, ownership and career growth. Freelancing is one way to make it happen, but there are many alternate careers which are likely to be mainstreamed. There will be resistance, of course, but flexible and hybrid work on our own terms will become the norm.

Lastly, change will be accelerated, and we will need to make room for breaks and pauses to live a long, meaningful life where we take care of ourselves and our communities at large.

CHAPTER 17

MARX, ADAM SMITH AND BULLSHIT JOBS

In his *Song of Myself* published in 1855, American poet Walt Whitman remarked, 'I am large, I contain multitudes.' He may not have work in mind, but his statement does have implications for the all-pervasive generalist vs specialist debate of the 21st century. There are myriad interesting versions of ourselves which seldom get a chance to manifest at our jobs, internships and the way we carry on with our lives. We are quietly conscious of our unfulfilled destinies and wonder if there could be more to our lives than the mandates of our punishing work schedules and plans to live our lives.

The strongest critique against tinkering and dabbling with our various selves comes from the Scottish economist and philosopher, Adam Smith. In *The Wealth of Nations* (1776), he explained that the division of labour premised on deep specialization was essential for augmenting productivity in the capitalist system. He explained with great panache the brilliant efficiency that can be brought about if everyone focused on one narrow task and stopped indulging in what Walt Whitman's 'multitudes' are.

Adam Smith was prescient in many ways. Doing one narrow job made perfect economic sense in the industrial age. It unleashed great economic productivity, but to some extent it came at the cost of experimentation, tinkering and curiosity essential to the human soul.

One of Adam Smith's most serious readers was Karl Marx, who agreed with Smith's analysis as applied to the economic system. Where he differed with Smith was the overall efficacy of such a system focused on hyperspecialization. Marx said that we dull our lives and cauterize our talents by specializing without knowing why.

As you can tell, both Smith and Marx made sense. There was, at least in the industrial era, a clash between the demands of the employment market and the free, wide-ranging potential of our work lives.

In 1930, John Maynard Keynes, who we have discussed in great detail earlier, predicted that by the end of the century, technology would have advanced so comprehensively that we would all be working 15-hour work weeks. Well technology has advanced much more than Keynes's wildest imagination, but hardly anyone works 15 hours a week today.

One theory proffered by London School of Economics and Political Science anthropologist David Graeber is the emergence of 'bullshit jobs'. He asks: Why did the Keynesian utopia never materialize? The standard response to Graeber is the exponential increase in consumerism. Given the choice between less hours and more toys and pleasures, we have collectively chosen the latter.

Graeber says that it is as if some powerful force out there is making up pointless jobs just for the sake of keeping us madly busy. In old socialist states like Soviet Union where employment was considered both a right and a sacred duty, being busy was equated to doing actual work. It was only too common to find three clerks earning a pittance employed to sell a piece of meat. Tired of the woeful inefficiency, market competition was supposed to fix it, but even according to the latest surveys carried out in countries ranging from the United Kingdom to Sweden to America to India, somewhere between 35 and 60 per cent of employees believe that their work makes zero difference. There is clearly a crisis of meaning, even though these 'bullshit jobs' pay the bill for the time being.

The answer, Graeber believes, isn't economic: It is moral and political. The ruling class/elites figured out that a happy and productive population with free time on their hands is a moral danger.

I believe that the time for 'bullshit jobs' is coming to an end. Coronavirus-induced pressures on economies will lead to a massive disruption in our work lives. Passion economy is not only a window to new kind of employment but also an emergence of an operating system where people will have to stop being busy for the heck of it, pause to figure out what problem really needs their attention and then plan to create more meaningful jobs that both pay the bill and propel us to explore our 'multitudes'.

In this pursuit, the ability to reinvent ourselves will be the most important skill. And it goes without saying that reinvention is not easy as a solitary pursuit. We will need our collective networks, combined resilience and a mind which questions pre-established systems which make no sense today.

It is hard to say whether Whitman, Smith, Marx or Keynes will prevail, but perhaps a new system will be cocreated by all of us. That is why Network Capital is committed to offering a full stack platform to all ideas, insights and intelligence which is personalized at scale. Technology and the much touted AI will no doubt be an important factor, but it will only make sense if contextualized at the human level not only for the big enterprises and big governments but also for micro-networks, micro-communities, micro-institutions and micro-cultures.

We don't have all the answers, but we are surely excited by the myriad possibilities which can be unleashed when we bring the smartest, most driven people on the planet to empower each other to do more, achieve more and create new avenues for those in urgent needs—the marginalized. It will happen in phases.

CHAPTER 18

DIFFERENCE BETWEEN INFLUENCERS AND CREATORS

In March 2021, the UK Parliament announced the launch of a public enquiry into 'influencer culture,'[1] calling for experts to help confused government officials understand what exactly influencers do.

Defining an influencer turns out to be harder than one would have assumed. Law scholars started with baseline contractual questions; business academics wanted to refer to the quality and effectiveness of their influence; computer scientists looked to influencers' relationships with algorithms.

In terms of tasks, 'influencer' and 'creator' aren't really different. Both are largely one-person companies which are independent and specialize in the production of content for social media platforms. Both influencers and creators are paid in similar ways, through a mix of platform revenue-sharing schemes, sponsorships and fan-funded models like Patreon. Why, then, are they made to sound like different things?

Of late, the term 'influencer' is referred to as someone who typically specializes in creating advertorial content with the clear intent of selling products. Creators, by contrast, get a lot more respect, as the assumption is that they are driven by the pursuit of art. Their content is considered more authentic. Revenue is a by-product, not the core purpose of their activities.

A 2019 *WIRED* piece by Emma Grey Ellis argued that women are more likely to be called influencers and men are more likely to be called creators.

1 https://committees.parliament.uk/work/1126/influencer-culture/

According to Ellis, this gendered distinction between influencers and creators shapes power dynamics in the industry. Influencers, despite their massive reach, are considered frivolous and lacking substance because they don't create anything new. They sit below creators within the value hierarchy of Internet culture, despite the fact that creators feature themselves in their work and make money through advertorial content. Creators are accidentally commercialized.

In an article for *The Atlantic*, Taylor Lorenz rejected Ellis's gendered thesis—'that men are more likely to self-identify as creators, while women more often call themselves influencers'—as incomplete. For her, corporate branding is a more defining factor.

YouTube started growing its partner programme over a decade ago by pouring its marketing and advertising might into branding its top content producers—both women and men—as 'creators'. The YouTube creator programme gave wings to the creator movement by creating stars beyond what we usually saw on television (TV).

Soon after, the term 'creator' was co-opted by other platforms like Tumblr to describe the burgeoning group of bloggers who were gathering scores of followers on the sites. In Lorenz's view 'influencer' stands against 'creator' as a 'platform agnostic' term which is applied to newer, up-and-coming content producers with less experience, less early-adopter cache and less legitimacy.

In my experience speaking to thousands of independent media professionals running one-person companies, I have seen a clear move towards the term 'creator'. In the last two years, I have not come across a single person who introduced themselves as an influencer. One person I interviewed for the book said that she created content. Influencing others was a by-product, a by-product she craved for, nonetheless.

An influencer can create compelling original content, and a creator can influence millions, but as of writing the book, the term 'creator' has gained serious traction as a profession, while influencer has lost sheen.

At this point, it might be worth exploring the roots of the word 'profession'. To be a professional is not a wild goose chase of a designation or power. It is to join a profession. Once we join, we 'profess'—declare publicly—that we intend to perform our craft to serve others.

A professional joins a tribe. As new kinds of professions spring up in the passion economy, one of the first things professionals will do is to find like-minded individuals on a similar path and a sense of community. Once they do, emphasis will soon shift to evangelizing their craft to get respect.

Just a few years back, it would have been unimaginable for young professionals to say that their profession is YouTube vlogging or TikTok content creation at a family gathering. Today, millennials wear it as a badge of honour.

This subtle shift can also be attributed to changing paradigms in the society. Wild successes of many start-ups, multiple relatable role models, social media and increasing household income of middle-class households have collectively created an ecosystem where influencers are tolerated and creators are respected.

What is interesting about creators is the wide range of content they are creating. There is education, travel, technology, food and beverage, news analysis, film and sports. Practically anything you can think of, there are a few creators who have made it huge.

SECTION 3

ALTERNATE CAREERS, PASSION ECONOMY PLATFORMS AND THE NEW WORLD OF WORK

CHAPTER 19

SOLVING UNEMPLOYMENT BY PLAYING VIDEOGAMES

Almost 0.5 billion people[1] lost jobs during the pandemic. Unemployment rate in the Philippines[2] crossed the level of unemployment during the Great Depression. There seemed to be no recourse in the short term—the government was clueless, the private sector was in shambles, tourism had come to a standstill and there seemed to be no hope apart from hoping against hope for things to get better. Surprisingly, video games came to the rescue of young Filipinos.

Axie Infinity is a blockchain-based game which draws heavily from Pokémon: Players form a team of three creatures called Axies with various skills, which you compete with against either computer-controlled opponents or other real-life players.[3]

Players control Axies, fantasy creatures based on axolotls and Mexican walking fish which can regenerate. The game's title is a reference to this quality and to the fact that players can create infinite types of Axies on the platform.

The Axies live in an environment called the Terrarium, where players can feed their team of Axies, take care of them and direct them to engage in battles. They can also visit a marketplace to buy and sell Axies.

Essentially, Axie Infinity is a 'play-to-earn' game. The key focus for gamers is to play to get the chance to earn tokens or breed monster non-fungible tokens (NFTs), which they can sell and earn real money from. Basically, the goal is to win battles with

1 https://www.globalpolicyjournal.com/projects/gp-e-books/alpha-century-viral-world-raisina-young-fellows-speak
2 https://digitalnative.substack.com/p/how-people-in-the-philippines-are
3 https://digitalnative.substack.com/p/how-people-in-the-philippines-are

your Axie so that you earn an in–game resource called Small Love Potion (SLP) which can first be exchanged for the cryptocurrency ETH and eventually converted to real-world cash.

WHO CREATED AXIE INFINITY?

Trung Nguyên started his career at the age of twenty years, serving as the chief technical officer and a co-founder of Lozi, a popular social network for food bloggers which received investment from Golden Gate Ventures in 2015.

As it often happens in start-ups, the co-founders fell out and Nguyên left the company. Thereafter, he spent nearly three years in Ho Chi Minh City working as a software engineer for Anduin Transactions, a Silicon Valley-based investment platform. Around that time, he got interested in the crypto world via CryptoKitties, one of the world's first blockchain-based games, where players bought, sold and bred virtual cats which were unique by virtue of being validated by Ethereum network's architecture. He was hooked and soon realized that he could create a similar block-chain-powered play to earn game himself. With the support of his friends, he got the company off the ground.

The game's beta version was released in mid-2018 and turned out to be a massive hit, generating enough cash to pay everyone and create a healthy runway.

AXIE INFINITY'S ANSWER TO THE UNEMPLOYMENT CRISIS

This blockchain-based game has empowered an entire generation of Filipinos to venture into the passion economy and create a meaningful living doing something they enjoy. All this when literally every other seemed to be shut.

Not only in major cities like Manila but also in small villages, millennials and Gen Zs started making double the minimal wage by first familiarizing themselves with the Axie Infinity ecosystem and then finetuning their skills to win. This turned out to be baptism by fire. Anyone playing the game needs to get a basic understanding of blockchain and cryptocurrency. Playing the game is both educational and fun. More importantly, it makes the participants connect with the larger digital economy where one does not need to be defined by one's physical location.

Axie Infinity has become an age-agnostic movement which started out with teens and younger millennials but soon spread to boomers. There are digital records of entire families, including grandparents, becoming gamers and making a solid living together. This is perhaps the 21st-century equivalent of quality family time.

Thirty per cent of all Axie Infinity users are Filipinos, and the game has become so vital to survival there that everything from medical expenses to education and training expenses for families comes from this blockchain-powered videogame economy. Countries like Lebanon with flailing governments and social structures should consider exploring avenues like Axie Infinity. Waiting for the systems and procedures to be set right may be too little too late.

THE AXIE INFINITY UPFRONT COST CHALLENGE

One problem with Axie Infinity is that upfront cost is high. An Axie costs about $100 today, and you need three Axies to play the game—that's $300 in upfront cost or almost two times the monthly wage for many Filipinos. Realizing this problem, a company called Yield Guild Games (YGG) has started buying up and leasing game assets across various online games, including Axies. YGG has hired community managers to raise awareness about the leasing programme and laid out clear systems in place. Their goal is simple—to get as many people as possible to play the game and keep 30 per cent of the money for themselves (20% for the community managers and 10% for the platform). It is a win-win situation for everyone involved. Without their leasing programme, most Filipinos would not have the upfront capital to play the game.

YGG also offers training to upskill the gamers. In a way, YGG is a university, a leasing company and a fintech platform rolled into one. In technical terms, it is a decentralized autonomous organization (DAO)—essentially a community-owned organization built on a shared set of blockchain-enforced guidelines. YGG's vision is to allow anyone to earn income through play-to-earn games across the metaverse. It recently raised capital from a16z, a premier VC firm in Silicon Valley.

Play-to-earn games started because people needed cash, and unemployment was huge. Today, however, the digital economies are becoming a lot more nuanced with jobs like fashion designers for digital avatars emerging. It is a phenomenal start for labour to be as free flowing as capital. In the post-pandemic world, you can be sitting in Beirut, Mumbai or Manila, and still work at a metaverse company in Tokyo.

What's most exciting about play-to-earn games is that they incentivize players who have skills rather than those who have money, thereby creating a relatively more meritocratic digital economy.

CHAPTER 20

THE MYSTERY OF ONLYFANS: INDUSTRY DISRUPTOR OR SLEAZE PLATFORM?

If you haven't heard of OnlyFans, it is understandable. It is a privately held company which makes tens of billions of dollars in gross merchandise value and billions of dollars in net revenue. It was set up just 5 years back in 2016 by Tim Stokely and has more than 130 million users. It rose to prominence and popularity by providing a platform for content creators, largely from the adult entertainment industry, to connect with their audience, build a community and create a business on their terms.

ONLYFANS MILLIONAIRES

OnlyFans stars like Aella have made multiple millions of dollars building on the features of the product. She writes essays, shares her business model strategies on well-known podcasts like Means of Creation and has built a massive community of followers who pay to join her network for greater access.

Pornography is exploitative. Is OnlyFans changing that?

Mia Khalifa is a Lebanese-American woman who had a brief stint with the porn industry and achieved worldwide stardom and unwanted fame which completely changed her life. In no time, she became the most-searched adult entertainment star on the planet.

As it turned out, Khalifa received a paltry $12,000 for about a dozen exploitative shoots. This happened over three months which left her traumatized, and she left the industry for good in 2015. In the pornography industry, almost all profits from subscriptions and advertisement revenue go to the production companies. OnlyFans is attempting to change that by letting the adult entertainers set the price, define the terms of access and keep majority of net monetary gains for themselves.

Without getting into a moral argument, it is an alternative worth reflecting upon not only for the industry but also for the implications for the creator/passion economy.

POWER TO THE PERSON

As newsletter writer Packy McCormick puts it in his piece 'Power to the Person',[1]

> We're on the precipice of a creative explosion, fueled by putting power, and the ability to generate wealth, in the hands of the people. Armed with powerful technical and financial tools, individuals will be able to launch and scale increasingly complex projects and businesses. Within two decades, we will have multiple trillion-plus dollar publicly traded entities with just one full-time employee, the founder.
>
> That sounds bold, but it's kind of already happened: Bitcoin, which has no employees, crossed the $1 trillion mark.

ONLYFANS'S BUSINESS AND PRODUCT STRATEGY

OnlyFans's business and product strategy has been realizing the power of subscriptions in shaping the 21st-century creator economy. They figured out that both companies and individuals can run successful subscription-based services.

The company has enabled a wide range of professionals to productize themselves. Yes, a vast majority of the early adopters were from the adult entertainment industry but eventually major companies, entrepreneurs and creatives joined to leverage the vast popularity of the OnlyFans platform.

1 https://www.notboring.co/p/power-to-the-person

They realized that it could enable them to build a community and add a new revenue stream. The live streams, videos and pictures could be used for e-commerce and education as well. After all, if there is a community, adding a subscription layer on top is the way most businesses are going anyway.

WHY SUBSCRIPTIONS WORK? HISTORY AND RATIONALE

American rapper Kanye West is popularly called the first software as a service (SaaS) musician. In 2016, he launched *The Life Of Pablo*, an unfinished album, where he kept tweaking the lyrics based on the feedback from fans and constantly changed the order of songs. In Tech Speak, he launched a MVP and reimagined his customers into subscribers and creative participants.

Research shows that companies that run on subscription models grow their revenue more than nine times faster than S&P 500 firms. There are three reasons subscriptions work for businesses in the digital age.

First, they expand optionality for the customer. If customers aren't satisfied, switching to another service provider is straightforward.

Second, subscriptions transform transactions into meaningful relationships. Instead of focusing on one-time sales, entrepreneurs need to provide value over an extended period of time. This is a win-win scenario. Entrepreneurs work hard to understand unmet customer needs and figure out innovative means to provide services which go beyond the expectations of the underlying contract. This makes the service provider better and enhances customer surplus.

Lastly, subscriptions ease out the financial burden of customers. Instead of committing a sizable chunk of their savings to acquiring assets, they can avail the desired services for a fraction of the cost.

While subscriptions are not a new idea, ubiquitous Internet connectivity coupled with decreasing infrastructure cost and high levels of customer awareness have made subscriptions the perfect complements to businesses in the digital age.

In 2002, commenting on the decline of iTunes downloads, Steve Jobs said that the subscription model was bankrupt[2] and destined to fail. The same year, songwriter David Bowie made a far more prescient statement: 'Music subscriptions are going to become like running water of electricity.' While Jobs got several things right, he underestimated the power of subscriptions, the heart and soul of businesses in the digital age. Bowie saw what Jobs couldn't.

OnlyFans has enabled anyone selling anything online to create a subscription-based business. While there are other platforms which have the same functionality, OnlyFans took a strategic (although morally grey) approach to go after one industry where it would achieve a solid product–market fit.

THE FUNDRAISING CHALLENGE

Despite significant growth and revenue, OnlyFans has struggled to raise funds. Institutional investors are uncomfortable with funding a platform which is largely associated with adult entertainment. Also, payment providers like Mastercard and Visa have stringent rules about serving as a platform for adult content. Owing to these challenges, OnlyFans recently decided to ban such content.

The ban didn't last long. The backlash from early adopters was so strong that the company was forced to change its decision. The future isn't entirely clear. Maybe the platform will go down the decentralized cryptocurrency path, making it less dependent on existing financial institutions. Maybe it will try and create its own transaction platform.

Given the sheer size and popularity of the company, it is unlikely to go down without a fight. For a privately held company which spends barely anything on advertising, what it has accomplished is noteworthy. Some might argue that it even empowered a massive number of adult entertainment professionals who were exploited financially and otherwise, others might disagree and say that it

2 https://www.theverge.com/2015/6/8/8744963/steve-jobs-jesus-people-dont-want-music-subscriptions

inflicted even more sleaze onto the world and made tons of money through the process.

You should feel free to arrive at your own conclusion. The reason I put this company forward was to highlight the power of individual creators, emerging business models and an offbeat company trying to change the dynamics of one of the oldest industries since the beginning of time.

CHAPTER 21

THE ECONOMICS OF NEWSLETTERS AND MILLIONAIRE NEWSLETTER WRITERS

In the past 15 years, more than 25 per cent of American newspapers have gone out of business. Those which have survived are smaller, weaker and more vulnerable to hostile acquisitions and takeovers. As of writing this book, 50 per cent of all daily newspapers in the United States are controlled by financial firms, according to an analysis by the *Financial Times*. The number is likely to grow.

These numbers are the cause for worry. Research suggests that when a local newspaper fades away, it tends to correspond with lower voter turnout, increased polarization, misinformation, corruption and a general erosion of civic engagement.

While the newspapers as institutions are unlikely to resurrect in the short term, newsletter writers are emerging as alternate voices in business, politics, culture and society. News is becoming unbundled, and people are beginning to trust individuals a lot more than institutions.

Ben Thompson got his MBA at Kellogg, worked at Microsoft and today lounges in Thailand/Southeast Asia writing a newsletter on technology trends, making more than $3 million in profits every year. He started by charging $100/year and at the last officially reported count in 2015, he had 2,000 monthly paying subscribers. It is a conservative estimate as Ben has not talked about numbers since 2015.

Ben's product hasn't changed. He has been consistent with his writing, and his writing has become better every week. He isn't focused on reporting every deal and every new product but expends all his energy filtering signal from noise.

Paul Jarvis, the author of *Company of One: Why Staying Small Is the Next Big Thing for Business,* explains that the future of business is being better, not bigger. Scale is a consequence, not the end goal. Like Ben Thompson, you can build a company of one where you can scale up revenue, fans, engagement quality and experiences without compounding payroll, expenses and stress levels.

Ben Thompson is a newsletter entrepreneur who runs a profitable company of one on his terms. Let's look at the financial viability of such newsletter entrepreneurs.

To make $100,000/year (~₹80 lakh/year), you need 800 subscribers paying $10/month.

To make $1 million/year (~₹8 crore/year), you need 8,000 subscribers paying $10/month.

NEWSLETTER ENTREPRENEUR VS MCKINSEY PARTNER

People who want to become McKinsey partners should do so and those inclined to become newsletter entrepreneurs should go right ahead. We do not suggest one over the other. We are a career intelligence community—our goal is to empower you with insights and mental models.

According to Morgan McKinley,[1] a junior partner at McKinsey in the United States makes between $0.5 million and $1 million every year.

Now compare the life of a McKinsey partner with the life of Ben Thompson. If you feel that Ben Thompson is an exception, think again.

So we should all start newsletters, right?

Starting a newsletter is simple. Two clicks and you are all set. Given below are some popular options:

- Ghost
- Substack

1 https://www.morganmckinley.com/au/article/how-much-can-partner-mckinsey-bcg-or-bain-actually-make

- TinyLetter
- Contentful
- Medium
- Revue

To be clear, there is nothing fundamentally new about newsletters. These are articles delivered to your inbox. There are minor tweaks in presentation and language but that is about it. The real power of newsletters lies in the community which organically builds up (it does in successful newsletters).

I spoke to one of the co-founders of Substack who explained that they had deliberately designed it to be a no-frills affair. GIFs and clips and colourful margins are distractions for many readers. More importantly, writers sometimes confuse presentation with substance.

Some of the most famous newsletter entrepreneurs such as Ben Thompson and Andrew Sullivan have simple, no-frills design which cuts the clutter and gets to the point. There is no/minimal advertising, and they are living reminders of why subscriptions are the future of all businesses.

Subscriptions are also straightforward to set up. You can use Stripe internationally and if your business is India focused, there are a bunch of local alternatives like Razorpay and Instamojo. So far so good.

So what is the hard part?

The biggest challenge of becoming a successful newsletter entrepreneur is knowing who you are writing for. You need to be able to surprise and delight your reader. If you don't remember the surprise–delight framework, it will be worth your while to read Elizabeth Gilbert's advice on great writing.

The next roadblock is community. Subscribers first come for the trust factor/brand of the newsletter entrepreneur and stay for the network or the community they have created. Community takes a while to build. It is a by-product of relentless hustle and fierce consistency.

Unless you are Mark Zuckerberg who can build a Facebook or Elizabeth Gilbert that your writing will make you an overnight sensation, you will need an organically grown community to become a successful newsletter entrepreneur. You can either start one and invest the years it takes to build or be part of one and create your category of one within it. The important thing to keep in mind is that no one will pay you a single dollar if there is a close alternative.

Lastly, consistency is a bottleneck. Starting a newsletter is easy. Writing daily/weekly/fortnightly is hard. There will always be a reason not to, and if such reasons keep cropping up, you should think long and hard before starting your newsletter.

IMPORTANT METRICS

Subscribers: Those who pay you for your offering

Open rates: Percentage of subscribers who open your email to read

Churn rate: Percentage of subscribers who unsubscribe

How to get started?

I recommend a trial period. Write for a reasonably well-established newsletter and ask for the above-mentioned metrics after 24 hours. If you are able to get 5 new paid subscribers with open rate of 35–40 per cent, you did great. It is a strong indicator that your content resonated with your community.

Repeat.

Do this thrice. If you enjoyed the process and felt a rush of adrenaline, you could consider starting a newsletter of your own. Once you start, consider bundling with other established newsletters. Competition is for losers. Collaboration creates a win–win scenario.

Amidst the COVID-19 pandemic, there has been a surge in the number and quality of newsletter entrepreneurs like Ben. Not everyone will go on to make millions of dollars, but many will be able to carve out a meaningful job which provides financial security.

The newsletter economy is blossoming, and newsletter platforms have been adding to their portfolio of products. Take a look at the acquisitions of Substack.

1. They are betting big on comic creators.
2. They acquihired Cocoon.
3. They acquired Letter.
4. They acquired People & Company.

What does all this mean?

Writing and creative expressions will be major economic engines in the times to come. Companies like Substack are building a portfolio of offerings to make the process of writing as simple as possible. While they aren't teaching writing, they are taking care of everything else. And who knows, they might just launch a CBC on writing, along the lines of Network Capital and Maven.

Morning Brew, another newsletter focused on business, is going down that route.

CHAPTER 22

HOW WRITING CAN PAVE THE WAY FOR VENTURE CAPITAL CAREERS

Andrew Chen is a General Partner at a16z, one of the world's leading VC firms. Recently, he led[1] the $20 million investment Maven, a platform which helps creators build CBCs. I also invested in Maven because cohorts and communities will be key pillars of the future of education. I see many areas of collaboration between Network Capital and Maven and hope that CBCs become the default mode of learning online.

You can read more about why I invested below in the later sections of the book.

I got a chance to meet him in the middle of writing this book and learned about his work, investment thesis and career at large.

Given below are some takeaways from our discussions and broad reflections on his career principles quite applicable to creators and passion economy builders.

Focus on identifying the problems that need you the most. Andrew graduated from the University of Washington with a degree in applied maths at the age of nineteen years. He was obviously great at maths but soon figured out that he was more interested in solving real-life problems than abstract research. Having that clarity helped him start his first entrepreneurial venture. He focused on exploring what he could solve uniquely based on his curiosity and skill set. Andrew was interested in consumer tech and consumer behaviour. That was what he ventured to solve.

Build something and try for a reasonable amount of time. Andrew worked on his first start-up for five years but despite the

1 https://techcrunch.com/2021/05/20/maven-series-a-a16z/

virality, strong funding from leading venture capitalists and millions of app downloads, it didn't quite achieve the product–market fit. He and his team soft landed at Uber, but it wouldn't be considered a ravishing success. The key point to remember is that he tried consistently for half a decade. One should pick carefully and stick diligently for career choices to reveal themselves. Jumping ship too quickly doesn't provide depth of learning required to bounce back stronger.

Treat every job you take as the most important job. Andrew led Uber's ride growth product teams which achieved hyperscale. He got this job because of his customer insights, product sense and willingness to go above and beyond his job description. A less discussed aspect of his time at Uber was his willingness to adapt to a different culture. Cultural change is hard to navigate after acquisitions. Andrew understood that his start-up was a very different ball game and he needed to change the strategy to make meaningful impact in his new role.

Reflect and write. He has been writing consistently for over a decade—successes, failures, reflections, market trends, observations and opinions. This led to strong awareness about his way of thinking. Andrew carved out a strong brand by the power of his words. His consistency helped compound his brand over time.

In fact, he got his job at a16z largely due to his writing. a16z co-founder Marc Andreessen sent him a cold email to talk about some of his blogs.

Marc obviously knew about his product and operations expertise but what helped create his category of one was his writing. At that time, there were very few techies who also wrote prolifically. a16z often refers to itself as a content company which monetizes through VC. Andrew was someone who created great content and had a following which amounts to access to deals, strong brand awareness and operating chops. Together it made him an ideal addition to the a16z team.

It was 2007 when Marc first wrote to him. Andrew got the a16z job in 2018, a good 11 years after. Great outcomes take a while to manifest.

When you are trying to venture into a new industry, it helps to demonstrate synergies with where you are trying to go. Andrew did that through writing. You could choose videos, audios, tweets or memos. Pick the format you feel most comfortable with and stick it out. The result will not be instant, but it will surely follow.

Study history and industry cycles. Andrew isn't a big proponent of advertisement-supported business models these days. To explain this, he often cites the evolution of click through rate in advertising from the early days of the Internet (which was a whopping 70%—70% of people clicked ads they saw) to the paltry 0.05 per cent today. At the hyperscale of Google, it works but will it work for newer companies, Andrew is uncertain.

More than the fact that he knows this, what strikes me is his ability to go back into history and explore trends from first principles. This is something that good investors and smart business folks do as well. To get a sense of the future, one often needs to dive deep into the past. It clarifies your thought process and helps uncover insights which can easily be overlooked.

Develop a clear point of view of the world. When you speak to Andrew, his clarity jumps out. He is able to explain why he believes what he believes—whether it is an opinion on politics or the way the ed-tech industry is evolving. You may disagree with his conclusion, but it is hard to argue with his rationale—again, the result of first principles thinking. I like the fact that he combines data with stories and observations.

He subscribes to the 'strong opinions weakly held' way of life. I noticed that he doesn't couch his opinion but is perfectly willing to change his mind. This became clear to me in a discussion where he was talking about a deal (I can't mention the name per his request).

Speak to others like you want to be spoken to. Our structured meeting time was one hour, but he hung out with a medium-sized group for three more hours. There I noticed that he was as interested in listening to others as he was in expressing his opinions. Everyone felt heard. I think each person who was there felt as if they were the most important person in the room. Sincerity cannot be faked. He was genuinely interested.

Connect meaningfully by asking thoughtful questions. Take a look at his note: 'I moved to the Bay Area in 2007, as a first time founder with a lot of energy and a lot of questions. I spent the first year meeting everyone I could, reading everything about tech, and writing down all that I was learning.'[2]

This hasn't changed even today. To write his book, he started by setting a goal of interviewing 20 founders. He ended up speaking to 200. His superpower? Asking great questions. Energy and enthusiasm aren't enough for building meaningful relationships. We need to learn the art of engaging people in questions they care about answering and know something about.

To do serious work, you don't need to be serious all the time. Andrew reads, travels, chills and doesn't take himself too seriously. He is purposeful about whatever he does but keeps things light for everyone around.

To conclude, I would just like to add that Andrew is amazing but you don't need to be like him. Be your best self and take inspiration from whatever you find relevant to your personality and your vision for life. Andrew has done pretty well in life not trying to imitate or impress anyone—just following his curiosity, finding his superpower and writing about his experiments consistently.

2 https://www.linkedin.com/pulse/update-im-joining-andreessen-horowitz-andrew-chen/?articleId=6369967616165056512

CHAPTER 23

SPOTIFY'S JOE ROGAN EXPERIMENT

Joe Rogan is an American stand-up comedian and TV host turned provocateur, who launched his podcast in 2009—among the first movers of the medium.

He invites a wide array of guests (some controversial), including actors, musicians, comedians, politicians, entrepreneurs (you might remember Elon Musk's on-set adventures) and conspiracy theorists on to the show.

Rogan has previously advocated for 'long-form media' and has 8.42 million subscribers to his YouTube channel.[1] (This will stop when the new Spotify deal kicks in. We will analyse it in this chapter.) He has a Reddit community with 500,000+ members, a Twitter with 6 million followers and an Instagram with 9.5 million followers.

He is among the most consumed media products on earth— with the power to shape cultures, politics and medical decisions. (He decided to weigh in on the coronavirus situation. It wasn't the smartest comment but accuracy isn't what he always optimizes for.)

FIRST MOVER ADVANTAGE

He began building the Joe Rogan Experience in 2009 with a microphone in his garage. Podcasts were unheard of at the time. Today, that experiment has evolved into a cultural phenomenal, downloaded 42 million times more than CNN in its best month.

Being an early adopter of YouTube helped Rogan get to 1,000 hard-to-find die-hard fans (you will remember our previous discussion on the subject).

1 https://www.bbc.com/news/entertainment-arts-52736364#:~:text=
Rogan%20has%20previously%20advocated%20for,new%20Spotify%20
deal%20kicks%20in)

Consistent effort paid off for Rogan. Fans found other fans through word of mouth, community started building and the show's appeal kept increasing bit by bit, play by play. This helped Rogan game the algorithms. There was barely any competition because he had created a category of one. (Remember Peter Thiel's golden rule: competition is for losers.)

CATEGORY OF ONE

Rogan differentiated himself by flipping conventional norms.

1. Episodes were two–three hours long.
2. Distribution was built into production design: YouTube's recommendation algorithm prioritizes videos with high percentage completion.
3. He knew how to mix quality content with reasonable doses of controversy. Simply put, he seemed interesting and 'real' to his followers.

SPOTIFY'S $100 MILLION JOE ROGAN EXPERIMENT

Rogan signed an exclusive deal with Spotify (a former adversary as Rogan never put his podcast there due to paltry advertising gains) for 100 million dollars. 'All' his podcast content will now disappear from all other platforms.

Let's analyse numbers.

If you don't like charts and numbers, remember this: Rogan makes 30 million dollars a year. Spotify will recover its 100 million dollar investment in 3 years and also make a ton of money converting Rogan's followers into paying subscribers.

Every company is a subscription company, including Spotify. Read my Mint article – https://lifestyle.livemint.com/news/talking-point/opinion-why-millennials-are-willing-to-swipe-right-on-subscription-models-11164145583425.html

In 2002, commenting on the decline of iTunes-style downloads, Steve Jobs said that the subscription model was bankrupt and destined to fail. The same year, songwriter and actor David Bowie made a far more prescient statement: 'Music subscriptions are going to become like running water of electricity.'

While Jobs got most things right, he underestimated the power of subscriptions, the heart and soul of businesses in the digital age. Perhaps Bowie saw what Jobs couldn't.

Even if 5 per cent (in all likelihood the number will be much higher) of Joe Rogan's followers subscribe to Spotify at $12/month, that is an annuity of $6 million.

Not only does Spotify recover its 100 million investment in 3 years, it adds an ever-increasing, reliable revenue stream to its mix.

Spotify's Masterstroke

The term 'masterstroke' is a bit of a joke in politics these days but indulge us in this context, please.

Since the deal was announced, Spotify's stock has risen by 11 per cent. Why?

1. Concrete strategy to grow paying subscribers
2. Unparalleled content acquisition
3. Podcasts are the fastest growing advertisement medium, growing 40 per cent in 2019 to $679 million in the United States alone. Media pundits say that Spotify could do for advertising on podcasts what Google did for advertising on the Internet.

It is a win-win situation for both Joe Rogan and Spotify—financially and strategically. More importantly, it is a noteworthy moment for content creators, micro-entrepreneurs and passion economy enthusiasts.

Now you can potentially become a billionaire doing what you love as long as you do it consistently, find a niche and create a category of one.

Was Joe Rogan's Spotify deal worth it? It depends on what you value.

Spotify's market cap jumped by ~$4 billion within a day of the announcement. On paper, the deal looked like a win-win situation. A new report from The Verge suggests that Spotify got the better end of the deal.

Since going exclusive, Rogan has lost influence.

Spotify hasn't revealed Rogan's listenership numbers, so the report looked at a variety of secondary metrics before and after the signing, including the following.

- **Twitter followers:** Pre-Spotify, Rogan's guests averaged 4k new followers after an appearance on the show; since going exclusive, that number has dropped to 2k.

- **Google Trends:** In 2020, Rogan maintained steady interest and regular spikes; since going exclusive, his baseline interest has dropped and he's only spiked 2x.

- **YouTube subscribers:** Pre-Spotify, Rogan averaged 265k new YouTube subscribers per month; post deal, he's averaging 100k.

Rogan isn't the first big name to lose influence after going exclusive.

When the deal was announced, Andrew Wilkinson of Tiny compared the move to Howard Stern's deal with Sirius, arguing that Rogan got ripped off.

Citing Stern's waning cultural influence, he questioned whether Rogan's payout was worth the trade-offs of going exclusive, specifically

1. Losing a direct relationship with subscribers
2. Building Spotify's recurring revenue instead of his own
3. Serving a smaller audience and having less impact

Who needs influence when you can get the bag?

Seeing the downsides of exclusivity first hand will likely influence up-and-coming podcasters facing similar decisions.

Both Alex Cooper of Call Her Daddy and Dax Shepard of Armchair Expert signed exclusive deals with Spotify recently; will others be so fast to follow suit?

In Rogan's case, it's hard to argue with a $100+ million payday, but there's still a good chance he sold himself short.

ECONOMICS OF PODCASTING

The number of podcasts offered tripled in a year, from 700,000 in the final quarter of 2019 to 2.2 million at the end of 2020.[2] The pandemic unleashed a whole army of podcast creators and listeners with a quarter of all Spotify users engaging with podcast content in some way.

Spotify ventured into podcasting only in 2019. It recorded a doubling in podcast listening hours in the fourth quarter of 2020. It now has over 155 million paying customers for all its services of the total monthly user base of 345 million (growth of 27% year on year). It is on track to reach as many as 427 million monthly active users and 184 million paid subscribers.

CEO Daniel Ek said, 'We have increasing conviction in the causal relationship between growth in podcast consumption driving higher [value] and retention among our user base.'

The company's podcasting strategy helped it outperform expectations of advertising income, which grew 29 per cent year on year to €281 million. This is huge by any standards and augurs well for Spotify's ambition to become the 'Google of the audio world'.

Despite Spotify's advertising success, the main driver of its business continues to be subscriptions, up 15 per cent year on year to 1.89 billion.

Can you make a living hosting a podcast?

The short answer is yes. If you need a $100 million inspiration, go back to our analysis on Spotify's Joe Rogan experiment.

When we aspire to be something of somewhere, we usually end up as nothing of nowhere. There are of course exceptions to this norm. After all, the 'Uber of Middle East' Careem did make it work, and there are other examples as well. As a general rule though, it is

2 https://www.theguardian.com/technology/2021/feb/03/spotify-podcast-popularity-24-percent-growth-subscribers

usually not wise to follow someone's lead in an established category. Creating your own pays off better over the long term.

Austen Allred, the founder of Lambda School, an ed-tech company, thinks that there are more podcasts than podcast listeners. Austin may be right. Many podcasts struggle for listeners. The truth of the matter is that top podcasts usually get all the listeners, while upstarts struggle for a long time before seeing tangible results.

Network Capital started its podcast adventure in the second half of 2019. By that time, we did have a large, trusted community but didn't know how things would pan out. We were experimenting with different forms of content and long-form audio seemed to be a worthy shot.

We approached podcasting like we approach everything. Start small, be consistent and let the community decide whether our endeavours our worth their time. We focused on careers but looked at timeless principles, often-forgotten mental models, nuances which glitzy media tends to miss and launched a new podcast every five days.

The results have been encouraging thus far. After 86 episodes, this is where we stand.

Apple Podcasts: 4.9/5

Chartable: Top 2.5 per cent of podcasts globally

So how much did we make through our podcasts?

Our podcast adventure has turned out well on most metrics, but we have not made a single dollar from it. That is not because popular podcasts like ours are financially unviable. We simply chose to keep our audio content free from advertisements, co-branding opportunities and subscriptions.

Hundreds of brands reach out to us for advertising slots, perks and promotions, but thus far we have said no to every single offer. We are focused on subscription-enabled video content and live cohort-based fellowships which you find on Network Capital TV. That is our strategic choice. You don't need to go down our path.

Feel free to try out additional/alternate podcast revenue sources. For example, Erik Weinstein, MD of Thiel Capital, promotes brands he likes on his podcast without asking them for any money. Once the brands start seeing tangible increase in traffic/revenue from Erik's podcast, his team broaches an advertising offer.

These days, investor Naval Ravikant invites interesting guests from the field of science and uses his podcast followers to financially support the guests who come on his show. His guests these days aren't big celebrities but people hustling to solve difficult problems. By supporting them through his clout, he redirects advertising income for social good in a way.

PLATFORMS

Podcasting platforms such as Apple, Spotify and Google are well known, but we are also witnessing the emergence of YouTube as a platform for podcasters. Why? Simply put, it is creator-friendly, easy to discover and makes monetization simple.

Despite YouTube's many positive attributes, it doesn't work so well for most podcasters. To give you a statistic, this is what 1 million YouTube hits every month amount to:

1 million YouTube views/month = ₹1 lakh/month income (some say it is ~₹60,000 in India)

1 million YouTube views/month = Top 3.5 per cent YouTube channels

Simply put, that is too small an earning for way too much social capital.

1 million followers are more than the population of Amsterdam. Someone with a following greater than the population of Amsterdam should be entitled to more than ₹1 lakh/month.

The problem with YouTube-enabled podcasting isn't the number 1 lakh (which is pretty solid by Indian income standards) but the fact that a 'very' small percentage of podcasters will ever get there.

Relying on YouTube-propelled advertising dollars isn't a robust podcasting strategy. It can be a good complement but not the only source.

One way to look at podcasting is a useful community engagement tool. Leverage podcasts to give a flavour to your community what your larger endeavours are all about. If they like your podcast, they are likely to consider exploring your other suite of products on which you can build more stable, substantive revenue sources.

This is what we do on Network Capital. We curate our podcasts in a way that the listener feels intellectually nourished after an episode and then explores our website, our masterclasses and fellowships. In almost all cases, once people listen to few of our episodes, they end up subscribing to Network Capital TV.

Could we also monetize our podcasts? Sure, but it would deprive someone unfamiliar with Network Capital to check out what we really do. Keep in mind that our Facebook group is closed, our masterclasses are available only to subscribers, our newsletters also go out only to subscribers and our fellowships are offered only to subscribers. Given the context, podcasts allow us to share what we do broadly and also help those who can't afford to pay with enough information to build a career they truly care about.

What if you didn't go down the Network Capital route?

For us, podcast is one product of a larger suite of services we offer. That may not be the case for you. Perhaps you want to create a podcast and make your living with that. How might you approach it?

To those budding podcasters and hustlers trying to hack it, there is hope in the podcasting world, but you need to look east for inspiration.

THE CHINESE DRAGON

China's Internet users have long relied on creativity to produce and consume the content they want. Twitter, Facebook, YouTube and Instagram are blocked. Podcasts are the source of creative expression with slightly less censorship. Chinese nationals use podcasts to advance free speech as much as possible there and also use them to augment their knowledge.

There are more than 542 million podcast users, part of the online audio industry, also called the 'ear economy', in China, which includes podcasts, audiobooks, audio live-streaming (precursor to Clubhouse in the West) and other forms of online audio content. The market of China's online audio industry was RMB17.58 billion (US$2.5 billion) in 2019, with a solid year-on-year increase of 55.1 per cent compared to 2018, and is estimated to continue on its growth in the years to come.

China is one market which has made subscription-powered podcasts work. This is possible because of low cost of smartphones and cheap data plans, but the biggest reason is the maturity of fintech ecosystem in China. Indian fintech ecosystem is also pretty good, but subscriptions aren't the norm yet. Very few companies have made it work, and they are all massively large behemoths. Hardly any small/medium-sized company is propelled by subscriptions.

There are various podcast platforms in China, but Ximalaya FM, QingTing FM and Lizhi FM are leading the industry in terms of paid subscriptions for podcasts.

Lizhi complements its subscriptions by selling virtual items through its live, interactive audio sessions. This is something Clubhouse might take inspiration from in the near future.

One adjacency which has fascinated us is audio-based classes for education. Think of Network Capital masterclasses delivered in an audio-first format. Zoom gloom is real. We notice that many of you don't turn on your video during fellowships. We understand that being online and looking your sharpest self is challenging if you are glued to your screen all day for work.

Zoom gloom may evolve into the mainstreaming of audio-first educational content delivered like a full-fledged course. There are some platforms already doing that. Knowable, Feedcast and Listenable are some examples.

CLOSING REMARKS

Podcasts are here to stay. There is a lot of promise in the 'ear economy', but you need to be in it for the long haul. There aren't any get-rich-quick schemes, but if you are persistent, carve your niche and figure out a way to add value to your listeners consistently, monetization will not be a distant dream.

Remember that advertising is one of the many ways you could make podcasting your living. There are so many experiments you could conduct.

CHAPTER 24

BTS: THE KOREAN BOY BAND THAT BUILT A MULTI-BILLION EMPIRE

BTS, also known as the Bangtan Boys, is a South Korean boy band which was formed in 2010 and has gone on to become the most popular music group in the world. Big Hit Entertainment, the agency behind BTS, went public in the middle of the pandemic. In less than 60 minutes, nearly $2.32 billion flowed into brokerages handling the 2-day public subscription. According to *The New York Times*, Big Hit 'has positioned itself as a "content creator" in the vein of Disney, with BTS essentially playing the role of Mickey Mouse—a priceless intellectual property that can be spun off in almost limitless directions.' The 10-year economic impact of BTS on the Korean economy is estimated to be $50 billion. And yes, the Bangtan Boys are now a Harvard Business School case study.

BTS is not your typical boy band. Their understanding of the passion economy, their approach towards monetization and audience connect are more nuanced than some of the largest companies in the world.

Streaming constituted 85 per cent of 2020 sales in the US music industry, but BTS made a large chunk of money selling physical and digital copies of their songs and albums. Even though their popularity online is skyrocketing, their uniqueness lies in the way they engage and connect with their fans known as ARMY (Adorable Representative MC for Youth). They demonstrate fierce loyalty and organizational cohesiveness which ensures sales and outreach of a different order of magnitude all together.

THE BTS ARMY

Today, anyone with an Internet connection can become their own media company. Many BTS ARMY accounts have millions of followers and play a big role in scaling the community, recruiting new members and sharing relevant information. They come together to raise funds for social causes, buy BTS merchandise, translate songs from Korean to English and other languages, and do everything in their power to augment the brand every single day. Such level of ownership is unheard of in most companies. The important question is: How did it happen?

From the beginning, BTS lyrics focused on being authentic, relatable and empathetic. Self-care, love and personal growth are recurring themes in their music. They have never tried to project a larger-than-life image. Each member of BTS has cried on camera and talked openly about the challenges in their lives.

Even with stratospheric online popularity, BTS has remained true to its Korean roots and scaled relatability through the process. BTS ARMY thinks of the band as their true friends and goes out of their way to protect the brand image of the creators, thereby suggesting substantive 'emotional capital', a sociological term which connotes the fulfilment of emotional needs. Today, influencers, both micro-celebrities and megastars like BTS, are all about cultivating friendship and generating emotional capital with their following or fanbase.

BTS ARMY: PARASOCIAL RELATIONSHIP?

There is a term in psychology to describe this one-sided bond which is built with media figures, first coined in 1956 by Donald Horton and R. Richard Wohl: parasocial relationships. While this type of one-sided relationship existed long before TV and radio, the growing prominence of social media has made parasocial relationships fairly common.

Even though 'parasocial relationships' are not mutual, the psychological effects of the relationships can be significant. The Korean pop industry, especially BTS, has built these parasocial relationships with fans to a degree rarely seen in Western societies until the recent rise of Gen Z influencer culture icons like Charlie D'Amelio. Parasocial relationships create a strong sense of belonging and play a crucial role in building a community.

The seven men of BTS have a remarkable voice, and they come together as a group in a charming way, but that is not why they have achieved this level of success. BTS ARMY and an intimate understanding of what modern-day fans want have catapulted them forward. Their business strategy, community design, sustained consistency and constant evolution all the while staying true to their roots have helped build their category of one.

CHAPTER 25

14TH MOST POPULOUS COUNTRY: PEWDIEPIE

CAREER PRINCIPLES AND OF COURSE PEWDIEPIE VS T-SERIES

For decades, people have idolized the Marilyn Monroes and the Marlon Brandos around the globe, associating with them an ethereal, other-worldliness which could never be achieved by mere mortals.

The power of an influencer, on the other hand, lies quite on the opposite side of the spectrum. While the Met Gala and Victoria's Secret after-parties will always retain their unattainable glamour, the relatability quotient of an influencer holds a degree of power which is as fascinating as it is dangerous.

WHO IS PEWDIEPIE?

One of the most obvious examples of the authority of an influencer is PewDiePie, a 32 year old YouTube mega-sensation with over 104 million subscribers. With his spontaneous charisma, easy-going charm and ability to cater to the large audience of edgy teenagers, PewDiePie has developed into a brand of his own (and he started out merely filming his gameplay).

EARLY CAREER

When Felix Kjellberg aka PewDiePie started his channel in 2010, YouTube culture hardly existed and passion economy was a topic unheard of. He was like many other twenty-one-year-olds who liked playing video games in his apartment. He realized that he was good at it, in fact really good.

Eventually, he took his game footage, superimposed some running commentary in the corner and started uploading it on YouTube—early examples of a genre which became to be known as 'let's play.' As Kevin Rose puts it, thanks to some combination of goofy charisma and algorithmic luck, Kjellberg's channel blew up in a way no YouTube channel ever had. In 2012, he hit a million subscribers.

BUILDING THE WORLD'S 14TH MOST POPULOUS COUNTRY

Eight years since his start, PewDiePie has effectively emerged as the emperor of the world's 14th most populous country. He is not only paid over $10 million annually but also shapes the culture of the infinite YouTube universe, especially the 'inner circle'.

His channel is at the epicentre of YouTube's cultural divide: it's loud, passionate gaming community and the milder, more old-school users who use the site for other forms of content such as sitcoms, music videos and TED Talks.

PewDiePie's long-time girlfriend and now wife Marzia is also a passion economy icon with her work on pop culture and fashion.

PewDiePie's videos may not feed everyone's intellectual or entertainment desires, but with the cult of fans he already commands, his success is unquestionable.

PEWDIEPIE VS T-SERIES

In 2018, a hacker started a global movement to unite his fans to defeat T-Series, Bollywood movie and music production studio, in terms of highest number of YouTube subscribers. He hacked into printers around the world and sent a document with a five-pronged agenda:

1. Unsubscribe from T-Series.

2. Subscribe to PewDiePie.

3. Share awareness to this issue. #SavePewDiePie.

4. Tell everyone you know. Seriously.

5. BROFIST!

It worked for a while, but the very fact that one person could potentially overcome the combined might of a corporate is worth reflecting upon.

WITH GREAT FAME COMES GREAT CONTROVERSY

Being associated with a fair share of controversies (jokes, pranks, silly statements and comments taken out of context) has merely scratched the surface of his fame. As long as his content resonated with people, cancelling him would be a futile task.

At different points in time, YouTube, Disney and others considered cancelling or distancing themselves. Eventually, they realized that messing with an edgy millennial who commands an army of over 100 million die-hard fans wouldn't be a great idea for their brand or their cash flow.

MONETIZING YOUR PASSION

The most impressive facet of PewDiePie's intense stardom is the fact that he managed to turn his generic interest into a global movement. Following are the steps he followed. We will dive deeper into them in later sections of the book.

1. Chose pursuing something he was very good at and enjoyed doing

2. Built a community around his passion/vocation

3. Got better at his craft with feedback from his community

4. Got 1,000 true fans and kept scaling them

5. Built a revenue source—advertising, subscriptions and closer 'access'

6. Hit refresh: Stayed true to his origins but adapted to changing context

7. Learnt from his mistakes
8. Kept enhancing his luck surface area by getting better at his craft and sharing with larger audience

WHY THIS MATTERS TO YOU

The key lesson for you is that PewDiePie's career reinforces the cardinal rule of exponential success in the passion economy: Pick something you are great at and care about; if you build a community around it, you are likely to succeed.

CHAPTER 26

HOW PELOTON IS BOOSTING THE PASSION ECONOMY

Peloton is a subscription-powered company which sells state-of-the-art bikes and fitness equipment at more than $2,500. While the bikes and fitness accessories are popular, what makes Peloton unique is its content engine. In this chapter, we will explore how it is propelling the passion economy.

What is Peloton at its core?

Founder John Foley calls Peloton a software, hardware and content company. Foley is an engineer and competitive cyclist who started the company in 2012 because he and his wife couldn't find the time to go to the gym. They felt that existing at-home workouts didn't quite make the cut, so they were stuck between a rock and a hard place. Around the time Peloton got started, there was a massive uptake in the demand for spin classes. People were looking for new ways to get fit and have fun through the process. Foley's genius was pairing indoor cycling with progressive technology and high-energy rides which users could access on demand at their convenience. Customers bought the super expensive bike and then took group fitness classes delivered over video. These videos have now transformed into highly curated immersive learning experiences, much like CBCs in the ed-tech space.

MEMBERSHIPS AND GROWTH

Foley's bet on home workouts combined with top-notch content has paid off handsomely. Let's look at the growth metrics.

Peloton defines a 'member' as any individual with a Peloton account.

According to a company shareholder letter, Peloton had over 4.4 million members on the platform (as of 31 December 2020). The total number of members had grown 22.22 per cent since the previous quarter, up from 3.6 million users.

Peloton has added an average of 560 thousand new memberships each quarter since Q1 FY 2020.

Peloton also offers a subscription for those who don't have Peloton equipment. These users can access the content library at roughly the same cost as a Netflix subscription.

Peloton had 625,000 paying digital subscribers (as of Q2 FY 2021). That's an increase of 22.55 per cent over the previous quarter, up from 510,000 paid digital members.

Peloton generated $1.06 billion in quarterly revenue (Q2 FY 2021). This is the first time they surpassed $1 billion in a single quarter. Things have been rough for Peleton towards the start of 2022 but its content game is worth analyzing.

PELOTON'S CONTENT STRATEGY

Peloton's equipment is great, but it isn't the first home fitness bike. In fact, even today there are many other products which offer similar features in terms of hardware. Their real distinguishing factor is their content.

Their marketing executive Anke says, 'Peloton music is one of our strongest concepts.'[1] Peloton has started releasing exclusive music and playlists on the platform. They have recently had a partnership with none other than Beyoncé.

The Peloton Artist Series currently features 74 different artists. In most cases, the Peloton content library features more than one workout per artist.

During Q2 FY 2021, 3.6 million Artist Series classes were taken. In a single quarter, 1 million people completed workouts featuring music by Beyoncé.

1 https://blog.dcmn.com/pelotons-marketing-strategy-growth/

PELOTON INSTRUCTORS AND PASSION ECONOMY

As of February 2021, Peloton had 35 instructors offering classes ranging from strength training to yoga to cardio. On Instagram, they have a combined follower count of 6.62 million. Among Peloton instructors active on Instagram, 23 (67.65%) have more than 100,000 followers.

In many ways, Peloton is a content studio which happens to sell fitness equipment. The quality of fitness videos on Peloton feels like movies or Netflix productions.

PELOTON AND THE PANDEMIC

While the pandemic forced many gym instructors to start fitness classes via Zoom, Peloton took it to a whole new level. Every Peloton video has a script, much like a TV production. The scripts are due 36 hours before shooting.

The Peloton fitness instructors are leveraging the passion economy wave. Many look like movie stars, are in great shape and have signed with top talent agencies like UTA and CAA.

These fitness instructors, much like star newsletter writers and podcasters, are using digital platforms to create strong brands for themselves. Of course, they earn money from Peloton, but thanks to representations from talent agencies and their social media presence, they get multiple brand deals and cross-promotion opportunities.

Peloton could choose to strike exclusive contracts with top Peloton instructors but that would cost a sizeable amount of money. The financial upside for the instructors will provide a strong fillip to the passion economy.

In a way, the elite Peloton instructors are a lot like top-notch teachers online. Similar to how a great teacher can either make you fall in love with a subject or hate it with vengeance, a solid fitness instructor can certainly make or break your workout. Learners/ fitness enthusiasts recognize their value and are ready to pay for it.

The larger point is that whether you are teaching productivity techniques or calculus or Pilates on the Internet, passion economy makes it possible for you to monetize what you love and what you are good at.

Massive companies such as Peloton, Spotify and Facebook have recognized the power of creative individuals in shaping their future strategies. Not everyone needs to build a platform, some people can use existing platforms to build their category of one and reap handsome financial rewards and massive influence online.

Success is obviously not a given, but it is feasible, especially if you are exceptionally good at your craft.

PELOTON'S 100 MILLION MISSION

'100 million subscribers, we believe is a reasonable goal,' Foley said during Peloton's first investor meeting as a public company, which was held virtually due to the pandemic. 'There's close to 200 million gym-goers in the world. That's 200 million people paying hard money, month after month, to access what we believe to be inferior fitness equipment in an inferior location.'

Peloton is looking to grow much larger on its home turf, the United States. In the United States, Foley said, there are 35 million households with a treadmill, 'and they're not used because they're just pieces of hardware and they're not fun.' He said that he believes tens of millions of homes in the United States could be Peloton customers in the coming years.

Peloton is currently in the United States, Canada, the United Kingdom and Germany. But it is looking to launch in new countries in the coming years. It means that there will be new instructors who will teach classes in new languages. We won't be surprised if Bollywood actors like Ranveer Singh and Deepika Padukone are roped in to produce Peloton content.

Not everyone can afford to pay $2,500 for a home fitness bike. It is likely that Peloton will launch a rental service or a product + content subscription for emerging markers. It could also consider adding financing options like EMIs and 'buy now, pay later' schemes. The lifetime value of customers in the Peloton ecosystem is high. The company is likely to keep that in mind in its pricing model.

In addition, Peloton content is now available on Apple TV, Amazon, Android, etc. We can expect a wider digital distribution strategy, given that the content is their ultimate asset.

CONCLUDING THOUGHTS

Peloton isn't a fitness company. It is a subscription-based content company which gets a foot in the door with its quality equipment but wins the hearts of its customers with immersive content produced by massive stars like Beyoncé and also upcoming passion economy creators—the slightly lesser known but influential fitness instructors—thereby creating a win-win situation for everyone.

Many other companies operating in different industries might adopt the Peloton playbook—starting off with a solution and then creating content and community to carve out a holistic offering. What is likely to be common among all such experiments would be the role of the passion economy in shaping future outcomes. Creators are likely to have a role in almost every new technology and cultural change. That is good news for anyone thinking about venturing into this space. No longer will it be an afterthought; it will be front and centre of business strategy and execution design.

CHAPTER 27

CASE STUDY ON LIL NAS X

To understand the subcultures on the Internet, let's start by looking at the year major tech platforms were born. As you will notice, something changed in 2007.

Company Name:	Founding Year
Microsoft:	1975
Google:	1998
iPhone:	2007
Twitter:	2007
Kindle:	2007
Android (Public Beta):	2007
Spotify:	2006–2007
Facebook:	2006–2007 (opened to everyone over 13, launch of pages)
YouTube:	Purchased by Google in 2006–2007
Instagram:	2010, acquired by Facebook in 2012
TikTok:	2016

WHO IS NAS X?

Montero Lamar Hill, also known by his stage name Lil Nas X, is an American singer, songwriter, rapper and media personality. He rose to prominence with the release of his country rap single 'Old Town Road', which first achieved viral popularity in early 2019 before climbing music charts internationally and becoming diamond certified by November of that same year. 'Old Town Road' spent 19 weeks atop the US Billboard Hot 100 chart, becoming the longest-running number one song since the chart debuted in 1958.

In 2021, he had achieved the unimaginable, a feat only dreamed of by some of his peers who had gone from anonymity to the top of the charts—he made another hit song, and a brazenly gay one at that. He sings well and has strong stage presence, but a part of his success comes from intimately understanding Internet culture. He has leveraged online platforms to master virality and composed content—not just music but memes, videos and tweets—which complement his style.

Lil Nas X is one of the first digitally native megastars. He was born before Google. When Facebook launched, he was four years old. When the iPhone came out in 2007, he was eight years old. He built his category of one online, thanks to his fluency in digital culture.

THE YEAR 2007 AND FINANCIAL CRISIS OF 2008

The converging of mega-trends in 2007—lowered cost of devices, ubiquitous Internet connectivity and digital platforms that made cost of content production close to zero—propelled Gen Zs to play a pivotal role in shaping the digital sphere.

Along the time of this digital revolution, a massive global crisis was about to unfold. Many Gen Zs saw their parents getting fired in the financial crisis and suffer intense economic and psychological agony. Suddenly, the promise of the 9–5 job and a stable life with predictable income through 'regular' employment seemed hollow.

That is perhaps when they started exploring careers and lifestyles where they would have more autonomy on the outcomes. The context of the generation growing up around 2007–2008 changed their perspective and that changed perspective played a huge role in shaping the online world we know today.

CULTURE ISN'T PREORDAINED

Culture is built, strengthened or weakened with actions. The Internet culture is being shaped with every new tweet and every new podcast being uploaded online. There is no digital Mecca.

How the Internet evolves and what it becomes is a function of the choices of the digital natives. Nothing is preordained.

Instagram became a household name because back then, perfectly curated images were all the rage (a lot is still the same but a lot is changing). People wanted to project success, beauty and all the wonderful things in life. There was one problem: It got so disconnected from reality that it became the ultimate envy tool. People started competing with each other on everything. Pleasure became performance, and the result was anxiety.

While much of this is still the norm, there is one age group which has taken back control, at least some of it—the Gen Zs, part of the generation Nas X belongs to. They seem to prioritize spontaneity and authenticity over performative curation.

The emergence of new social media apps like Be Real and Dispo point us to the new Gen Z-led culture on how things are in reality as opposed to what might be in our imagination. It is more focused on real engagement as opposed to 'likes'.

There are economic implications of this trend—likes don't translate to dollars if you are not already a mega celebrity with a massive following. Real engagement builds a community which is a precious economic resource. Liking online has become a mere symbol of acknowledgement; engagement is a conversation. It is far more active and actionable.

NAS X' DIGITAL STRATEGY

As a teenager, Nas was part of Barbz, a community of hardcore Nicki Minaj fans. According to Urban Dictionary, 'stan' is a portmanteau of the words 'stalker' and 'fan', and refers to someone who is overly obsessed with a celebrity. Nas X was a Minaj stan.

He created an avatar on Twitter and dedicated every waking hour making content which did two things—cheer her work and build a brand for himself. He gamed Twitter and figured out a way to make content viral instantly. In the process, he also built a loyal community of followers. However, in 2018, Twitter banned his account. All the work he had done so far was reduced to zero.

Around the same time, he broke up with his (secret) boyfriend at the time, failed a maths class in college and lost his beloved grandmother. It was a dark period, and he thought that he would die as well.

Then one day, while toiling away on his maths homework, he wrote a song titled 'Shame' and posted it on Twitter. It became massively popular and gave him confidence to write more. He started building a Twitter base all over again. His genius was combining his music with viral tweets he had the knack for creating.

In December 2018, he bought a $30 beat on YouTube, wrote down lyrics and posted it, like his other songs, to SoundCloud. Thereafter, he leveraged Reddit to create virality for his creation. He posted 'What's the name of the song that goes "take my horse to the old town road"[1] (in order to spike curiosity for his creation) on a subreddit focused on helping people track down songs they liked but couldn't place. That's when things started to get seriously viral. Eventually, his song made waves on TikTok, and a new music sensation was created.

Many sceptics call this luck, but this is far from being the case. This is what he said: 'No, this is no accident. I've been pushing this hard.'[2]

Not too long ago, Nas X came out as an openly gay man who embraced his sexuality. There were many detractors online and, in many quarters, he was mocked and ridiculed. However, he was celebrated and cheered for much more loudly in most pockets. Being the savvy digital native he is, Nas X managed to make the most out of this controversy. His songs became even more popular, and his fans felt a deeper sense of connection with his persona.

Nas X's brand, despite all the fanfare and success, is built on keeping it light, sticking true to the authentic self and not pretending to have it all figured out. There are parallels to BTS.

1 https://www.oprahdaily.com/entertainment/a27073704/lil-nas-x-billy-ray-cyrus-old-town-road-lyrics-meaning/
2 https://www.nytimes.com/2021/07/07/magazine/lil-nas-x.html

NAS X STANS

Just the way Nas X stan accounts of Niki Minaj, today there are hundreds and thousands of Nas X stans trying to replicate what he did. In a way, he shaped online culture more strongly than most established media outlets. His new song 'Industry Baby' broke the Internet—not only because of his significant musical prowess but also because of his understanding of how culture scales in the online world in the 21st century. This is specific knowledge—it can't be taught, it can't be mimicked but it can be learned by tinkering and experimentation. That is the essence of Internet subcultures and how you can create something valuable in the online world—be it business or art or music.

CONCLUDING THOUGHTS

In early 2019, Lil Nas X was a college dropout ashamed about his sexual identity, sleeping on his sister's couch, with −$5.62 in his Wells Fargo account. 150 days later, he'd broken Mariah Carey's record for the most consecutive weeks at #1 on the Billboard Hot 100.

As Nas X explains, this didn't just happen. Yes there was an ounce of luck and the touch of good timing but this popstar studied Internet subculture like an anthropologist, scaled content like a digital entrepreneur and built his category of one doing something he loved—creating music and being unabashedly himself.

CHAPTER 28

BURGERS, FRENCH FRIES AND A MULTI-MILLION-DOLLAR YOUTUBE EMPIRE: MRBEAST

Jimmy Donaldson, better known as MrBeast, operates six YouTube channels which collectively have close to 100 million subscribers. His videos have been watched more than 13 billion times. His ultimate aspiration is to be the Elon Musk of the passion economy.

He has productized himself and created multiple revenue streams which include a world-class content creation and dissemination strategy, a mobile gaming app, a cloud kitchen chain MrBeast Burger (Burgers and fries were the core products. It's estimated that the brand made ~$8 million just on burger sales in three months[1]) and an investment vehicle which offers creators up to $250,000 in exchange for equity in their YouTube channels. His approach towards the passion economy is a lot more nuanced than playing the elusive game of online fame. There are many pranksters on the Internet, but there is one MrBeast. In no shape or form do I endorse his views. All his controversial takes on issues of social importance should be evaluated carefully. Exploring his career is not endorsing his strategy. I trust the reader to keep that in mind.

He started his YouTube career as a thirteen-year-old by posting videos of playing online games, sharing satirical content and live-streaming some of his stunts. It took him a while to figure out the art of going viral, but he mastered it in no time. Brand partnerships came his way from early days and that made his content quality and distribution even better. He even started giving out money to strangers and recording their bewildered reactions. With the

1 https://www.restaurantbusinessonline.com/financing/breaking-down-mrbeast-burgers-first-1-million-burgers

advertisement and partnership revenue growing, he more than just made that money back.

Today, MrBeast employs about 50 writers, editors and production assistants who curate his YouTube channels which collectively make almost $5 million a month, according to data from Social Blade, a YouTube analytics service. He is on track to overtake PewDiePie as the most subscribed YouTuber in the world by 2022.

In the times to come, the line between creators and brands will continue to blur, and the ways in which creators productize and monetize their passions will diversify. This will create new types of jobs, unleash innovation at the level of the creator and also the platforms and infrastructure required to support them.

That's the exciting part of passion economy. Creator innovation puts a flywheel in motion driving platform, infrastructure, culture and business model innovation.

What we need to keep in mind is that while creators like MrBeast have a major role in influencing change, the smaller players can feel drowned out. Creator economics follows the power law and we need to figure out ways to level the playing field to ensure broader participation. For the passion economy to be truly democratized, we don't just need one MrBeast. We need a wide spectrum of creators to figure out ways for sustaining their livelihoods using the platforms driving the passion economy.

CHAPTER 29

ALI ABDAAL: CAMBRIDGE DOCTOR TURNED YOUTUBER

When a Cambridge educated doctor quits his job to create content, it makes news. Ali Abdaal is the son of an immigrant single mother living in the United Kingdom. Early on in his life, he realized the importance of passive income. He learned to code in school and worked on a wide range of projects with different degrees of success. For a while, he was confused about pursuing computer science or medicine.

He chose medicine after earning an admission at the University of Cambridge. There he found some classes to be interesting, but a large chunk of them were just about okay, boring often. Leveraging his love for coding and tech, he built a side hustle to help students get into medical schools. That took off and gained serious traction. He kept working at it over and above his college work. Even after becoming a junior doctor, he kept at it. Revenues were good, and Ali started creating a bit of a name for himself.

As you can imagine, being a doctor means a busy life. Despite that and the pressure of a successful side hustle, he started tinkering with YouTube, essentially creating content about the stuff he found interesting.

He started with exam preparation because he already had an audience, thanks to his side hustle. But soon after, he started getting into content related to productivity techniques, great books, tech products and gadgets, among others.

For the first few years, the growth of his YouTube channel was slow. There were barely any subscribers, but he persisted and kept producing new material. The YouTube algorithm rewards two things:

1. Consistency

2. Completion rates

For Ali, both these metrics worked well. He created a regular rhythm and stuck to it no matter how busy his work got. His audience, however small, enjoyed the videos and completed them. That is how Ali started cracking the YouTube algorithm.

Ali has always been open about finances. When he made zero dollars, it was public. When he made thousands of dollars a month, that was public as well. In fact, he shared the salary he made as a junior doctor and showed the dashboard of his income via YouTube.

He realized that he had found a strong content–market fit. YouTube was paying him handsomely, advertising contracts came in and multiple cross-promotion opportunities made his monthly income significantly larger than the managing director of an investment bank.

Not one to settle for that, Ali became a teacher. He created a course on Skillshare which helped other YouTubers monetize their channels. That was a smart decision, one that anyone interested in passion economy should take to heart: Create something you have legitimacy in and can do exceptionally well.

Ali's Skillshare adventure became a great source of passive income. Thousands of users watched his course, and he made a ton of money with that. The beauty of Ali's approach was that he monetized his work at scale without putting in additional effort. It was a win-win situation for everyone. It was a win for Skillshare because Ali brought so much traffic to their platforms. His course was only available to Skillshare subscribers, which meant massive incremental revenue for them. It was a win for Ali because Skillshare paid him a percentage of the platform earnings. It was also a win for the learners as they got to learn YouTubing from one of the best in the world.

In the middle of the pandemic, though, Ali decided to repivot his strategy. To understand why, one has to explore a new wave in ed-tech called CBCs. To demonstrate what CBCs are, let me share why I invested in Maven along with some more context.

WHY DID I INVEST IN MAVEN?

I am an early investor in Maven, a platform which helps creators build CBCs. Maven raised $25 million from a16z and Andrew Chen in May 2021.[1] In its first four months, instructors did over $1 million of course sales on their platform.

Cohorts and communities will be key pillars of the future of education.

I see many areas of collaboration between Network Capital and Maven and hope that CBCs become the default mode of learning online.

On Network Capital we constantly keep an eye on the content, community and career intelligence trinity.

Content + Community + Career intelligence = Future of learning

Maven has been an inspiration for shaping Network Capital fellowships, which now serve thousands of subscribers around the world. The Network Capital Summer School will also be structured as a CBC.

What CBCs do is that they make learning a communal activity. They make the student more invested and the instructors more accountable. They transform learning from a passive content consumption scenario to an active, outcome-oriented process by focusing on three key elements.

1. A thriving community

2. A set of instructors hyperfocused on learning outcomes

3. A formal system of checks and balances

Webinars conclude with generic motivation (also important), while good CBCs conclude with outcomes students care about. These outcomes could range from upskilling, changing sectors and seeking side income to launching new products/communities.

CBCs, unlike other forms of online learning, are binary. Either students meet their goals or they don't.

1 https://www.networkcapital.tv/blog/why-i-invested-in-maven

Traditional online learning and massive open online courses (MOOCs) are self-based, while CBCs are time-bound. You need to keep up with the classes, work through assignments, take feedback from peers and instructors, and work through holidays. Case in point is that Network Capital community building, investing and policy fellowships go on till few hours before Holi and restart right after.

While this may seem intense, it works for busy people. This schedule does not go on in perpetuity. It functions in short bursts of intense activity followed by a break. This is not very different from how athletes train for big competitions.

In a CBC, there is intentionality, a time-bound goal and a cohort of peers who keep you motivated by their sheer presence.

You may wonder what is so innovative about this? Aren't classrooms of any kind meant to function this way?

In theory, yes, but not so much in practice. In traditional classrooms, student goals evolve organically, motivation levels vary and students go through many classes because they have to, not because they want to.

Motivation is contagious. For good CBCs, the average motivation level of a learner is substantially higher than that of someone in a classroom. Further, peer and faculty accountability make motivation higher as classes progress. This augments student achievement and makes learning fun for all.

As the CEO of Network Capital and an investor in Maven, I hope that this movement to democratize cohort-based learning propels student outcomes across age groups.

ALI ABDAAL'S CBC

While Ali's course videos are still present on Skillshare, his largest share of income comes from live cohort-based classes. He has more than a million followers on YouTube, out of which over 1,000 pay anywhere between $1,500 and $5,000 to join a six-week course. Today, he earns over $100,000 every month doing what he loves— with the flexibility he wants, living anywhere in the world.

CHAPTER 30

MILLION-DOLLAR FACEBOOK ENGINEER WHO QUIT TO BECOME A YOUTUBER

Patrick Shyu started his career creating apps in 2008. His first app was a game called 'World of Blood' which got more than 1.5 million users at a time when the app ecosystem was nascent. Thereafter, he built a social network and a bunch of interesting software products. His corporate career started in 2014, and he spent half a decade coding at Google and Facebook. By the time he left in 2019, his salary was close to half a million dollars. This isn't uncommon in the Silicon Valley. Deep technical expertise is handsomely rewarded, but it comes at the cost of personal freedom. You can't say or do whatever you want, whenever you want. Perhaps that is a good thing for some people. For others, it just doesn't feel right.

Shyu belongs to the latter. Evidently, he was fired from Facebook for having a YouTube channel where he would put out funny videos and ironies of the tech industry.

Today, he is among the most polarizing figures talking about technology on YouTube and as of writing this book has over 1.2 million followers. He provides funny and insightful commentary about his experience at Google and Facebook; is radically open about his personal life, including but not limited to his divorce; and shares controversial and polarizing views on social justice issues like Black Lives Matter. I do not subscribe to his views and no part of this chapter should be considered an endorsement of Shyu's belief system. In fact, I thought long and hard about including him in the book but decided to go ahead because we can learn from everyone, including those we disagree with.

His polarizing views notwithstanding, Shyu has built an interesting one-person company with millions of fans, doing what he loves, on his terms. Two years back, he shared a video titled 'How I make $1 million a year. (not clickbait)'. 'Something interesting happened to me recently. My income has surpassed a million dollars this year,' he said. 'I've just been sitting around here in this toolshed drinking my coffee while you've been prancing around in a business suit, your Banana Republic clothing, driving your Jaguar cars, acting all self-important.'[1]

At the time he was still working at Facebook. Half a million came from his software engineering job, the other half million came from his YouTube videos. Interestingly, he considered his engineering job his side hustle and YouTube video creation his main gig. He worked 80 hours a week and didn't take any breaks on weekends and holidays.

Fast forward to 2021, his YouTube channel continues to grow and much like other popular creators, he has created new income streams from mentoring, teaching and cryptocurrency trading. While his income information isn't public, it is safe to assume that Shyu earns significantly more than the million dollars he made in 2019.

Income is not the only remarkable aspect on Shyu's story. His lifestyle design seems to be the ultimate millennial dream. While he is a good coder and can easily find another corporate job if he wants, I will be surprised if he goes down that path again. He has figured out a way to creatively combine his curiosity, expertise and passion in a way which makes financial sense. In a way, he has carved out his dream job, reinvented himself and propelled thousands of other young professionals to reconsider their career choices. Many professionals have tried to mimic his style and create videos about their stories of quitting the corporate life. A large chunk of them got famous on the Internet for a few days and then fizzled out.

That's another thing to remember—authenticity is your best friend in the passion economy. You need to create your own path and find people who will pay a premium to listen/be part of your story.

CHAPTER 31

LEBANON AND THE UNEMPLOYABLE PROFESSOR TAKING PHILOSOPHY BACK TO THE MARKETPLACE

Lebanon is in freefall. The GDP has been plummeting, and the unemployment rate is alarming. Children don't have milk to drink, and people have to que up for four–five hours every morning to scamper for gas. Last year, in the middle of the pandemic, there was a massive bomb blast in the capital city of Beirut. Till date, the perpetrators have not been identified.

Only God can help the country, said the outgoing head of the State when he resigned. For a short period, new leadership was instituted before it crumbled, and the old guard was back again with no plan, no alternative and no scheme to revive the tanking economy and the ruptured society.

International organizations have offered aid but on the condition that the rotten political leadership make way for something new. Nobody knows how that will happen so the status quo continues, worsening the state of affairs every day.

The salaries of teachers have now been reduced to $200/month, doctors earn about $350/month and engineers earn somewhere in between. Every single educated youth is craving for one thing—move out of the country. Given the state of the pandemic, no one knows if and when that will happen.

Amid all the chaos and hopelessness, there is one professor who offers a way forward. Mahmoud Rasmi tried long and hard to get tenured at various universities in Lebanon. His classes were interesting and engaged the students to think for themselves. Despite strong ratings, his career didn't advance. He was barely making any money, and his job satisfaction reached an all-time low.

With no option in sight, he decided to quit. He knew that he was unemployable in Lebanon, but he wondered if he could create an opportunity for himself on the Internet.

The Internet allows anyone to build, scale and monetize curiosity and passion to create something interesting. This movement is broadly referred to as the creator economy or the passion economy, as we have discussed earlier. Creators don't necessarily have to build one product which instantly finds product–market fit. They can create a portfolio of small bets, build their audience step by step and find multiple streams of revenue to support themselves. That is what Mahmoud did.

SARDONICALLY SPEAKING: MAHMOUD'S SELF-PUBLISHED INTERNET SENSATION

Mahmoud started by combining his strength—philosophy—with a clear gap in the market—the way philosophy was taught. He decided to write a book which captures the core concepts in an accessible way, sprinkled with relatable references to pop culture and spunky illustrations.

Instead of chasing publishers, he used a creator monetization platform Gumroad (I am an investor in Gumroad) to sell his book. Initially, it was priced at $5, but seeing the popularity of his work, he made it free. That turned out to be a smart decision, as it expanded his reach overnight. More importantly, it gave him the idea to launch a live CBC on philosophy.

TAKING PHILOSOPHY TO THE MARKETPLACE

With his CBC, he now had the opportunity to monetize what he had spent learning for years. He picked topics which would appeal both to ambitious corporate honchos and students trying to figure out what they want to do with their lives.

If he priced his course keeping Lebanon in mind, he would have had to keep it under 1$. But the Internet and digital tools enabled him to charge a premium for quality content and delivery. The advantage of premium pricing for creators is that it allows them to focus on their craft instead of marketing and sales. Mahmoud didn't need thousands of paying members.

Today, he prices his cohorts between $100 and $150 and caps his class at 30–40 students. That makes his monthly revenue between $3,000 and $6,000. That is good money by most standards, but in Lebanon that is a fortune today. Remember that doctors earn $350/month there.

Mahmoud managed to invite legendary investor Nassim Taleb for one of his CBCs. It turned out to be a delightfully interesting class. Most students tweeted their experience, and Mahmoud's next cohort filled up instantly.

That is the power of delighting your captive audience. Mahmoud has mastered the craft of focusing on few people and giving them a phenomenal learning experience. That has helped him cut through the clutter and create his category of one.

BUILDING A COMMUNITY

If you analyse Mahmoud's portfolio of products and services, you will find merchandize, discussion groups and CBCs. What isn't explicit is his community, the most important component for any creator.

He is able to sell effectively because he has managed to build a reasonably large, engaged community which is willing to invest time and money to learn philosophical concepts. Without his community, he would have to find new audience from scratch for every new launch. That is challenging for everyone, especially for one-person companies which are largely built on the personality of the creator.

CONCLUDING THOUGHTS: LEBANON, CREATOR ECONOMY AND FUTURE REVIVAL

Lebanon is a resilient country. It has witnessed countless wars, emergencies and fatalities. Every time it has managed to emerge but this time, locals say, it is far worse than they have ever seen. Miracles happen but not just by hoping for it. For Lebanon's revival, individuals will need to create opportunities for themselves online. Waiting for the economy to bounce back and for local jobs to return could be disastrous.

'Unemployable' professors like Mahmoud demonstrate that the creator economy opens up new vistas for employment. All one needs is the Internet, grit and commitment to experiment till the portfolio of small bets add up. It takes a while and success isn't guaranteed, but isn't that the case for everything we try?

We see Mahmoud's philosophy adventures transform from being a one-person experiment in a small room in Beirut to a global community of professionals interested in engaging with rich, timeless content. After the pandemic, he could plan in-person meetups, conferences, retreats, corporate coaching and leadership modules, among other things. The possibilities are infinite, and we are confident that Mahmoud will emerge even more anti-fragile in the times to come.

CHAPTER 32

KIRAN GANDHI: HARVARD MBA TURNED MUSICIAN AND ACTIVIST

Kiran Gandhi's stage name is Madame Gandhi. She is a Harvard Business School MBA graduate, who built her category at the intersection of music and activism. She went to Harvard to try and explore the business aspect of creativity. During her time there, she got the opportunity to meet the British-Sri Lankan star M.I.A. and popped the idea of her band having a drummer. Nothing happened for a while.

Then one fine day, the product marketing manager on set sent a video of Kiran playing the drums to M.I.A. That was how Kiran started performing live. She would attend business school from Monday to Thursday and then tour with M.I.A. from Friday to Sunday. There was a time when she had to go to New York (where M.I.A. was performing) on week days, perform live and return late at night to Boston to be ready for case studies to be discussed in the MBA classroom.

Side hustles often scale in short bursts of intense activity. The key is to plan and prepare in advance for such opportunities and complement them with good old, consistent micro-actions.

Kiran has always loved the stage. Her parents saw her talent early on and provided lots of opportunities for public speaking and performing arts. Her undergraduate education was in maths and political science at Georgetown University, after which she briefly considered becoming an Obama Fellow. At least her father wanted her to go down that path.

Despite her impressive academic record and solid public service credentials, she followed her intrinsic curiosity. Around the time Spotify was becoming a leading music platform, she decided to become an analyst at InterGlobe. This combined her quantitative skills with her passion for music.

Through the process of repeated experimentation, trial and error, and listening to her true calling, she combined activism and music in a way that satiates her creative hunger and provides financial stability.

As an emerging star in the passion economy space, she has created multiple revenue streams: selling merchandise, performing live, high-profile talks and conferences, among others. Pursuing a wide range of projects augments her creativity.

This is another point to pay close attention to. There are some people who feel burned out by context switching, others find it energizing. You must strive to find what works for you.

In the times to come, Kiran could start teaching live CBCs, build a community, create intimate offline experiences for the most ardent lovers of her music, invest in other creators and launch an accelerator. The possibilities are infinite for creative professionals like Kiran, but the opportunity cost for every new project must be calculated by the creator herself. Prescriptions and playbooks need to be personalized. Everyone needs to find their creator–community fit one experiment at a time.

Kiran's career choice is not one-off. We are witnessing a large number of ambitious, highly accomplished professionals who are venturing into the passion economy, creating a niche and scaling it step by step. This broadening of the professional landscape creates new avenues for young professionals to apply their skills and curiosities. Their futures are not preordained; they don't feel obliged to follow a script for their careers and their lives. It is the uncharted exploration of new economic and social possibilities which provide hope for everyone.

Passions and curiosities don't need to be saved up for retirement. They are the hope for a world where people actually care about the work they do instead of thinking of it as a means for making ends meet.

CHAPTER 33

HOW GEN ZS ARE TRANSFORMING THE CAREER NAVIGATION SPACE

In the last three years, job postings with the word creator in the title or description have soared 4,645 times, to 92,900 positions, according to data firm Thinknum, which crawls more than 3 million job postings on company websites every day.[1]

Amazon is the leader of the pack, with dozens of senior roles including but not limited to vice president of creators at Twitch focused on increasing streamers' earnings and audiences, and influencer marketing manager for Prime Video to work with online talent.

THE LARGE SHIFT

This shift can be traced to the way Gen Zs saw their parents deal with the various financial crashes in the last two decades. These parents worked hard in strict cultures, but when adversity struck, it became obvious that there was almost no cash left to pay the bills. Something didn't quite add up. So much effort, so little reward.

This disenchanted the Gen Zs from the traditional nature of employment. The money, the flexibility, the saving and the output seemed to make less sense with each passing year. Fuelled by adversity and the burgeoning of new tech platforms and tools, Gen Zs started exploring ways to build projects which might generate some passive income.

1 https://www.theinformation.com/articles/creator-related-job-postings-at-amazon-google-spike

Being a large market, some of these passion projects started exploding in popularity. Advertisers followed suit. This age group became too large and too economically important to ignore.

The power finally starting shifting from institutions to individuals. With each passing day, barriers to creation reduced. One reason why TikTok became so popular was that it made high-quality production—with effects and subtitles—possible for millions without them having to spend a single dollar on anything. Just 10 years back, producing one TikTok video would have costed hundreds of dollars and weeks of production time. Now it became zero dollar production cost ready to launch in a few seconds.

The cost of failure reduced. The cost of tinkering became zero. Finding the product–market fit finally seemed possible without investing a ton of money on sales and marketing.

Some Gen Zs started earning more than their parents who had gone to college and business school spending hundreds of thousands of dollars. The more they earned, the more disillusioned they became with the choices their parents' generation had taken.

BIG TECH AND CREATOR ECONOMY

The top 10 companies hiring for creator roles included Facebook, Google, Amazon and TikTok parent ByteDance. What's interesting is that the jobs available are in strategy and other core corporate functions, not just content creation. The message is clear: Creator economy is top of mind for big tech.

Essentially, any business which has power over culture is going big time into the strategic side of creator management. That's led to a new subset of jobs which straddle operations, strategy, media and tech.

What is making all of this happen?

TikTok is the global go-to platform for short-form videos. What started out as a place for cat videos, teen dance numbers and beat boxing has transformed into the destination of choice for the digital natives aka Gen Zs to hang out, connect, create, educate, learn and even invest.

Gen Z influencers like Charlie D'Amelio are opening up the realm of possibilities when it comes to creator monetization. She is a regular American teenager who cares about a wide range of issues and loves to sing, dance and chill. She has 120 million followers on TikTok and has amazed almost 10 billion likes for her creative work. D'Amelio's appeal is in her regularity. She is the quintessential girl next door, with a following equal to the population of many European countries put together.

This following isn't a vanity metric. She has built a thriving, financially lucrative career which includes brand partnerships, digital marketing, venture investing and content creation. She charges upwards of $100,000 for putting up a single post on her profile. Her net worth is tens of millions of dollars.[2]

Josh Richards, 19, is the fifth-highest-paid TikTok creator, with 25 million+ followers. Despite his influence and reach, he doesn't rely on brand deals.[3] He launched various brands and co-founded a $15 million VC fund, Animal Capital. He is also co-writing a book to teach his young audience about financial literacy.

Teens like Josh and D'Amelio are living examples of alternate careers which Gen Zs are building in the passion economy space. These aren't random celebrities who have become famous overnight. They are young entrepreneurs who first built a community online and then figured out multiple streams of revenue. They also inspired an entire generation of Gen Zs to look for alternate career paths.

HOW GEN ZS ARE TRANSFORMING THE CAREER SPACE

Realizing the market potential, TikTok launched a job portal for Gen Zs. There is a clear difference between how teens think of careers and the way their parents did.

2 https://www.cosmopolitan.com/entertainment/celebs/a33275435/charli-damelio-net-worth/
3 https://www.bloomberg.com/news/videos/2021-04-22/fifth-highest-paid-tiktok-creator-launches-venture-capital-fund-video

LinkedIn is the world's largest professional network, but it hasn't really caught up among the Gen Zs. That is one age group where LinkedIn has consistently struggled. The primary reason isn't technical. It is cultural. Most power users of LinkedIn are middle-aged professionals. Their take on careers, way of looking at jobs and advice don't seem to resonate with the younger population.

TikTok is venturing in the career discovery space for Gen Zs to capitalize the passion economy. These are early days, but the way they are posting jobs on the platform and the creative job application forms augur well for the future.

Not to be left behind, LinkedIn has also launched a wide range of tools for creators including but not limited to newsletters, new tools for monetization, customer acquisition channels and community building services.

Facebook is launching newsletters as well, Twitter has just acquired a newsletter platform called Revue and every other day we hear of large tech behemoths creating economic opportunities for solopreneurs, creators and small business operators. Both Twitter and Facebook might launch job-centric products in the near future. They may not directly compete with the loyal audience of LinkedIn, but the Gen Z career navigation industry is massive and open to disruption. No one company has figured it out yet, which is why it will be interesting to see the evolution in the product strategy of these tech companies when it comes to becoming the go-to platform for Gen Zs seeking career support.

It is also possible that top influencers launch their own job/career services. They already have massive following, exponential growth and multiple streams of income. They might directly reach out to their communities and create an alternate source of income. All these new models may not work, they may not scale and people could find better alternatives, but they are to collectively alter the alchemy or career exploration.

CONCLUDING THOUGHTS

Gen Zs are already major drivers of culture, economy and society. The way they look for jobs, the way they shape their careers and the platforms they choose to build their work life will impact big tech, big government and civil society. While it is interesting that some massive platforms have realized the trend, it is still an afterthought for most companies. Such companies are likely to struggle in the 21st century.

CHAPTER 34

TREVOR NOAH, REID HOFFMAN AND THE FUTURE OF ONE-PERSON COMPANIES

In September 2021, I witnessed Trevor Noah deliver a hilarious masterclass (yes, it was one, far more nuanced than a regular comic gig) on international relations, bias at work and the power of Indian curry. It was mesmerizing and left me wondering if he was a comedian, a public intellectual, an influencer or a satirist. Perhaps he is all of these identities weaved into one. Walt Whitman was right. We are all multitudes.

He is the host of 'The Daily Show' on Comedy Central, but I am not sure if that is his primary identity. I think 'The Daily Show' leans on Trevor Noah a lot more than the other way around. Let's take a look at the Twitter followers for reference. Noah has 11.5 million followers, while 'The Daily Show' has 9.4 million.

Without 'The Daily Show', Noah may not be as well-known as he is today, but things have turned around from the time he started his job. At a macro level, power dynamics have changed from institutions to individuals. We are witnessing the unbundling of work from employment and the emergence of scalable one-person companies. Basically, if you are good at your job, you don't necessarily need to find your identity with your employer. You can choose to do the same work on your terms using new technology platforms with a wide range of companies. I am not suggesting you to do that. That should be your decision. You have the option, and that option has emerged because work is getting decoupled from employment.

Noah's comedy show/masterclass had 32,000 Londoners pay an average ticket price of $60 over two days. That is approximately $2 million just in ticket sales. If you include food, beverage, merchandise, sponsorship and media, the total revenue for these two days would be close to $4 million (based on back of envelope calculation).

London is one of over a dozen live shows he was doing in 2021, a year largely lost to the pandemic. His annual salary is approximately $16 million. To give you a comparable number, the annual salary of the executive chairman of Ford Motor Company (the highest-paid person at Ford) is $16 million.

The difference between the executive chairman of Ford (Bill Ford) and Trevor Noah is that of identity. Noah would thrive even if he decided not to be associated with 'The Daily Show'. His personal brand and pull have more than enough leverage in the world today.

ONE-PERSON COMPANIES

Noah could go on to build a billion-dollar one-person company without leaning on any institution. Today, he has a Netflix show, a podcast, a series of live performances and a bestselling book. He could easily add new products and services to his portfolio.

As we discussed, people pay a premium for deeper access and experiences. Imagine Noah offering a live CBC. People would pay any amount of money to learn from him and, more importantly, to get access to him.

Joe Rogan, the biggest podcaster on the planet, sold his company to Spotify for $100 million. One-person companies won't be exception but the norm, as work and employment get unbundled further.

Earlier, institutions gave identity to their workers, but the tables have turned. In China, for example, many star professors of major universities have quit to create online courses, audio content and live CBCs. They now earn millions of dollars doing exactly what they did before with two small differences.

First, they are customizing their offering to new means of consumption aided by emerging technology and media platforms.

Passion Economy and the Side-Hustle Revolution

Second, they are breaking down the work they did into smaller parts and creating new products and experiences for their customers. Instead of looking for students within a university, they now have the Internet to find their niche and monetize it.

BUILDING YOUR PORTFOLIO OF CAREERS

This trend is being observed even among hypersuccessful technology entrepreneurs like Reid Hoffman, whose day job is that of an investor at Greylock, a Silicon Valley-based VC fund, but most people now know him as the curator of the most successful business podcast 'Masters of Scale', which has recently been turned into a book.

After reading *Masters of Scale*, I realized that additional content and access to Reid would be enabled through a subscription-based app and CBCs. Yes, 'every company is going to be a subscription company.'

Reid is a billionaire. He has more money than most of us will ever have, but his hunger to keep growing is admirable. Even at his level, he is working relentlessly to unbundle work from employment. The larger lesson is that this unbundling isn't just about money or fame or influence. It is indicative of our changing relationship with work.

The innate desire to find work at the intersection of our curiosity, conviction, passion and market trends is becoming universal. That is why I believe that there will be a lot more one-person companies in the coming decade, some of which will become massive—perhaps unicorns and decacorns. Crypto analysts suggest that there will likely be the first trillion-dollar company run by one person in the not-so-distant future.

This in no way means that traditional corporates will fade away or that teamwork will become less important. All this trend alludes to is the fact that people will monetize their creativity, individuality and intrinsic motivation in more deliberate ways, often without the institutions they are affiliated with. They will build a portfolio of skills and match it with market need as and when they like.

This isn't my techno-utopian fantasy but a considered view based on what I am observing around the world.

I am optimistic about people building a portfolio of careers because it will prepare them well for a world of work where disruption will be the norm, not the exception. Some might follow a sequential path in that they will hop sectors, industries, functions and eventually do something completely different. Others might split their week, month or year into things they enjoy doing and are good at. They might even pursue three different jobs a month not because they need to in order to survive (although that could happen and does happen among gig workers) but because they want to experiment, figure things out and build their category of one at the intersection of their curiosities.

Time has come for all of us to reimagine our work lives. Start by asking the following: What would your work unbundled from your employment look like? What would you spend your time doing? What activities and projects would you love to pursue? What are the ones you would avoid or outsource? I often do this exercise looking 10 years ahead and then working backwards. The answers give me clarity about my present and the future I want to shape.

CHAPTER 35

HOW TONY ROBBINS CREATED HIS 'CATEGORY OF ONE'

Tony Robbins is 6 feet 7 inches tall and could easily pass off as a heavy weight champion or an athlete. In fact, he tried but life had other plans. He barely finished high school, but his impact in the world of business, finance and personal transformation is noteworthy. He is worth hundreds of millions of dollars, and scores of Fortune 500 CEOs have attributed their success directly to Robins. He had a Netflix movie about his adventurous life.[1]

By the age of twenty-six years, he was already a millionaire with a bestselling book and today he is one of the world's most well-known motivational speakers. He has worked with high-profile individuals on a one-to-one basis, such as Bill Clinton, Serena Williams, Oprah Winfrey, Hugh Jackman and Marc Benioff, among others. How did someone with no fancy credentials or diplomas accomplish so much for business and society? Our associate, Jenya, analyses that.

It didn't just happen.

He created his category of one with persistence and generosity. After managing to escape an abusive home and having endured a difficult childhood (growing up with four different fathers), he went on to become a janitor and helped people move on the weekends, all to support his family. This was until his life changed at the age of seventeen years.

1 https://abcnews.go.com/Business/tony-robbins-11-things-superstar-life-coach/story?id=29513846

He spent a week's pay cheque and attended a seminar by Jim Rohn, an American motivational speaker. This seminar mesmerized and inspired him to change his own life. Tony described Rohn and his speeches as follows: 'A man takes everything he's learned in 20,30 years of his life, and he pours it into like four hours.' Thus, he approached Rohn to work for him. He agreed and things started to change. Tony found a mentor, even though his job in the early days was to fill the room for Rohn's speeches.

This relationship would not have blossomed—in fact, they wouldn't have managed to meet—without Robbins investing in his learning and development at a time he had very little. You will notice this pattern over and over again. Those with insatiable hunger to learn prioritize it over everything else. They don't believe in the 'life deferment' plan which involves waiting for the mythical perfect day to arrive.

MOVING ON, STARTING UP

Tony learned a ton from Rohn, but he realized something while trying to manage the community for his seminars: He could do what his mentor did, perhaps even better. He knew that he had to try.

He started applying lessons from behavioural psychology, adopted a more personalized approach and started delivering his own speeches. He attended several hundred seminars (nothing significant happens until you perfect your craft and know your playground) across North America to gain deep customer insights and launched his career knowing reasonably clearly how we wanted to serve them.

Many people are sceptical of Tony because they say that he is just simplifying what scientists have already said. Others say that he is performer or a snake oil salesman. Everyone is entitled to their opinion, and I am not trying to change anyone's mind. All I am saying is that one can learn from anyone and everyone. Also, there doesn't need to be any hierarchy of achievement. Why must we compare researchers and entrepreneurs, or ones with fancy diplomas and those without? Comparison is a natural but silly emotion, best avoided as much as possible.

SIX FUNDAMENTAL HUMAN NEEDS

He built his category of one by developing a strong understanding and communication of six fundamental human needs. This isn't just a framework. If it were, it wouldn't be memorable. Business people create frameworks every day, but how many do you remember?

Tony's fundamental human needs approach is drawn from real-world experience of growing up in complete disarray with no relatable mentors, no food on the table and still figuring out a way to give and serve.

SIX CORE HUMAN NEEDS BY TONY ROBBINS

Following are six core human needs by Robbins.

Certainty: Having the assurance that you can avoid pain and derive pleasure

Uncertainty/variety: The need for pursuing the unfamiliar or unknown, the need for change or new stimuli

Significance: Feeling validated, important, loved and needed

Connection or love: A feeling or bond of closeness or forming a union with someone or something

Growth: The increase or expansion in one's capacity, capability and/or understanding

Contribution: A sense of serving and the need to help, support or give to others

PERSONALIZING THIS FRAMEWORK

For each person, these six needs are ranked and prioritized differently, and it shapes their character and behaviour. For example, if your top need is uncertainty, it will be hard for you to find happiness in stability or sticking to one thing. You may feel the need to keep changing your personal relationships or your career/job choices in order to feel like there is variety in your life, or you may undertake risks just for the sake of risking something. On the other hand, if your top need is certainty, then you would minimize the risks you take in all spheres of your life and constantly seek stability. Thus, it is important to maintain a balance and understand all of these six needs to find out where you are lacking and modify your behaviour accordingly. Each of these needs is equally important; however, it is equally important to avoid extremity in any case, and this is where dysfunctionalities arise. When we focus too much on one of these and neglect the rest, we are bound to fail.

KNOWLEDGE = POWER ?

'Knowledge is not power—it's only potential power. It is the application of knowledge (action) that leads to power,' Robbins explains in one of his podcasts called 'The Psychology of Success'. He says that one of the most important reasons for his success and what makes him smarter than other people is that every time he learns something new or significant, or when he decides to go through with an important decision, he does something in the moment that makes him commit to the task and follow through. The key is to not hesitate and maintain your pace and to act upon what you have decided to take up. It can be something as simple as sending an email or scheduling an appointment which you have been putting off. Most people think that acquiring wisdom and knowledge is enough and that is how people succeed. Robbins thinks otherwise and believes that people are extraordinary because they succeed in taking practical action. This is how he believes people can create their category of one and escape being average or indulging in finite thinking.

Robbins himself practised this at the age of seventeen years when he gained wisdom from the words of Jim Rohn, and then decided that he wished to work with someone like him, and he acted upon this. This helped him carve out his own career path as well. Thus, feeling inspired and enlightened is not enough, and your learnings will be rendered worthless if you do not make good use of them. Coming from a background in which his family could not afford Thanksgiving dinners at some point, a stranger helped Robbins one day by giving him a meal. This made him develop an unwavering sense of faith in humanity, and he decided that since strangers have been kind to him, he would be kind to them as well. For this reason, he aims to donate enough funds for 57 million meals for those in need through his partnership with the Feeding America Foundation and wishes to raise public funds to increase it from 57 million to 100 million meals. He believes that the true essence of living is in giving, and this is one of his core principles that he lives by.

OTHER KEY LESSONS FROM TONY ROBBINS

We can learn to master the art of consistency without stagnation or rigidity from Robbins. He chose something he was passionate about and stuck to it for over 40 years. Time flies when we chase our curiosity and understand our motivation. Throughout these four decades, he has been immensely successful and has maintained his wealth, and the only reason for this can be his ability to adapt to new times and circumstances while still maintaining his core values and personality. His contribution to people's lives is immense, and he has even helped improve lives of high-profile individuals who at some point lost their path in life. If Robbins did not help inspire Marc Benioff at a time when he needed it, Salesforce would probably not exist as the multibillion-dollar company that it is today. Benioff himself has credited Robbins for being the reason he created Salesforce.

Robbins also points out an important thing that we all need to change about our mindset: He teaches us to prioritize fulfilment over achievement. There are people who are by all objective standards successful, financially or otherwise, but in reality, underneath all that success and everything they have achieved, they are quite miserable. 'Success without fulfillment is the ultimate failure,' explains Robbins. Most people are always in a competitive rat race to 'achieve' the most in their lives and seldom focus on self-development, and this leaves them empty and dissatisfied with their lives, even if they manage to attain success. This is what finite thinking is, a concept given by James Carse in 1986. When people focus on short-term goals and neglect the more important things by focusing on what is urgent, they lose their sense of self and create an illusion of purpose.

Robbins also believes that there is a difference in being rich (having monetary wealth) and being wealthy (having true wealth). He thinks that while monetary wealth gives us the purchasing power, only true wealth can give us genuine and permanent happiness. For being truly wealthy, it is important to align your financial pursuits and decisions with your passions. To learn more about this subject, I recommend reading 'Building Wealth' on Tony Robbins's website.

He has established himself as the world's top life coach with a net worth of $600 million and has learnt to balance the six human needs and attained true wealth. I hope that while reading about Robbins and learning from him, we can all start acting on our aspirations and manifesting them into reality instead of treating them as merely far-fetched ambitions.

CHAPTER 36

CURATION AS A SERVICE

I am one of the first 100 curators of Faves along with Marissa Mayer (Former CEO, Yahoo!), Deborah Liu (CEO, Ancestry), Sean Kim (Head of Products, TikTok) and Ksenia Se (CEO, Sequence) at Faves, an interesting media platform trying to reimagine curation for the passion economy.

Like Faves, there are other curation platforms such as Pocket and Matter, among others. These are technology-enabled services which try and personalize your content consumption. Today, there are way too much content. Readers can get lost in the miasma of information. To counter that, they use services which make the Internet manageable.

While technology has an important role to play, individual or small groups of people have also started playing the role of a human Google. Most of my friends only go through content referred to them by a trusted source, someone relatable and aspirational.

I am observing two trends gaining more traction—people subscribing to other people and people subscribing to communities and micro-media houses for information and insight.

The Browser is a newsletter where the editorial team goes through hundreds of articles every day, pick out the top five and email it to the thousands of subscribers who pay to receive this curated list. All the articles they send are public. You can find and read all of them for free. Why do people pay for a service which is essentially finding interesting free stuff online, packaging it and sending it out?

I was struck by the testimonial of Ishita, a Network Capital subscriber and a student at Stanford's MBA programme. She said, 'I've subscribed to many newsletters but the Browser is the only one I consistently open and read, it's undoubtedly my favorite and highest-ROI newsletter subscription.'

What we are witnessing is the emergence of curation as a service. The world's most influential technology newsletter writer Ben Thompson who we have discussed earlier wrote an essay about the future of careers and economy at large. He suggests,

> I believe that the economy of the future will, if we don't stifle it along the way, look considerably different than the post World War II order dominated by large multinational corporations whose differentiation is predicated on distribution. Instead, the future looks more like a rainforest, with platforms that span the globe and millions of niche businesses that sit on top.
>
> I am, given my career, biased in this regard, but the rise of platforms like Shopify, Etsy, Substack, and the App Store are evidence that new careers can be built and untold niches filled when the entire world is your addressable market. The challenge in a worldwide market, though, is finding the customers who are interesting in the niche being filled.[1]

Curation is all about finding customers interested in your niche. You can demonstrate the value to your customers by a wide range of ways. The key is to add consistent value to them in ways that don't burn you out and leave your customers delighted. Ishita, referenced above, is a bright and successful professional. She can find five interesting articles to read on her own, but she finds value in the curation service of The Browser.

Ben Thompson writes a long-form analysis of technology trends, but there are thousands of other writers, analysts and mainstream media houses that provide solid commentary on tech. Ben's success can be attributed to delivering important insights regularly. Consistency builds trust and once trust builds, unless a serious breach happens, it sticks.

Curation combines consistency, trust and user delight. Passion economy builders need to understand the unmet needs of their

1 https://stratechery.com/2021/facebook-political-problems/

communities, remove fluff and separate signal from noise in order to create memorable experiences for the users.

Curators are emerging in all sorts of fields: from beauty to biochemistry; from entertainment to e-sports; and from product management to rocket science. The Internet enables all sorts of niche interests to scale. That is fundamentally what this book is about.

The hobbies of the past are emerging as mainstream professions. Even a few years back, it would seem ridiculous for a job to exist where all day long a person would read interesting articles and then send out the most interesting ones via email. But this is precisely what Robert Cottrell's team from The Browser does. It is a privately held company, so its revenues cannot be verified. Estimates suggest that over 10,000 people pay $5 every month to read their curated list of articles. They have a tiered subscription model where a small percentage of subscribers pay $30/month or $120/month for greater access to the core team. We discussed access economy earlier, and The Browser's pricing model is an interesting demonstration of what that looks like.

In addition to the subscription-based offering, The Browser also makes advertising revenue by promoting other newsletters and digital products. Overall, I will be surprised if the annual revenue of the company is less than $1 million. Let that sink in.

There is so much more that a company like that can do. Imagine Browser cafes, city-based subgroups, offline meetups—all propelled by the power of human connection and curation.

I have no direct or indirect connection with The Browser. I don't read it every day or every week. Occasionally, when I am looking to diversify my reading, I go through its content. We did, however, discuss it as a case study in Network Capital's Community Building Fellowship.

Many companies have tried to provide customized reading recommendations based on algorithms. So far, their success has been modest at best. In the years to come, AI will be able to get more sophisticated and new technologies will come up to personalize reading/learning experiences. That said, the role of the human curator in making such experiences come to life will be available at a premium.

Curator economy will be a major component of the passion economy. In the early days, I was more of a curator and connector at Network Capital. Doing that job gave me a flavour of what our community members wanted. Curation is more experimentation than anything else. A good curator is one who is trusted by his/her community to conduct experiments and arrive at the right curator–community fit.

All of us must strive to become better curators in our own networks, offices and families. Doing so will make our life more interesting and work more meaningful. It is very much an acquired skill which is honed by experimentation. Tinker away! That's the key.

CHAPTER 37

THE TIKTOK FACTOR

TikTok, a short-form video app, mastered the attention economy, made billions of dollars, grew faster than any other technology product and navigated complex geopolitical relationships to redefine what culture means in the 21st century.

Chris Walker is a London-based journalist who has chronicled the entire TikTok story in seven parts:

The dream of a global video app

ByteDance welcome

Growth of TikTok

Inside ByteDance

Creativity in the 21st century

Geopolitics

Future

'In the future, everyone will be world famous for 15 minutes.'

This is a quote by Andy Warhol from 1968. It was an outlandish prediction but seems to be coming true in today's Internet culture dominated by attention-grabbing apps. On TikTok, for instance, whether you have 1 follower or 1 million, you can become an overnight celebrity and then slip back into oblivion.

This happens because TikTok's algorithm works on what's called a 'content graph' which looks at previous engagement rather than social graph which explores who you follow. Social graph has been the core of most social networks (Facebook, Instagram and Twitter) in the last decade, but TikTok's algorithm has redefined fame as influence. But fame does not always translate to capital. The book explains the skewed economics of creators and documents how millions of likes can sometimes translate to enough money to purchase a hamburger in New York. The rise of TikTok has led to immense hope and immense scepticism. Hope should not drown out scepticism. Both need to be analysed in detail.

Let's start with 2016.

Alex Zhu and Louis Yang co-founded an app called Musical.ly, which allowed people to record 15-second snippets miming along to popular songs. It became such an Internet sensation that 7 out of 10 users had real-world friends on the app.

That said, the app was not designed to hyperscale. They struggled with growing-up pains—security, privacy and community integrity, among others. However, the co-founders kept iterating and eventually served hundreds of millions of teenagers. Their genius was understanding the pulse of how Gen Zs express online and connect with one another.

Eventually, Musical.ly would become TikTok, which is now close to having 3 billion users on its platform.

How did it happen? How did TikTok grow so fast?

The key factors of TikTok's hypergrowth include the following:

Ease of content creation: This includes adding music, editing and giving it a professional feel.

Video length: Attention spans are at an all-time low. TikTok understood that and wanted to give users the tools to watch hundreds of videos every hour, should they want to. They cracked the perfect video length for the modern, distracted Gen Z.

Finding audience at scale: Thanks to its content graph, it made every user believe that they could make it big online. And it delivered on the promise. Everybody from seventeen-year-old girls who knew how to mime to eighty-five-yea-old retired grandfathers who work out joined this global attention economy. A small chunk of them made fortunes.

Oodles of cash: TikTok has invested huge sums of money on marketing and finding and supporting creators.

This turned out to be a huge difference from Vine, a similar company of yesteryears which failed because it could not crack monetization and because the popular Viners felt that they were not getting a fair deal. Basically, Vine was getting a much better end of the bargain.

A similar case can be made for TikTok, but with the launch of their billion-dollar creator fund, they have at least in part allayed the frustration of their most important users—the content creators.

THE BYTEDANCE EQUATION

Have you heard of ByteDance? Most people haven't. Founded in 2012 by Zhang Yiming, it is valued at over $180 billion. Its suite of apps is used by more than 2 billion people, and its 2020 revenue was $34 billion.

Zhang came up with the idea of the company while observing how newspapers in subways were being replaced by smartphones. Smartphone sales were through the roof in 2011, and newspapers were dwindling.

'I thought smartphones would replace newspapers to become the most important medium of information distribution.'

His key insight was deploying AI at the core of its app and enabling personalization to suit the tastes of its users. Again, content graph based on people's interests was the key, unlike the social graph popularized in the West.

Even though he was not familiar with the technicalities of the personalization engine he wanted to develop, he figured it out by identifying people in his network who could help. The important insight from Zhang's career is that one can learn anything or figure out how to solve the most complex of problems if one knows the important questions to explore.

ByteDance wanted to be 'borderless as Google' from the start. It started by publishing an app for sharing memes: Neihan Duanzi. It became viral and led to the creation of a closely knit community which would also meet offline.

Then came ByteDance's news app, Toutiao, which personalized tailored stories likely to capture the interest of users every time they opened the app. Its data needs were huge—identifying what a user wants isn't an easy problem. ByteDance deployed some of its smartest engineers to figure out the problem and, by 2018, the app was processing 50 petabytes of data every day. That is roughly equal to streaming 11 million 2 hour-long HD movies on Netflix—every 24 hours.

THE ACQUISITION SPREE

Musical.ly wasn't the only acquisition which paved way for TikTok we know today. There have been more than 17 acquisitions to augment its technology base and broader user base.

Flipagram turned out to offer both. It had powerful content creation tools, but it didn't know how to serve it up to users within the app. People would create content on Flipagram and share it on other social media platforms. The videos had a watermark which helped its popularity, but there was no incentive for users to remain engaged.

By then, ByteDance had built a solid recommendation engine for its news app. Flipagram had the content, ByteDance had the technology. Conditions were ripe for an acquisition and that's what happened.

TIKTOK ONLY HAPPENED IN 2017

Even today, TikTok doesn't operate in China. A remarkably similar, slightly more sanitized app Douyin serves up China's users. Only in 2017, having observed the kind of popularity Douyin enjoyed, ByteDance made an early version available on Google Play Store. TikTok relied heavily on Douyin's code.

From its inception, it wanted to capture the global market. TikTok was happy to pay for popularity. In India, for example, they started targeting tier 4 and tier 5 cities, often paying the most popular creators to move from other platforms.

TikTok is designed for addiction in a way. Because people use it as much as they do, it has copious amounts of useful data which can be mined for advertisements and censorship (somewhat of a growing worry these days), most importantly for finetuning its own algorithm. It does sound a bit dystopian, and the scepticism of Western countries and that of countries like India is understandable. However, based on Chris's analysis, TikTok doesn't seem to be created as a global domination tool by the Chinese government. It is an incredibly sophisticated product which like most things coming out of China goes through lots of checks and controls.

Yes, that makes it at odds with Zhang's vision of a borderless Google, but it is hard to get rid of your origins.

CONCLUDING THOUGHTS

Whether you like TikTok or not, there is no denying that it is a critical piece of technology which is changing culture faster than we can keep up with. We can panic, criticize or be part of it in order to shape it. The choice is ours. Nothing is preordained.

SECTION 4

MENTAL MODELS AND PRINCIPLES FOR MAKING PASSION ECONOMY WORK FOR YOU

CHAPTER 38

FIND YOUR
FRUSTRATION AND START
A SIDE HUSTLE

In March, 2021, my team and I hacked together a small project called London Stack, with the simple mission of revitalizing serendipity in the post-pandemic world with outdoor brunches in groups of six. If the experiment goes well, we will scale it to all cities where Network Capital is active. If it doesn't, we will learn from the experience.

We can safely see that every single person on the planet has been frustrated by something. The difference between doers, procrastinators and naggers is that doers have a bias for action, procrastinators tend to push forward deadlines to a mythical date when things will be perfect (spoiler alert: things will never be) and naggers find comfort in complaining incessantly.

Most of us happen to be procrastinators. We don't want to do things that don't work or don't scale. There is a reputation to protect and there is comfort in status quo.

I want to make a case for rapid prototyping and taking micro-actions towards your frustration. Perhaps you find the way people network silly, perhaps your neighbourhood is too polluted or perhaps you are tired of fake news. Whatever your frustration is, there is light at the end of the tunnel.

All you need to do is to march ahead and do something small to address it. Who knows where that path might take you, who cares if the result is favourable, you owe it to yourself to try.

The beauty of weekend projects and side hustles is that they propel us to scale down our vision into something tangible in a few hours of hacking. Instead of whining about why conditions aren't conducive, weekend projects help you figure out how badly you want to do something.

Scaling down is important at times. It teaches you more about yourself than you realize. If you are curious about starting a bar of a pub, you should try to host a weekend pop-up and see how it goes. Perhaps you will love the experience or perhaps you will realize that it is way too much work and the end result leaves you unenergized. Instead of paying for rent, getting F&B licence and seeking permission for music from local authorities to run a massive establishment, try something scaled down.

We know of our community members who wanted to work in investing but realized that their true passion is venture building, aspiring writers who always wanted to write a book but realized they didn't really enjoy sitting for hours typing out words on their laptop. They liked the idea of writing, not the craft itself. Again, you will know where you stand only if you conduct micro-experiments over weekends.

OBSESSION WITH PERFECTION

There is fear of failure and an obsession with perfection which stops many ambitious, capable and curious people from trying. You should be wary of such a mental trap. Your goal is not to prove a point to someone but to enjoy the process.

Perfectionism creates bottlenecks for execution. LinkedIn co-founder Reid Hoffman often says that if you are not embarrassed of the first iteration of your product, you launched too late.

Is Reid saying that we should all do embarrassing things? Of course, not. He is making a case that embarrassment is a natural by-product of experimentation, and creative people should wear embarrassment as a badge of honour.

LATERAL THINKING

Weekend projects and side hustles make us better thinkers by sparking lateral thinking. We are able to develop a broader perspective on the way the world works and what our unique role is in shaping it. Essentially, we are able to connect dots better.

London Stack will teach Network Capital about a wide range of unfamiliar subjects: complex coordination, food, pricing strategies and trying out an invite-only model, among others. Hopefully many learnings will help scale our local Network Capital chapters. Again, we don't know but we are excited to see where it goes.

Even if there are no tangible benefits, we would have become smarter through experimentation. Economist Sanjeev Sanyal, in his Network Capital masterclass, said that there are no failed experiments. We test hypotheses through a process of trial and error; we can't go into them expecting the result we want.

The joy of discovery is indescribable. Weekend projects propel practical innovation, stuff that actually moves the needle. In addition, they add colour to our coronavirus-fatigued stay-at-home existence.

Gumroad, a company I invested in, was built over a weekend. Patreon, which recently raised $155 million at $4 billion valuation, was set up in a few weeks of hacking.[1] The first version of YouTube was ready within days, as three former PayPal employees decided to act on their frustration of struggling with sharing videos online. The YouTube of today is far more sophisticated, but its origin can be traced to a few weekends of trial and error.

You may or may not build a gazillion-dollar company over a weekend project or a side hustle but indulging your curiosity has a massive upside.

PICKING THE RIGHT PROBLEMS TO SOLVE

Naval Ravikant once asked, 'What feels like play to you, but looks like work to others?' I reflected on this question and jotted down my responses. Take a look.

---

1 https://www.npr.org/2021/01/08/954876726/patreon-jack-conte-and-sam-yam

Community building

Public speaking

Writing

Building deep relationships with large groups of people

Mental maths

These are not only my strengths but also activities which energize me. I would pursue them even if no one paid me.

This question is pivotal for all of us, especially if we want to build our category of one.

In order to do meaningful work which makes a real dent in the universe, we need to do three things:

Be consistent: We need to show up and put our work out there regularly. Certain days will be hard, and there will always be competing forces vying for your attention. The difference between people who are able to get a lot done and those who don't comes down to consistency. Talent doesn't differ too much. Neither does intelligence. Ability to deliver output despite odds is the key differentiating factor.

Be persistent: Grit matters. Overnight successes are massive lies. No one is an overnight success. Years of rejections, preparation and deliberate practice lead to exponential success. If you want to dive deep into this subject, I recommend listening to the Network Capital podcast[2] with Northwestern University's Professor Benjamin Jones.

Focus on micro improvements: Compounding is the eighth wonder of the world. To excel at something, we need to become 1 per cent better every day.

I didn't become good at mental maths overnight. I remember going to bed thinking of numbers and patterns as a kid. I found it interesting, so I kept enjoying the pursuit. Without realizing,

2 https://www.networkcapital.tv/course/podcast-with-professor-benjamin-jones

I kept getting a tad better. With time, compounding revealed its magical effects.

If we consider the above-mentioned points, it will become clear that success is a long-term game. And the first rule of long-term games is that we need to keep playing. No one wants to be a one hit wonder. Shortcuts, prescriptions and hacks don't really work, so we need to follow our curiosity and create our own path.

CHAPTER 39

WHY PRESCRIPTIONS AND PLAYBOOKS DON'T WORK

FIGURING OUT 'WHAT FEELS LIKE PLAY TO YOU, BUT LOOKS LIKE WORK TO OTHERS?'

We explored this partially in the previous chapter. Let's dive deeper. The beauty of this question is that it contextualizes our skills and strengths. A regular strengths finder/personality assessment test is useful in that it gives us a flavour of what we are good at but it fails to put that in perspective to market realities.

Also, many of us are great at things we don't really love. The case in point is engineering entrance exams in India. There are thousands of Network Capital community members who studied at top engineering institutions but dislike engineering. Should they work as engineers just because they were good at taking an exam?

IMAGINE YOU WON A LOTTERY

What would you choose to do if you won a lottery and didn't have to earn a living to make ends meet?

Perhaps you will want to travel the world, buy things that you always wanted and give a ton of money to charity. Let your imagination run wild. You have all the money in the world for this thought experiment.

What would you do after three years when the novelty of being wealthy has been normalized. Hedonic adaptation is our tendency to quickly return to a relatively stable level of happiness despite major recent positive or negative events or life changes.

Even after winning the lottery, you will at some point have to grapple with the existential pangs of meaningful work. Remember the AMP framework?

We can't do great work without being intrinsically motivated, so we need to define what autonomy, mastery and purpose mean to us. Let's assume that winning the lottery gives us the autonomy. Even then, mastery and purpose need to be contextualized.

What would you like to master? And what should the deeper purpose of your work be?

Answering these two questions will be the first step towards figuring out 'What feels like play to you, but looks like work to others?'

Next, observe how you enjoy spending time on weekends. Leisure is revealing in that it tells you how you like to energize yourself. I built a moderately successful acting career and a decent debating career by understanding what leisure meant to me.

I like being out and about immersing myself in new adventures. Knowing this helped me figure out major work and life decisions. I don't debate and act as much as I used to, but a large chunk of my work at Network Capital is communicating complex ideas to large groups of people. It is play for me, and I reckon that it would be a ton of work for many people.

Lastly, reflect on the top three projects/experiences which fulfilled you the most. Most likely there will be common recurring patterns. Observe them. Your superpower is hidden somewhere in that data. It is the time to find it.

**If you can't find your top three, it is time to rethink your career strategy.

CHAPTER 40

PRODUCTIZE YOURSELF

AngelList founder Naval Ravikant often tells us to productize ourselves.[1] He explains that we should figure out what we're uniquely good at and apply as much leverage as possible.

Productize yourself = Specific knowledge + Leverage

Let's unpack specific knowledge and leverage.

SPECIFIC KNOWLEDGE

Specific knowledge is the knowledge you care most about. It is a function of genuine curiosity. I find communities fascinating. I have spent a large chunk of the last five years thinking about them, experimenting, reading, learning, hustling and iterating. That specific knowledge (about communities) helped me build Network Capital, write a bestselling book, teach CBCs on community building, invest in a platform for CBCs, get a column with *Harvard Business Review*, *Mint* and World Economic Forum, give TED Talks and much more. Every single item in this list can be traced back to my curiosity and specific knowledge about communities.

Naval says that specific knowledge is found much more by pursuing your innate talents, your genuine curiosity and your passion. It's not by going to school for whatever is the hottest job, it's not for going into whatever field investors say is the hottest.

LEVERAGE

Now let's get to leverage. Basically, it means scaling your specific knowledge with the help of labour, capital, code, media and, most importantly, community.

1 https://www.youtube.com/watch?v=wICGnoYtciA

CASE STUDY: SAHIL LAVINGIA OF GUMROAD

I invested in Gumroad and recently topped up my investment. The founder of Gumroad, Sahil, is an interesting character. He wrote an evocative article 'Reflecting on My Failure to Build a Billion-dollar Company'.

The article got great traction online and Sahil's personal brand (despite the supposed failure) started soaring. People appreciated his vulnerability and authenticity. They were also inspired by the fact that despite having to fire all employees and return money to investors, Gumroad kept going.

His Twitter followers grew exponentially, and realizing the potential of his story, he decided to diversify. This is what he did:

1. Kept building Gumroad in an unorthodox way
2. Leveraged his Twitter following to launch a rolling fund and read the thesis of his fund

> I have access to high-quality companies from around the world, because:
> - I have a fast-growing audience of founders who respect me because I operate a successful business in a burgeoning space (the creator economy).
> - I have a strong network from living in Silicon Valley and tweeting from afar.
>
> Founders want me on their cap table, because:
> - I am a designer and engineer. I help my investments solve real problems
> - I am a founder. Founders want to raise money from founders.
> - I have an engaged audience that can move the needle for them, in an organic way
>
> I will look for founders who:
> - have a deep understanding of the space they are in—they typically read a lot

- haven't waited for permission to get started—they have hard skills if not degrees
- don't have access to the traditional startup ecosystem—they may be younger, URM, etc

I am interested in products that are:
- soon-to-be obvious but only recently possible
- solving a difficult, boring, complex problem with an easy-to-use, elegant solution

I'll look at anything, but especially B2B SaaS, e-commerce, future of work, video, and developer tools. I'll avoid music, DTC, and gambling. I do plan to make some international investments.

I am investing $100K–250K checks in early-stage companies that have the potential to 100x. I will take my pro rata almost never—and likely through SPVs. My primary focus will be helping these companies get to their next financial milestone, often a Series A.

3. Started teaching online with Maven (a company I invested in)
4. Wrote a book with the same title as his online course, *The Minimalist Entrepreneur*

Basically, Sahil failed forward, productized himself and unbundled his experiences to become an unorthodox entrepreneur, investor, teacher and writer.

From the outside, these might seem like unrelated activities, but if you dive deep, you will realize that Sahil is creating these new opportunities for himself based on the specific knowledge developed by building Gumroad.

Genuine curiosity has the power to catapult you forward in the toughest of times, so your challenge is not to look for the hottest new trend but to seek the question(s) that sparks fascination. It should ideally be something you would do even if you were not to get paid. Even if you fail like Sahil, the insights gleaned and networks developed are there to serve you forever if you are smart about it.

SUGGESTIONS FOR PRODUCTIZING YOURSELF

1. Ignore almost all 'hot new things'. You will reap the benefits of specific knowledge, not cursory purviews of Twitter feeds and newspapers. If you try and stay on top of everything, you will burn out.

    Remember Don Knuth?

    Dr Knuth says that he has been a happy man ever since he abandoned his email, one that he had been using since 1975. In his typically witty voice, he says that it seems to him that 15 years of email is plenty for one lifetime.

    > Email is a wonderful thing for people whose role in life is to be on top of things. But not for me; my role is to be on the bottom of things. What I do takes long hours of studying and uninterruptible concentration. I try to learn certain areas of computer science exhaustively; then I try to digest that knowledge into a form that is accessible to people who don't have time for such study.[2]

    Develop specific knowledge, read what sparks your curiosity and feel free to ignore other things.

    Unbundle your skills and experiences. Ask yourself what you can write about, what you can talk authentically about, where you can invest and what you can build. Your first iteration won't be an award-winning publication or a billion-dollar investment or a trillion-dollar company. And that is a good thing. Wait it out, keep building and keep unbundling. Once you have enough specific knowledge, you will notice how opportunities keep trickling down to you.

2. Your recall value is your brand. Be intentional about it. Generally speaking, it will be hard to build a strong brand in a crowded space. Build your category of one.

Productize Yourself

3. Try to be among the best in the world at something. It doesn't need to be massive or profound. It is a winner-take-all market. The best in any category gets to do it for everyone. For example, if you are a top-notch Clubhouse/Twitter Spaces moderator, everyone in your circle will ask you to join their club and speak. If you are consistent in upping your game, you are likely to be paid handsomely in the long run.

This is what my unbundled career map looks like.

Key curiosity: Communities

Building: Network Capital

Investing: Maven, Gumroad, Backstage Capital, Etsy (all community-driven companies)

Writing: Books, magazine + newspaper articles about communities

Speaking: Mostly about communities and their applications to education, learning, skilling, etc.

What's interesting about all these initiatives is that all of them support each other. Writing, speaking and investing help Network Capital scale, and Network Capital scaling brings about interesting avenues to write, speak and invest.

CHAPTER 41

TEACH SOMETHING

Towards the end of 2020, I invested in an unnamed education company which was keen to unbundle the university experience. I liked their community-based approach and found their CBCs remarkably similar to the fellowships we run on Network Capital. The founders seemed to understand that education was so much more nuanced than just test preparation and other FOMO-fuelled techniques to drive up the collective anxieties of parents and students.

Few months after my investment, that unnamed company found a name, product–market fit and a massive investment round from Andreessen Horowitz. In just 120 days, teachers on Maven made $1 million by sharing what they know to a bunch of serious, motivated learners.

THE UNDERPAID, OVERWORKED TEACHERS

In Finland, teaching is considered among the most prestigious jobs. It pays well and offers steep career growth and strong social capital. Breaking into teaching involves a series of fairly competitive exams. Only the very best make it.

This is not the norm in most countries. Most teachers are overworked and underpaid. Here we are only talking about serious teachers, not the ones who take up the profession only to slack off. Go to lower-income schools in any country and you will see how classes really work. There, students succeed not because of teachers but despite them. Yes, there are some exceptions, but there are exceptions to everything. Let's focus on trends, not outliers here, shall we?

COVID-19 put inordinate administrative overload on teachers. They not only had to redesign their lesson plans and keep students engaged but also figure out ways to track progress, submit clunky performance updates and make do with budget cuts across the board.

Two things happened.

First, 'star teachers', teachers loved by students, realized their importance to keep the education system running amid unbridled chaos.

Second, it occurred to them that they didn't really need institutions. In fact, institutions made things slower and more bureaucratic. Also, institutions kept most of the money for themselves. There was no financial incentive to go the extra mile.

While many teachers don't get into the profession to make money, there is nothing wrong with teachers trying to create new income streams for themselves.

Who is a teacher?

Network Capital started with the fundamental belief that every single person on the planet has something to learn and something to teach. All we need is a community for enabling skill sharing at scale. The first time I saw this in action was during my internship at The Grameen Creative Lab, an initiative of Nobel Laureate Muhammad Yunus. There, we trained beggars to become sales agents for a protein yogurt. Beggars were perfect for the job, as they wandered about cities looking for alms and knew every street. We just had to complement their specific knowledge—knowledge which cannot be taught but can be learned—with training that made sense.

So who is a teacher? Is it someone with institutional affiliations? Someone with fancy degrees? Someone who enjoys knowledge sharing? Simply put, anyone with specific knowledge can be a teacher. That person just needs to figure out ways to make their students smarter in stipulated periods of time.

Some of our favourite teachers are ones we end up having long-term relationships with, but that happens over the long term. The seeds of curiosity are planted in the early days of interaction and instruction.

The teachers of the 21st century will be Internet-powered and community-oriented. Students will come to them despite their institutional affiliations.

Suppose someone has mastered enterprise sales but doesn't want to sell anymore. No university teaches stuff like this, but being good at sales is a life skill, even if you are a poet. Influencing, motivating, negotiating and getting to specific outcomes come in handy, whether you are negotiating your book deal or figuring out ways to get more signups for your online course or webinar.

If the person who is known in their circles as being good at sales, they might decide to translate all learnings into a CBC and create a channel to complement their monthly income. One day, that person might quit their job and commit to it full time. We have so many incredible examples of people who have done that on Network Capital.

Take a look at Mahmoud Rasmi, a former university professor in Lebanon who quit to teach an online CBC on philosophy. His online class is so much more interesting than his offline one. He has a smarter cohort, doesn't have to deal with university politics and controls his fate. Given the state of affairs in Lebanon, what Rasmi has built is nothing short of inspiring. He is earning thousands of dollars and having a blast doing it. Contrast that with the salary of a law associate in that country who earns $100 every 35 days or an engineer who earns $150/month, if lucky. Yes, that is how bad things are.

How will star teachers become millionaires?

On Maven, teachers charge around $1,200 for a power-packed 4-week course. These teachers are usually the absolute best in their fields.

Normally, CBCs admit anywhere between 20 and 80 students. So if you are a star teacher, you can expect to make $24,000–$96,000 for the month you teach on a platform like Maven. Maven is just one example. There are myriads of other platforms like that. Further, there will be many more in the making.

At $96,000, if you teach a CBC every month, you will be a dollar millionaire after the first year. This won't be easy, and very few people will actually get there, but it is very much possible.

Teaching is fun and immensely educational—for the teacher.

Richard Feynman, one of the most renowned physicists, had a four-pronged strategy for learning anything. Take a look.

1. Identify a subject that piques your interest

2. Teach it to a child

3. Identify gaps in your knowledge

4. Organize, simplify and 'teach'

Teaching crystalizes your knowledge. With tools like Stripe, Zoom, Maven, Teachable, LinkedIn, Facebook, Twitter, Network Capital, Skype and TikTok, you hack your mini university and create a job you love. If you do it well, money will not be a problem. More importantly, you will get smarter every single day. There is nothing quite like it.

Write

Writers are becoming millionaires at scale. To understand how and why, one has to go back to 2011 when *The New York Times* was thinking about pivoting to subscriptions instead of relying solely on advertisements. At the time it was unclear whether people would pay for quality writing.

After much back and forth, it decided to push the pedal on subscriptions. The rest is history. Bang in the middle of the pandemic, they added over 600k subscribers and generated over $130 million in revenue—in just 90 days.

When *The New York Times* does something, others usually follow, especially when it comes to taking inspiration from their most important strategic pivot. Slowly, most media companies started becoming subscription companies.

Understanding the power of subscriptions is critical to answering the question whether you should quit your job to write.

Subscriptions, in the context of media and writers, have enabled the smaller players to build something meaningful and financially lucrative. Back in the day, advertisements were the only source of revenue for media outlets, which meant that having a large audience was essential for success. In other words, if you don't work for a big brand, your writing career will be sprinkled with misadventures.

The ultimate leverage was with big brand media houses. Talented writers from around the world applied to a handful of jobs which paid a pittance and overworked to the bone. Want to see how competitive it can get? Watch CNN reporter and Network Capital member Aditi Sangal's masterclass.

The challenge of advertisement-based models even for big brands was unpredictability and uncertain return on investment (ROI). Further, when the economy is doing badly, the first budget that is slashed is advertising.

Interestingly, this larger movement towards subscription has worked well for both media companies and writers. *The New York Times* subscription revenues make things super clear. At a smaller scale, even Network Capital makes 'all' its revenues from subscriptions. We don't pay for advertising and don't take money from brands, even though hundreds of them approach us to reach our community members.

How does this relate to you?

Should you quit your job to write is an interesting question. What's clear is that in the 21st century, you don't need hyperscale as a writer to begin with. You don't need to have the following of a J. K. Rowling or *The New York Times* to make it. Few hundred or a thousand would do. At least, that would be a good start.

Take a look at Sam Parr's subscription-based newsletter 'Trends' which is making millions in revenue based on the power of words. He has a simple four-pronged strategy which got him to this point.

1. Pick a tiny but growing audience whose members truly care about what you are saying.

2. Write utilitarian content which helps readers accomplish specific goals—be in monetizing, career advancement, social capital or simply the feeling of being interesting at a dinner party.

3. Charge between $500 and $1k annually. Basically, that means focusing on few people who will be willing to pay a bit more than expected because they are deeply connected to what you have to say.

4. Grow your subscriber base via ads and free viral written content.

Writing, like product design or development, is hard but learnable through deliberate practice, for example, software, media (aka words) and scales. Once done, the marginal cost of replication is zero. For example, it takes the same effort to write an article or a newsletter for 100 people or 100,000 people. For example, if you google 'deep generalist', my *Mint* article comes up first. I wrote it keeping the Network Capital subscribers in mind, but it has scaled to reach millions of people with no additional cost or effort.

Getting to that point isn't easy or a one-day game, but it demonstrates the scale at which purposeful writing can operate. Of course, the quality of research and the clarity of writing matter, but the most critical question for emerging writers to address is the content–market fit.

Who are you writing for and what specific outcomes can the reader expect if they engage with your content?

WRITING STACK

Once you figure out your area of focus, you need to develop your ideas. They can't just be a summation of ideas present online. You need to combine them in interesting ways and add your own lived experience, your perspective to it. This is easier said than done because to write well regularly, you need to be a contrarian who comes up with non-obvious insights consistently in a way which is both surprising and inevitable. This surprise + inevitability framework is advanced by Elizabeth Gilbert, who we have previously discussed.

At the essence of it, you need to delight your readers in a way that doesn't seem formulaic but still manages to be relatable and remarkable. The 'Aha' moments are intangible but form the core of your writing stack. You can't design for such moments, but if you practise enough, you will understand the unarticulated needs of your reader in subtle ways.

Again, it comes down to intimately understanding your audience and developing familiarity with the ways they function. You can take inspiration from how anthropologists research and how iconic entrepreneurs bring new products to life. Repeated tinkering helps, so does curiosity—the art of being interested, not overtly attempting to be interesting.

Great writing comes down to paying attention, not getting attention. You can get thousands of eye balls by tweeting something provocative, but how long will it last? The Internet memory is short. You don't want to be a flash in the pan. Just as they say, build to last; writers need to write to last if they want to make a career out of it.

Invoking Shakespeare can seem intimidating, but humour us for a second. The Bard is as relevant today as he was hundreds of years back because he focused on things that don't change— human emotions, the primal nature of jealousy, lust, anger and betrayal. This is not a fundamentally different approach from Jeff Bezos who built Amazon constantly thinking of things that won't change. Customers will always want lower prices, faster deliveries and efficient services. A writer with the Bezos approach will direct their curiosity to fundamental things about human nature, even when writing about the pandemic or the ed-tech revolution or the way politics pan out at the grassroots.

Should you make writing your career?

You should, but you don't need to quit your job just yet. How about approaching this question like a scientist and conducting a bunch of experiments to test your hypothesis? Consider the following questions:

1. Do you actually enjoy the process of putting pen to paper?
2. What frequency of writing energizes you?
3. Are you able to build a loyal reader base over a period of six months?

4. If yes, ask them directly: 'Why do you read my work?' Your goal is to figure out specific reasons.

5. If you started paying people to read your work, will significantly more people read you?

6. How about if you decide to charge them? You will only know it if you try a controlled experiment.

7. Do you enjoy your own writing? When you go back to read your old work, do you feel a sense of pride or is there latent regret?

8. Do you have specific knowledge to share? This is true for both teachers and writers.

9. If not, how can you build your specific knowledge? Specific knowledge doesn't need to be related to what you studied in college or where you work. It can literally be anything.

CONCLUDING THOUGHTS

The time to write is now. You can set up your one-person company focused on writing in 20 minutes—Ghost/Substack/Revue/Convert Kit + Stripe will get it done. Whether you want to do it to think better or make millions (over time), you owe it to yourself to give it a shot. We only request that you approach it smartly. There won't be any perfect day or a macro epiphany coming your way tomorrow. You need an imperfect, clunky start. You need an MVP and, of course, you need to have something important to say. The good news is that every single person on the planet has an interesting story, an interesting perspective hidden somewhere. You just need to look for that story, start and be intentional about it for some time.

Even for iconic business writers like Ben Thompson who we covered in the newsletter economy, the start was choppy. He was turned down by every major news publication when he pitched. Today, the same newspapers run around to get a quote from him. This is not some revenge story, just a demonstration of how things compound over time. Ben is a far-better writer today than he was when he got started, but he persisted through all the rejections, quit his job at Microsoft and spent some time in anxious anticipation about his future. Today, the same Ben works out of a beach in Asia and makes multiple millions on his terms, doing something he loves.

You will 'not' be the next Ben Thompson, but you could build your category of one. It is the time to give it a shot, don't you think?

Afterthought: Competition is for losers. FOMO is for one-trick ponies. Peace out and build something you truly care about.

CHAPTER 42

AVOID THE FOMO TRAP

FOMO is the defining characteristic of our generation. We do our best to jump from one option to another, hoping to create impact, find meaning and lead change along the way.

WHAT IS LIQUID MODERNITY?

Liquid modernity is a powerful phrase coined by Polish philosopher Zygmunt Bauman. It refers to the state of affairs when we do our level best to not commit to any one identity, place or community. Thus, we remain like liquid—adapting to fit any future state.

The world around is liquid as well. Lawyer Pete Davis explains that we can't rely on any job or role or idea or cause for long—and they can't rely on us to do so either. That is liquid modernity: the infinite browsing mode for everything in our lives.

BEING STUCK BEHIND A LOCKED DOOR VS LIVING IN A HALLWAY

We are paralysed by the thought of commitment. No one wants to be stuck behind a locked door, but nobody wants to live in a hallway either.

We get stuck behind a locked door when we make important choices without giving proper thought. Living in a hallway is a metaphor for keeping all options open but refusing to commit to any. The upside of living in a hallway is that you get to observe and evaluate everything. The downside is that you are an observer, not a participant; you are a spectator, not a player.

Leave the hallway, shut the door behind and settle in.

Passion Economy and the Side-Hustle Revolution

I love micro-experiments. They form the core feature of our CEO Fellowship and the 'I don't know what I want to do with my life' Fellowship. These low-risk experiments conducted in a time-bound manner with the help of a supportive community play a pivotal role in figuring out the problems we care most about and people we want to partner with.

That said, at some point we need to transform our experimentation into outcomes. That is when we need to shut some doors—permanently—and give everything we have to achieving our vision. There is no guarantee of anything, but it is worth keeping in mind that unless we are all in, failure is the more likely outcome.

SUSTAINED COMMITMENT

Martin Luther King Jr is etched permanently in our memory for his iconic 'I Have a Dream' speech and his stoic determination confronting the fire hoses in 1963. While these are heroic acts without a doubt, his ultimate heroism was hosting thousands of tedious meetings to bring the community together.

Long-term heroism requires dedication to doing less glamorous things consistently. Interestingly, the word 'dedicate' has two meanings:

1. To make something holy (dedicate a song)

2. To stick at something for a long time (dedicated to the cause)

These two meanings seem to be connected in a way. Commitment—sticking to something for a long time—is holy.

'Tell me, what is your plan to do with your one wild and precious life?'

Poet Mary Oliver has a beautiful poem called *The Summer Day*[1]:

---

1 https://www.loc.gov/programs/poetry-and-literature/poet-laureate/poet-laureate-projects/poetry-180/all-poems/item/poetry-180-133/the-summer-day/

Who made the world?
Who made the swan, and the black bear?
Who made the grasshopper?
This grasshopper, I mean—
the one who has flung herself out of the grass,
the one who is eating sugar out of my hand,
who is moving her jaws back and forth instead
of up and down—
who is gazing around with her enormous and complicated eyes.
Now she lifts her pale forearms and thoroughly washes her face.
Now she snaps her wings open, and floats away.
I don't know exactly what a prayer is.
I do know how to pay attention, how to fall down
into the grass, how to kneel down in the grass,
how to be idle and blessed, how to stroll through the fields,
which is what I have been doing all day.
Tell me, what else should I have done?
Doesn't everything die at last, and too soon?
Tell me, what is it you plan to do
with your one wild and precious life?

You can read her poem with caution or hope. It might prompt you to think that you have one life. What if you get the big decisions wrong?

You could, however, also choose to interpret it this way— I have one wild and precious life. I will take many decisions. Some will turn out to be right and some won't. Instead of worrying about always taking the right decisions, I will try to 'make' decisions right, especially those where expectations and outcomes don't seem to align.

Trying to make decisions right with dedication, empathy and commitment is essential to make sense of the world. Hopping around like a butterfly can be fun over a few weeks in spring but as a lifestyle, it can get exhausting.

CONCLUDING THOUGHTS

Liquid modernity can get crippling if we lose touch with our community, identity and intrinsic curiosities. Being adaptable is a great asset, but that is different from trying to fit in everywhere by keeping options open. Shut some doors, move out of the hallway and find a room of your own. Build from there, browse from there—once a while.

CHAPTER 43

BECOME A DEEP GENERALIST

ART OF BEING A DEEP GENERALIST

Tennis star Roger Federer dabbled with basketball, handball, skiing, wrestling, swimming, table tennis and skateboarding as a kid. When he began to gravitate towards tennis, his parents cautioned him against taking the sport too seriously. Essentially, when they discovered his love for sports, they encouraged him to have what author Dave Epstein calls sampling period—low-risk experiments meant to organically discover what one loves doing and most want to succeed in.

Golf legend Tiger Woods, on the other hand, specialized under his father's tutelage before he turned three years old. Woods's learning path of early specialization has become the default template for schools and colleges who want to prime students for excellence. Even in most modern workplaces, a disproportionate emphasis is paid on having narrow skills which are marketable. While there is nothing wrong having an area of focus, one should be mindful of the perils of early specialization. There are three key reasons for that.

First, we tend to specialize without knowing why. More than 80 per cent of people work in areas which have nothing to do with their field of study. In India, for example, most students first graduate from courses like engineering and then figure out what they want to do with their lives. Spending four years of one's life getting deep into a subject one doesn't particularly care about is a colossal waste of time, energy and money.

Second, it hinders lateral thinking, a problem-solving approach which draws upon seemingly disparate concepts and domains. Most innovators are lateral thinkers. Their lateral thinking is a direct result of combining different strands of thoughts and learning from

Passion Economy and the Side-Hustle Revolution

different contexts. Leonardo DaVinci combined art and engineering, Steve Jobs built upon the interconnectedness of design, fashion and technology, and Richard Feynman, a Nobel Laureate in Physics, is known to draw upon references from music.

Third, people with a narrow set of skills tend to approach every problem through the same lens. This not only ignores loopholes in one's hypothesis but also amplifies biases. As investor Charlie Munger puts it, 'To a man with a hammer, everything looks like a nail.'

So if early specialization can backfire, should we all snack on an array of ideas, insights and interests? The short answer is no. The future belongs to deep generalists, a term popularized by Jotform CEO Aytekin Tank. These are people who combine two or more diverse domains and integrate them into something defensible and unique.

In the 21st century, with the mainstreaming of automation and AI, some jobs will be automated and some would become redundant. Even highly trained and accomplished professionals—radiologists, traders, programmers, etc.—might lose their jobs to algorithms if they are overreliant on their narrow set of specialized skills.

On the other hand, deep generalists will not only keep their jobs but also be able to demand a premium for what they bring to the table. These are the professionals who will push the boundaries for creativity and innovation in the AI era. Their competitive advantage—a unique combination of breadth and depth—will propel them to learn, unlearn and develop innovative solutions consistently.

One of the best professional decisions I took in my early twenties was to invest a year studying liberal arts. Studying anthropology, philosophy, history, literature, art and economics after a couple of years of work experience helped me understand what I wanted to do and why. Most importantly, it set me on the path to becoming a deep generalist by strengthening my lateral thinking ability. This is of course clearer in retrospect. I didn't pursue the fellowship to become a generalist or a specialist. I was simply following my curiosity.

I chose to take a year out to study before heading for my MBA at INSEAD, but there are many other ways to achieve the same goal. As long as we can figure out a way to build or be a part of diverse learning communities, we can conduct several low-risk professional experiments to sample various options and double-down on ones that interest us. I am not saying that sampling will make all of us like Roger Federer or Richard Feynman, but it will position us to take thoughtful career decisions.

In the age of widespread automation, learning and unlearning will be a lifelong pursuit. Tools and technologies will constantly change. While this might unsettle those with a narrow set of skills, it will empower deep generalists to create new opportunities they have nurtured over years of building lateral thinking and conducting repeated experiments to figure out how they want to contribute to the ever-changing world around.

POINTS TO REMEMBER

1. Sampling period is essential to discover areas that pique our interest. Once we conduct several rounds of low-risk experiments, we figure out what we are good at and what problem we wish to solve.

2. Specializing without knowing why or simply because someone said so could seriously backfire.

3. Future belongs to deep generalists, those who combine two or more diverse domains and integrate them into something defensible and unique.

4. Following one's curiosity is one of the most effective ways to become a deep generalist.

5. We can't become deep generalists on our own. In addition to following our curiosity, we need to create or be part of diverse learning communities.

CHAPTER 44

SEEK ALTERNATIVE CREATOR MONETIZATION PATHS

Web 3.0 will create new avenues to build careers, shape business models and carve out interesting niches online. It might unleash innovative ways of exchange of both labour and capital. Let's explore how the investing landscape might evolve in the Web 3.0 space and what roles you can play as you figure out what challenges to pursue in the times ahead.

Popular means for creator monetization include subscriptions from top fans, sponsorship for integrating their personal brand with that of a business, affiliate marketing and some form of teaching. While these strategies work well, a lot more can be done both by creators and businesses to create powerful alternate channels for revenue growth.

Ed-tech behemoth Unacademy founder suggests two ways in which individual creators can become more relevant in the investing world.

First, acting as talent scouts for companies. Hiring is one of the biggest challenges for most CEOs. It is expensive, time-consuming and often backfires because finding the right fit–capability–intent trinity is a lot more tricky than one might think. So far companies partner with executive search firms and companies in the HR space. Creators could be a high-leverage untapped opportunity for CEOs. They have wide reach, access to exclusive networks and an intimate understanding of sectors they specialize in. For example, YouTuber Marques Brownlee popularly known as MKBHD has more than 14.3 million subscribers who are mostly interested in technology. His follower base could be a potent source of tech recruiting not only in the United States but also around the world. With the post-pandemic world getting increasingly remote first, geographical location matters much less. MKBHD and other creators with massive followings could become talent feeders for 21st-century organizations.

Lenny Rachitsky, a former product manager at Airbnb, quit his job to write a newsletter in tech. Within a year, his income from his writing crossed his salary at Airbnb in Silicon Valley.[1] To complement his income and to add more diversity to his portfolio, he recently added a job board using a platform called Pallet, which was set up by Jake Berry, a Stanford wrestler turned tech CEO. Today, top companies pay Lenny to put their jobs on his job board. He curates opportunities which are appealing to his core reader base—twenty-five to forty-five-year-old ambitious and curious tech enthusiasts who want to build meaningful careers. In few months since its launch, the job board is making thousands of dollars in recurring revenue for Lenny. More importantly, it seems to be providing great value to both companies looking for top talent and ambitious professionals seeking whetted opportunities by someone they trust and look up to.

Sahil Bloom, an investor and a creator, also launched a finance job board for his followers on Pallet. The quality of jobs is significantly higher than on popular job search platforms where applicants often get lost looking for jobs they actually care about.

Second, creators could become deal scouts for funds/investing opportunities and get a carry (percentage of extra returns). Creators have started building and scaling communities. This gives them first access to interesting deals. They can of course pass them on to established firms like Sequioa, a leading venture fund which already has a scout programme in place. They can also choose to invest directly.

Creators becoming angel investors and investing in other creators is a trend that excites me. If things work out, they could get higher returns and new wealth creation opportunities to complement their existing income.

1 https://twitter.com/lennysan/status/1318940907824033792

Atelier Ventures founder Li Jin recently conducted a live CBC to teach creators the art and science of angel investing. Angel investing for creators is more than just about wealth creation. It is about ownership, she says.

While the emergence of creator funds from the likes of TikTok is a welcome trend, creators are still at the mercy of big tech platforms and their inscrutable algorithms. Ultimate power still rests with these tech companies who can significantly influence the means of production and distribution.

With creators investing in each other, there will be a shift in power structures—not completely but just enough to provide for a slightly more level playing field.

OWNERSHIP AND FINANCIAL UPSIDE

This larger trend of investing in Web 3.0 and the creator economy is about two critical things: ownership and financial upside.

We are already seeing some of it in action in the media world. Let's review how Mirror describes itself.

> Joining Mirror does not only make you a community member. It makes you a co-owner of the platform. As a result, our platform is a sum of our contributors. While we're eager to grow Mirror to a monumental scale, we'll first be granting access on an individual basis to ensure a quality foundation.

On Mirror, writers can raise capital to do research and draw a monthly salary for expenses in advance from readers to write the book/article/novel they want to read. And these readers/investors get a bigger stake in the pie. Essentially, it makes the relationship more horizontal and clear-cut. The outcome is tangible, the terms are well understood and the scope of failure is reduced. Unlike the VC world, there won't just be a handful of winners. Again, we aren't dismissing or taking a dig at VCs, simply pointing out the new emerging trend which will likely be influencing many other industries.

I fundamentally believe that in the times to come, no matter what your job is, you will also be a creator, perhaps writing a newsletter at nights and being a product manager during the day, perhaps being a chef during the day and a YouTuber at night. That is why you must start thinking and acting like one from today. Consider having real skin the game of your future.

Typically when you invest in an early-stage creator or a young venture, you expect to multiply your capital in case the company/creator goes public or gets acquired.

What if there were a new model where you could get a direct sense of ownership by opining on key decisions and enjoy the financial upside in case of the company getting to serious scale and size? This model of cooperative ownership will become mainstreamed in the times to come. Time has come for individuals to invest in each other and not leave that only to massive funds and platforms. That will be the ultimate legacy of the Web 3.0 world, one that would make Adam Smith, Karl Marx and even modern tech CEOs more fulfilled.

CHAPTER 45

KEEP THE 80–20 PRINCIPLE IN MIND

Eighty per cent of your most meaningful outcomes will come from twenty per cent of your actions. Choose your 20 per cent carefully. Not every project is created equal, not every hour spent will matter. Pick carefully, stick diligently. Don't feel the need to take up everything that comes your way because you feel the need to hustle. Pick problems to solve that you truly enjoy engaging with and have a unique perspective on. At the very least, it should be the epicentre of your curiosity. Striking the right 80–20 balance is essential for long-term success as a creator.

That involves picking the times of day you are most effective at, choosing the kinds of people who get the best out of you and the kind of projects that drive your creative juices. Your goal is to build a system where great projects find a way to come to you. You need to learn to augment your luck surface area which is a product of doing great things and telling lots of people. The essential element is to experiment purposefully. When you begin, it will be hard to tell which project will lead to disproportionate outcomes, but if you follow patters of your work, you will be able to predict and plan. That is the essence of maintaining energy for the long term, playing the long game.

CHAPTER 46

TAKE STOCK

Regularly take stock of where you are. Take refuge in philosophy and ask yourself why you are doing what you are doing.

Aristotle was born around 384 BC in Greece and grew up to be arguably the most influential philosopher ever, with influential jobs such as tutoring Alexander the Great, who soon after went out and conquered the known world.

He was fascinated by first-principles thinking and exploring how things really work. One of the questions that piqued his curiosity was exploring what makes a human life meaningful with society as a whole. For him, philosophy wasn't some abstract subject but a compendium of practical wisdom. Aristotle attempted to answer four big questions:

1. What does make people happy?
2. What is art for?
3. What are friends for?
4. How can ideas cut through in a busy world?

According to Aristotle, happiness consists in achieving, through the course of a whole lifetime, all the goods—health, wealth, knowledge, friends, etc.—which lead to the perfection of human nature and to the enrichment of human life. This requires us to make choices, some of which may be very difficult. Philosophy helps us figure out how to make these difficult choices which may include thinking about letting go of our co-founder or cutting off ties with a close confidant. As you can see, these are practical questions that no school prepares us for.

WHY ARISTOTLE MATTERS TODAY

Essentially, Aristotle saw theory as practice. His questions didn't have preordained answers; they had to be explored through micro-experiments and deliberate analysis. In this regard, he was a lot more of a scientist or a start-up founder trying to validate or negate his hypothesis.

Being a community builder and teacher at heart, he knew that both individuals and groups need to allow time for answers to reveal themselves and become accepted broadly. Entrepreneurs would call it finding the product–market fit.

Learning starts with asking the right set of questions, and philosophers like Aristotle began there. That is another commonality with entrepreneurs—they start by attempting to address stuff which the society hasn't quite figured out and complement it with solutions which have the potential to scale.

COUNTERING 'MAN WITH A HAMMER' SYNDROME

'To a man with a hammer, everything seems like a nail.' This one sentence explains the origin of all biases that permeate our society. It also explains why some entrepreneurs develop great solutions but struggle to explain the problem they are solving.

Studying Aristotle is an interesting way to train yourself to fight the 'man with a hammer' syndrome. Exploring his foundational message on experimentation and theory as practice helps uncover blind spots and enables discussions rooted in facts and observations, not dogma.

Unlike present-day religious preachers or loud politicians, he was more interested in figuring things out as opposed to overlaying an existing point of view on new things that emerge.

What makes Aristotle interesting is his emphasis on figuring out important truths by engaging with the society. In this regard, he seems a lot more like an anthropologist and an entrepreneur than a traditional philosopher who dispenses wisdom sitting in the ivory tower of knowledge.

TEACH, DEBATE AND LEARN

He founded a research and teaching centre called The Lyceum: French secondary schools, *lycées*, are named in honour of this venture. He liked to walk about while teaching and discussing ideas. His followers were named Peripatetics, the wanderers. Many of his books are actually lecture notes, and these lectures were far from being monologues. He trained his students to combine logic with observation to come with general causal claims.

Logic + Observation = Causal claims

The logic was discussed, debated and analysed as a group. This is what stress-testing an opinion looks like. Even observation is not set in stone. Context matters. Aristotle enabled observations to be dissected to its bare elements for clarity. Unlike the contemporary education system, Aristotle was not optimizing for conformity. Through his methods, he made thoughtful disagreement a core component of learning.

EUDAIMONIA

For Aristotle, *eudaimonia* is the highest human good, the only human good that is desirable for its own sake (as an end in itself), rather than for the sake of something else (as a means towards some other end). That is why he would have been baffled by the contemporary obsession with 'happiness'. *Eudaimonia* doesn't mean smiling all the time or trying to escape reality through filters but committing to finding meaning in challenging tasks. The pursuit of something consequential is *eudaimonia*. That is what we are striving for. Building a venture, training for a marathon and caring for an old relative aren't particularly fun tasks, but they matter and bring us closer to Aristotle's definition of human good.

CONCLUDING THOUGHTS

Philosophy should be a core component of school, college and life curriculum. Engaging with the likes of Aristotle helps us figure out what matters most to us and why. Lewis Carroll's *Alice in Wonderland* concludes with this: 'If you don't know where you are going, any road will get you there.'

The ultimate role of Aristotle is that of a life GPS. He has been giving us direction for more than two millennia and will continue to do so in the times to come. We just need to be intentional about carving the time and space for him.

CHAPTER 47

DON'T MANAGE YOUR TIME, MANAGE YOUR ENERGY

If you are trying to build something impactful, you will probably be racing against time. There will always be myriad things you need to attend to. Prioritizing important over the urgent is easier said than done. A useful mental model for going about it is the Eisenhower Matrix.

Dwight Eisenhower, the 34th president of the United States, famously said that the most urgent decisions are rarely the most important ones. The Eisenhower Matrix has four components, which we can use to grapple with the urgent–important conundrum.

Important, but not urgent: We can decide when to do such tasks. I often put such activities on my calendar and try to finish them off in one sitting.

Urgent and important: These are the tasks that require both focus and creativity. They also need to be attended to immediately. That is why I prioritize them over everything else.

Urgent but not important: These should be delegated to someone else. The cost of wasting your time on such tasks is far more than the cost of outsourcing it. I do such tasks usually on my way back from work.

Not important and not urgent: These things should be postponed without guilt. I have learnt to ignore such tasks.

The Eisenhower matrix made me realize that it is impossible to manage time. Considering all tasks equally important and spreading them through the day is a sure-shot recipe for disaster. Instead, we need to focus on managing our energy and attention on high-stake decisions. It seems intuitive, right? Then why don't more people follow it?

These days, everyone is burnt out. We are talking about work–life balance without getting to the core of the issue, and we are exhausting ourselves by taking inconsequential decisions that seem urgent.

An important addition to this framework is paying attention to energy. No matter what you are building, there will be aspects of your work which will drain you and there will be others which will energize you. I have observed that we get the optimum output when we figure out blocks of undisturbed time for tasks that energize us. Creative work should ideally be done in such time blocks.

Context switching is referred to jumping from one task to another. While it might give us the illusion of juggling time efficiently, it drains our energy and negatively impacts our creativity. Say you are writing an investment memo; it is far better to block three hours on your calendar and get as much done as possible, instead of taking six hours while checking social media, attending calls and replying to messages.

Your ultimate goal should be to manage your energy in a way that at the end of the day you feel excited for the next day instead of feeling depleted. If you optimize for energy, time will be managed as a by-product.

I have one big goal for each day. I focus on allocating most of my energy and creativity on that before attending to other priorities. Just to be clear, I don't just do one thing every day—as an entrepreneur, that isn't possible but having that clarity helps me allocate my energy in a way that works for me.

One can reasonably argue that if we manage our time well, our energy will take care of itself. You should feel free to do that as long as you don't stuff too much into your day. Slivers of time don't work well for deep thinking and rethinking.

In the times of the pandemic, managing time became hard for me. There were multiple medical emergencies at home, and friends and family needed help. New challenges sprung up every day. Managing the clock seemed beyond my control, so I started improvising. Even within utmost chaos, there were times during the week when I felt energized to create and build. That's when I focused on getting deep work done. It worked decently well.

Another mental model that I find useful for the passion economy comes from investor Naval Ravikant. He optimizes for freedom, not time. He suggests that an ideal work day is when we don't have to be beholden to a clock and to a location. Essentially, you can work on your terms when you want and from where you want. Isn't that a major reason why most passion economy builders embarked upon their journeys?

Escape competition with authenticity, he says. No one can beat you at being you. Authenticity is a pivotal asset in the passion economy, and with the right tools—code, media and social networks—you can scale yourself. I often wonder what unbundling oneself from work really looks like and what it means for the passion economy. Can passion economy builders really build systems that scale like software? Wouldn't that be great? The daily hustle might make way for an economic engine that makes money while we sleep.

On deeper reflection, it occurs to me that getting to such a state may not be possible. The core reason why passion economy is gaining traction is the power of stories. And what are stories without people? As someone who has worked at a large corporate like Microsoft for almost seven years, I have witnessed and contributed to scaling software that adds tremendous economic value and empowers billions to solve important business problems.

Even though efficiency is in vogue, passion economy builders must remember their core value proposition and not try to replicate the software playbook. Use software and productize yourself as much as possible but remember to keep the human aspect of your story alive.

GENERAL RULE OF THUMB

You don't need to split your day equally into all the things you pursue. The 80–20 split works. Spend 80 per cent of your time focusing on the one big goal of the day; the remaining 20 per cent can be spent tinkering, experimenting and generally keeping up with life. A small chunk of the 20 per cent time can also be used to generate passive income, the money you make while you sleep or by doing things you would anyway do. Previously we have discussed a few of those—newsletters, podcasts, YouTube channels, etc.

I build communities, write, teach and deliver public lectures. All of my activities help strengthen the Network Capital brand and product. That said, I also enjoy taking up new, challenging assignments as weekend projects. For example, I made some investments in 2020–2021, some of which turned out to be quite rewarding. This goes against conventional wisdom that entrepreneurs should focus on one thing at a time. Personally, I don't disagree with that. Focus is critical for long-term success, but it is okay (in fact welcome) to look for ways to expand your revenue sources.

This may not work for everybody, but it works for me. I enjoy stepping away for a few hours every week to partake of activities that complement my core job. The autonomy and flexibility spur my creativity. Sometimes it also augments my monthly income.

PASSIVE INCOME

Passive income is the money you make while you sleep or by doing things you would do regardless of the context.

Just before leaving for my Middle East book launch in August 2021, I listed my apartment on Airbnb. Although I had used the platform multiple times, this was my first experience being a host. Within a few hours, I had dozens of requests and managed to let out the property making a lot more than the average rent/monthly EMI of the area I live in. The people who booked my apartment included a primary school teacher, an international couple working at National Geographic and a wine maker from Bordeaux. These guests were not too different from the kind of people we have on Network Capital, so I decided to offer them subscription to our platform at a small discount. Soon after they subscribed, they connected with Network Capital community members in the city who offered to curate experiences for the guests using the 'Airbnb experiences' tab. It was a win-win situation for everyone. My guests got an incredibly personalized experience, Network Capital community members met some interesting people and made some money, Network Capital added new subscribers, Airbnb enabled a wonderful trip and I had the satisfaction of curating this adventure. Of course, the money I made didn't hurt.

The reason I am sharing this story is to highlight the power of passive income. Everyone immersed in the passion income should strive to create multiple revenue streams that work without too much incremental effort. To earn a few thousand extra dollars, all I had to do was connect a platform that I run—Network Capital—with a platform that I use—Airbnb—and figure out a way to create optimal outcomes for everyone involved.

Few weeks after listing the house, I had to be in Mumbai for a few hours to judge a large debating event for school students hosted by a TV channel (Zee TV). I was compensated for my time but more importantly, we got the opportunity to put the Network Capital brand in front of hundreds of thousands of ambitious school students and their parents—all this with spending zero on sales or marketing. Doing all this does take a toll on my body some days, but all factors considered, it is worth it. I keep my mind and heart open to new possibilities, especially those which are synergistic to the Network Capital mission.

As an entrepreneur who travels extensively for work, having a few thousand dollars of additional monthly income is helpful. I use most of my passive income from all platforms to experiment with new ideas and enable free access to Network Capital for those who cannot afford it. I firmly believe that talent is equally distributed, opportunities are not. My passive income allows me to take micro-steps towards addressing this problem.

The Internet allows everyone to generate passive income which can help you pursue passion projects, invest, donate or provide insurance in times of need. All you need to do is look for platforms that you are comfortable experimenting with. Like with everything, results won't be immediate, but with time you will figure things out.

THREE THINGS TO KEEP IN MIND

1. **Focus on things you enjoy doing and are naturally good at:** Experience curation and debating are things I love and am decently good at. When I started these pursuits, I got no meaningful reward for a long time, but after the gestation period, I started getting opportunities. Today, I get many such opportunities and have the luxury of choosing things that pique my interest. This is what we call 'luck surface area' on Network Capital, a product of doing great things and telling a lot of people.

2. **Figure out the right platform fit:** Not everyone will be a great experience curator, newsletter writer, YouTuber or debater. You don't need to excel at everything—just one would do. Keep an eye out on the new platforms, especially the Web 3.0 tools.

3. **Play the slow game:** Allow yourself the time and headspace to tinker. There is no point being in a rush to generate a certain level of passive income. This competitive signalling is a race to the bottom. Pick any dollar amount, and I will find you a person who generates 10x the passive income in 10 minutes. Our goal is not to prove a point but to improve (and let compounding work its wonders).

CHAPTER 48

AVOID THE ENVY TRAP
AND MAKE IT WORK FOR YOU

Like most high school students in India, my final schooling years were spent cocooned in books. I felt this invisible pressure of studying engineering or medicine but found myself drawn to theatre. There was no time for rehearsals amid the intense study schedule, so I postponed pursuing my passion for acting till I had cleared the engineering entrance examinations.

I enrolled for a theatre workshop in the summer before college. On the very first day, the workshop curator (a prominent theatre personality in Delhi) was late. I was among the students waiting outside when I saw a small group of three having a gala time mimicking each other. They were enjoying every bit of the wait in a way that made me realize I wasn't. I was standing alone in a corner, anxiously anticipating the start.

There was something about the way they were, the way they spoke to each other, how happy they looked together and how they practised their dialogues which magnified both my loneliness and my nervousness. They looked complete, and I didn't want to disturb them. I didn't resent them, but looking at them made me realize that they had something I desperately wanted. It was my first brush with envy.

Envy is secret admiration. It is an unintended compliment, perhaps an inexplicable emotion that cracks us open and reveals the things that we truly value. Nietzsche called envy and jealousy private parts of the human soul, Socrates said that envy was the ulcer of the soul and Aristotle went to the extent of stating that envy was the pain caused by the good fortune of others.

Was Aristotle right? Was I really pained by the good fortune of the three actors on the first day of my rehearsals? To understand this, let us try and understand how envy works and explore whether it can lead to growth.

THE GAZE OF ENVY

Relevance and similarity are two themes that keep recurring when we deconstruct envy. We tend to envy people whose work is similar to ours and those who are comparable to us. More often than not, they happen to be our peers. I worked in Microsoft for almost seven years but didn't see anyone being envious of Satya Nadella or Bill Gates. They inspired us; we admired them. Envy tends to be horizontal.

There are two types of envy: malignant and benign. Both are deeply personal and involve comparing ourselves to people we perceive are better off. However, with malicious envy, our focus is on wishing that the object of our envy didn't have the structural, cultural or positional advantages we wish we had. Perhaps Aristotle was talking about malignant envy when he defined it as the pain caused by the good fortune of others. Germans have a word for it—*schadenfreude*.

Benign envy is far more innocent. It focuses on the object of our envy but only to figure out ways to emulate it. People we benignly envy are a lot like us. We constantly think that with a little more luck and a little more effort, we could become them or better.

MAKING ENVY WORK FOR YOU

With a song on the lips, benign envy can drive us to positive changes, and usually it emerges as a useful self-help tool. It spurs constructive competition and sparks innovation.

That envy I experienced on the first day of rehearsals pushed me forward. Every time I got on stage, those three actors from my theatre class would become my invisible audience. I wanted to be as good as them. Every time I practised, I had three relatable role models. Thanks to social media, it was inspiration right in front of my eyes for years to come. Two of them went on to become well-known actors—one made waves in Bollywood and the other landed a mega TV show.

When I worked at Teach for India in Mumbai, I would often take a local train to work. Indian railway stations are works of art with a strange medley of music, food, Bollywood, bureaucracy and business coming to life inexplicably. Local delicacies are sold under massive bill boards, as crowds navigate their way amid thunderous announcements which are sure to make you shudder. Waiting for my train, I would often get some tea and snacks. I remember that once I had Vada Pao (a popular Indian street food) outside the station. Per tradition, it came served in an old newspaper which doubled up as a plate and a tissue. As I dug in, I realized that I saw a familiar face. That face turned out to be one of my peers from theatre class talking about her latest movie. In India, you know you have arrived when you start appearing in newspapers. It was a surreal moment. I felt proud. It was benign envy graduating to *mudita*, a word in Pali which roughly translates to vicarious joy or the pleasure that comes from delighting in other people's well-being. Interestingly, there is no English word for *mudita*.

So how might you make *mudita* part of your personal operating system? The answer is threefold.

First, make benign envy your teacher. The benign envy of the theatre world made me a tad more self-aware and a tad more emotionally resilient.

Self-awareness helped me translate the dance of envy into something constructive. Today, every time I feel envious of someone, I open the notepad on my phone and document three things:

1. What was the trigger?
2. How did I feel?
3. Was my envy following a pattern?

This simple trick which I call 'personal envy lab' has made me realize that there are undeniable patterns of my envious mind. It turns out that I feel most envious towards the middle of the month when I am waiting for projects to fructify. It so happens that my envy is mild and short-lived. I have trained myself to laugh it off and learn from it.

Having run this 'personal envy lab' for almost five years, I have no doubt in sharing that nothing reveals us to our own selves as the gaze of our envy. Instead of brushing past it, we should pause and reflect what made us envious of someone in the first place. Understanding the epicentre of envy is key to mitigating it.

Second, build your category of one and think of life as an infinite game. There is no 'winning' in practically anything that matters. You can't win a marriage, a partnership, a meeting or a friendship.

Competing for small wins shrinks the pie for everyone involved and makes us all victims of envious desire. Further, it distracts us into mistaking the goals of our peers with our own goals. After a couple of years of relentless practice, I realized that I enjoyed acting, but it wasn't my only love. There were other things I wanted to explore.

Today, I am an entrepreneur who also does some acting on the side. My peers from the theatre class are actors who also do some business as a side hustle. We collaborate on things and enjoy a wonderful friendship. I am building my category of one, and they are building theirs. Our relationship evolved from benign envy to admiration to *mudita* to friendship, largely because we weren't trying to beat each other in finite games.

Third, practise the *mudita* mindset. You are better off collaborating with those you envy instead of competing with them. It makes practical sense and also nudges you towards the indescribable bliss of *mudita*.

Once you get into the habit of celebrating shared wins, you will be known in your social networks as the person who helps shape win-win outcomes for everyone. Your luck surface area will increase, and many more new opportunities will come to you. Having a reputation as an envious person has absolutely no upside. You would be happier and more successful if your circle thinks of you as someone who embodies the *mudita* mindset and revels in the success of others.

Pursuing theatre seriously in my teens and early twenties was perhaps the best investment I ever made. I remember travelling daily for almost four hours on public transport to make it in time for rehearsals and auditions. I finished my college/office work on the way, and I remember going to bed exhausted and happy. I didn't go on to have an illustrious acting career but did well enough as an amateur. Recently, one of the movies I acted in premiered on Amazon Prime. Looking back, I would not have reached my potential as an actor without the dash of inspiration and benign envy from my peers. They catapulted me forward by showing me what unencumbered communication truly looks like.

What I didn't tell you earlier was that towards the end of high school, I had become a bit of a recluse. Benign envy of great communicators and actors helped me reconnect with the world. Today, when I look at my TED Talks and some of my movies, I can't help being thankful to all the inspiration which manifested in the form of benign envy along the way, especially those three gorgeous souls I admired quietly from a distance the first day I walked on stage.

CHAPTER 49

THINK BIG, ACT SMALL

Scale is the be-all and end-all of everything you hear about start-ups in the media. Without your product or service having scale, attracting VC money is impossible. That said, it is critical to do things that don't scale. This advice comes from Y Combinator co-founder, Paul Graham. Y Combinator[1] is one of the world's most successful start-up incubators with unicorn companies like Airbnb and Coinbase in its portfolio. Among other things, Graham explains that doing things that don't scale in the beginning gives you deep customer insights and equips you to figure out the problem you are solving with more clarity. Airbnb founders always wanted to build a massive company but early on they figured out that they needed to get the pictures of the houses they were trying to list on their website to be better so that more guests would book and, more importantly, more home owners would list their property on the site. To tackle this problem, they went to where most of their customers were (in New York at the time) and knocked on doors to speak to them. They even hired professional photographers to ensure that each listing was appealing enough to make the customer experience delightful. This was obviously not a scalable process, but it worked beautifully.

The larger lesson here is that even if you are attempting to build a massive company, start by acting small. The micro-steps that you take in the beginning don't need to be at odds with your larger dream, which by all means should be unrestrained.

The founders and creators who are ready to get their hands dirty and try out challenging operational stuff themselves develop an intimate understanding of the customer challenges and operational strategies which will be very useful at later stages.

1 https://www.ycombinator.com/

When I started Network Capital, there was just a simple form and Facebook group. A lot of mentors and mentees were signing up. They had many questions and doubts about the process, the next steps and the vision. I carved out time and spent hours answering them one by one. Doing this wasn't easy because I had a really demanding full-time job with Microsoft.

With the benefit of hindsight, I can safely say that the initial months I spent doing the non-scalable things gave Network Capital the foundation to grow. Even today, I personally take 1:1 calls with Network Capital subscribers. I do not know how big Network Capital will eventually become, but I am pretty sure that I always want to allocate a certain chunk of time doing that non-scalable work.

My ultimate goal is to scale intimacy which we have developed as a community over the last five years with the help of technology and good old human connect.

No matter what you are trying to build, ensure that you start by taking small steps consistently. Towards the end, let me share a useful mental model for your reference

GRADATIM FEROCITER

In June 2004, Jeff Bezos, the founder of Amazon and Blue Origin, wrote an 800-word memo, informally dubbed 'The Welcome Letter', which even today is given to new employees (of Blue Origin) as part of their orientation programme. These are snippets from the memo:

'We are a small team committed to seeing an enduring presence in space.'

Blue will pursue this long-term objective patiently, step-by-step. He described releasing new versions of its rockets at six-month intervals with 'metronome like regularity'.

'We have been dropped off on an unexplored mountain without maps and the visibility is poor.

You don't start and stop. Keep climbing at steady pace. Be the tortoise and not the hare.'

'I accept that Blue Origin will not meet a reasonable investor's expectation for return on investment over a typical investing horizon.

It's important to the peace of mind to those at Blue to know I won't be surprised or disappointed when this prediction proves true.'

He condensed the central idea of the company's strategy using the Latin motto, *Gradatim Ferociter*, which roughly translates to 'step by step, ferociously'

The document, signed by Bezos, took on the same sacrosanct space as Amazon's inaugural letter for shareholders which you would have read in our previous newsletter.

Why does this motto matter to you?

In today's 'breaking news' culture obsessed with dramatic success and failure stories, it helps to keep in mind that the most successful businessman in the world built his company step by step, ferociously. Success didn't just happen. It took a whole long list of embarrassing failures.

When pursuing challenging missions—such as trying to build your category of one doing whatever you do—remember that it will take effort, consistency and patience to flower.

CHAPTER 50

BUILD A MINIMUM
LOVABLE PRODUCT: MLP
(MVP VERSION OF AMAZON)

Minimum lovable product (MLP) refers to a protype, with remark-ability inbuilt into it. It can be a simple bit of code, a blog or a community which helps you test out your assumptions and give the people engaging with it an aha moment. Network Capital started out as a simple group on Facebook, but we ensured that every conversation added specific value to the community. Our curation created moments of delight for our users, and together we created a tiny civilization on the digital world map where people found a safe space to talk about their careers. It didn't cost anything in terms of setting up and allowed to carry out risk-free experiments which eventually determined the future course of the platform.

NPS or the net promoter score refers to the likelihood of someone recommending your product to others. From the beginning, Network Capital had a high NPS, all thanks to our MLP. Intuitively, I knew that mentorship wasn't accessible because of curation. There were a large number of technology-enabled mentorship platforms but barely any of them worked. Technology wasn't the bottleneck, curation was. This customer insight led us to first solve for curation, then build the community and then figure out the technology stack to scale it.

Start with the customer experience in mind, optimize for customer delight and then use technology to optimize it. This is not the only way to go about it, but through the course of my research and my own personal experience, I have come to the realization that having a sleek technological solution in search of a problem usually leads to suboptimal outcomes. The ideal scenario will be to be technology-first and customer obsessed from the get-go, but if you already have a busy job like I did or you are tinkering along to figure out if there is something unique about your idea, the MLP approach works well.

No one is stopping you from making your product perfectly sleek, but consider an iterative approach so that you can listen to what customers say and build a solution with them. In fact, even large companies like Amazon follow this approach. It allows them to experiment at scale. Take inspiration from the Amazon Playbook as you venture into the passion economy.

CHAPTER 51

SPEAK TO CUSTOMERS AND TRAIN YOURSELF TO THINK LIKE AN ANTHROPOLOGIST

Anthropology is the study of the human experience. Anthropologists are interested in figuring out what makes us human. They try to figure out different aspects of the human experience by taking into account the past, connecting them with the present and predicting trends for the future.

These days, anthropologists are hired extensively by technology companies. I was part of the team from Microsoft which helped build India's first smart village. One of our team members had a PhD in anthropology. She helped us develop a thorough understanding of the rural ecosystem before we started figuring out our strategy. This was a crucial step to ensure we didn't throw technology at a problem we didn't completely understand. With her intervention, we were able to figure out what the local villagers really wanted and co-create solutions which worked at scale.

Inculcating the anthropological mindset is an important step for passion economy builders. Understanding how your customers behave as a collective propels you to serve them in innovative ways. Objectivity, observation and contextual intelligence are three levers through which you can develop the lens of anthropology in your day-to-day work. When Network Capital sets up subgroups or launches in new cities, our team often starts by bringing people together in a shared space—first digitally and then in-person. Before we start deeper engagement, we attempt to step out and observe with as much objectivity as possible. The way our subgroups come together and engage with each other in Paris is so different from the way they do in Patna. Some of it is of course difference of culture, but there are deeper aspects than that, which can easily be

Passion Economy and the Side-Hustle Revolution

overlooked if one is not conscious of the larger context in which people operate.

In *Liquidated: An Ethnography of Wall Street,* anthropologist Karen Ho who worked at an investment bank herself attempts to understand the bankers' broader outlook to financial markets. With careful objective observation, she suggests that the investment banks and corporates are inseparable from the structures and strategies of their workplaces. She ethnographically analyses the voices of the entire chain—from those trying to break into investment banking to the stressed-out junior analysts and associates to the managing directors. By connecting the values and actions of investment bankers to the construction of markets and the restructuring of American corporations, her book reveals the particular culture of Wall Street, the incentives at play and the power structures that define the culture.

You don't need to get a PhD or write a book like Ho did, but spending your time studying the systems, culture, group dynamics, power structures and incentives, you begin to visualize how the tribe of your customers and community members truly engage and why. To design their experience with your community or product, you need to figure out their behavioural patterns, decision-making frameworks and collaboration techniques. The subtle nuances of group dynamics are integral to creating a culture that works and strengthens at scale.

If you impose your view of the world on a large group, community members will feel colonized in a way. Even if they appreciate what you bring to the table, they are unlikely to feel a sense of belonging.

CHAPTER 52

RESIST THE FUNDING TEMPTATION

Resist the temptation of thinking that your MLP cannot be built without funding. In almost all cases, it turns out not to be true. You can build an online university, launch a community, start a social network, curate a newsletter and build a media company with zero start-up capital. All the tools to make it happen are available on the Internet free of cost, so thinking that you need upfront external investment to get started is worth revaluating. Investor Naval Ravikant calls these tools permissionless leverage. Stitching together an MLP can be dauting, but it happens to be one of the most pivotal steps in your passion economy journey. It will be a long, challenging and adventurous journey, but having the MLP will give you the confidence to experiment, tinker and chart out your next steps.

Waiting for funding to start creates a chicken and egg situation. Don't let perfect become the enemy of good. A scrappy solution that gets the job done is better than an elegant idea resting inside your head.

Network Capital started with a Google Form, Microsoft Excel sheet and Facebook group. It was far from being an ideal solution for career experimentation and advancement, but it worked, at least for the first few thousand people. That traction made some investors interested in us and even though I had a full-time job, it seemed like they were intrigued enough to have a chat with me.

In the early days, I didn't know whether what I was building was fundable or not. I wasn't even sure it would scale. Had I waited for funding and external validation, I would have never started. I designed the Network Capital experience for remarkability. I wanted my MLP to become the go-to place for ambitious millennials to seek mentorship and genuine connection.

That is why I had a fairly hands-on approach. Any time I would witness the Network Capital culture spinning off in the wrong direction or conversations taking on a non-productive turn, I would gently nudge people to remember why we exist. I knew that this would not scale beyond a certain point but curating the MLP created multiple culture champions of the community. As we scaled, these culture champions played the role I played in the early days. They turned out to the foundations of our evolution into a more elegant platform. This didn't happen overnight.

After some trial and error, we managed to carve out a revenue stream in the form of subscriptions on our MLP, the Facebook group. This turned out to be a game changer in many ways. I could finally visualize how Network Capital would look and feel in the years to come.

Even today, with our platform in place, when we launch new products or features, we try and think in terms of MLP. We ask what would get the job done for the user. It proves to be a robust start, one that helps us refine things as we move along. Because we always communicate clearly with our community members, even when we slip up or make a mistake, people understand why we are doing what we are doing.

Evangelizing the MLP philosophy with your users makes them co-owners of your building phase. The key aspect of proceeding this way is to not stop product progress even if it serves the purpose. Consistent and compounding progress is the single biggest motivator for anyone building in the passion economy. There are bound to be hard days and days where the MLP will malfunction, but you need to pick yourself up and move forward.

CHAPTER 53

RELENTLESSLY FOCUS ON BUILDING A COMMUNITY

We discussed the importance of productizing in earlier chapters. Essentially, it is the combination of specific knowledge and leverage, two critical components of finding meaningful work in the 21st century. Specific knowledge cannot be taught but can be learned by following one's curiosity. In the passion economy era, your specific knowledge could literally be anything. With the help of capital, code and community, you can scale your specific knowledge, productize yourself and build your category of one.

It is useful to think of community building with the 'world-building' lens popularized by Alex Danco.

> Your job is actually to create a world that is so interesting and so compelling and has a reason for people to go walk in and explore this world that they can go spend time in it, without you even having to be there. There is an understanding of why they want to explore it. They have an understanding of why they want to be there and what's in it for them. And what's there to learn.
>
> It's not enough to tell one good story; you have to create an entire world that people can step into, familiarize themselves with, and spend time getting to know. Initially you'll have to walk them around and show them what's in your world, but your goal is to familiarize them with your world sufficiently, and motivate them to participate, to the point that they can spend time in your world and build stuff in it without you having to be there all the time.

Building a community is a lot like shaping a civilization with shared cultural values, code of ethics and even a constitution of sorts. In a way, a community is a country with citizens who co-create the shared values and norms. Some critical questions you should answer before you embark on this journey are as follows:

1. Why should your community exist?
2. What do community members get by being part of your digital civilization?
3. How can you enable community members to have meaningful P2P relationships?
4. What can you do to put accountability mechanisms in place?
5. How do you make community members feel like partners and co-creators of your mission?
6. When and how should you monetize?
7. How should you scale?
8. What can you do to ensure community culture strengthens with scale?
9. What does success look like? How do you measure community impact?

Answering these questions will give you the tools to transform a product/service you conceptualized into a fully formed entity which takes your mission to the next level. As I built Network Capital, I realized that even I built the perfect mentorship and career advancement tool, it will be restrictive in what it offers to its users unless the users themselves got involved in shaping the experience.

Managing a community is more complex than managing a tool/product, but the rewards are also exponentially higher. Giving up control is not something that comes easily to most founders. We want to manage every aspect of our passion project, but if we want to take things to the next level, that is, build a functional company, inviting others to be part of our 'world' and giving them power to shape it are vital.

Today, Network Capital is used for many more use cases than I had imagined. Every subgroup, every city chapter has a distinct identity. In fact, that is what helps us thrive in different markets. Network Capital Paris members are vastly different from say Network Capital New York or Delhi members. These subgroups have different personalities, but they are still aligned and committed to the overall mission. We couldn't enforce rules; we needed to explain why we exist clearly and repeatedly in a way which made sense to millennials around the world. This had to be done with no/limited authority. Hence, it was crucial to reiterate the reason for our existence.

Even today, I spend most of my time explaining the problem our community is trying to address. I do that with my writing, speaking and 1:1 conversations, and it propels other community members to do the same. The founder's role in shaping culture is critical, as long as they understand that it isn't a solitary job.

Building a community is perhaps the single most important component of shaping a meaningful career in the long term. Invest time and energy into it. The pay-off will be handsome as long as you are not impatient with results.

SCALE YOUR COMPANY WITH COMMUNITY FUNDING

We got funding from Facebook largely because we figured out a way to scale trust among millennials around the world and align them towards the shared mission of democratizing mentorship. From the beginning, there was a sense of ownership among our community members, but it was intangible. Was there a way to translate this into something more concrete, I wondered? Collectively our community members had helped design our strategy, strengthened our culture and defined our reason for being. That is why I took a call to raise additional capital from them directly.

EMERGING TRENDS IN FUNDRAISING

This trend of raising capital from community-based fundraising is gaining more traction these days. Gumroad, a company I invested in, recently raised money from its fans and users. It turned out to be one of the most widely subscribed equity crowdfunding rounds of 2021. Maven, another company I invested in, first raised money from a bunch of people they really wanted before raising $20 million from a16z, one of the top VC funds in Silicon Valley.

Historically, only those with significant access to wealth were able to invest in early-stage start-ups. Things are changing now. These days, a large proportion of companies are trying to rebrand themselves as communities. Their goal is to build a deeper connect with their customers and have a direct line of communication with them. One trend likely to emerge from this rebranding and repivoting will be community members becoming investors, brand ambassadors, board members and regulators. Essentially, many companies will become self-regulating, fully functional entities which thrive based on how well they serve community members. I see Network Capital going in that direction.

With start-up founders turning to their community for investment, any member of a fast-growing community can become an investor. Based on my conversations with community members who invested in Network Capital, I realized that financial upside was only part of their motivation. People wanted to have a play, a meaningful role in shaping the future of the company they invested in.

WHY RAISE CAPITAL FROM COMMUNITY?

My larger goal is to shape Network Capital into a platform which is co-created, co-owned and co-run by our community members. I plan to use the funding and strategic support from Facebook to advance systems and structures so that Network Capital becomes one of the most accessible, equitable and inclusive companies on the planet. For that to happen, stakeholders and community must have skin in the game. They must think like joint owners, not just passive participants.

I rolled out an initiative called '100 True Patrons', wherein I invited any community member who believes strongly in our mission to invest their time, money and resources in making career experimentation and advancement accessible to everyone.

I did not know whether the '100 True Patrons' initiative would work, but it helped that we didn't need the money to survive. Facebook had already decided to fund us, and Network Capital's monthly recurring revenue was growing robustly. It was time to accelerate, create new learning experiences and enable people from different social and economic groups to learn with and from each other.

One of our Seattle-based community members invested in us and decided to sponsor 10 students who could not afford the Network Capital subscription. A Bangalore-based member did the same and soon we had our community members from around the world joining the patron network. This set off a chain reaction. Within two weeks of launch, we had the backing of 100 patrons who had committed to serving the mission of Network Capital for the rest of their lives. Collectively we had pooled in a sizable amount of money and created a scholarship fund focused on expanding access. Thanks to their support and that of Facebook, Network Capital is now need-blind, that is, anyone with the hunger to learn can join our community and take part in all our CBCs.

HOW TO RAISE FROM YOUR COMMUNITY?

Based on Network Capital's offbeat fundraising approach, I have learnt three important lessons about raising capital from your community.

First, it is important to choose who you raise money from. Network Capital started out as a Facebook group, so being funded and strategically supported by them was a logical next step. Over the years, Facebook's community team had helped us launch many new initiatives and products, for example, an inbuilt mentorship tool within our group. Having their support was an important step for the company's growth.

When it came to raising from individual community members, I knew that I did not want to crowdfund. Let me explain why.

Raising capital through crowdfunding is different from raising from your true fans or strongest supporters. While crowdfunding means anyone from anywhere can invest, strategically reaching out to your community members entails offering them partial ownership of the company as gratitude for their past and future contributions. If they played a pivotal role in making your company successful, it is only fair they co-create the company and enjoy the upside as and when it happens.

Network Capital has three subscription tiers: monthly, annual and lifetime. With our '100 True Patrons' initiative, I put forward a simple criterion that those willing to invest must already be lifetime subscribers or become one before we take their money. I only wanted the support of the people who believed in building for the long term. One of my mentors once told me to play long-term games with long-term people. I have stuck to that advice ever since.

Through our '100 True Patrons' initiative, we wanted to thank our strongest supporters and lean on them to usher the company's future. While a start-up or a fast-growing community might have one CEO, it needs many partners who are invested in the mission to strengthen the culture and shape the future road map.

The real power of a company which has shared ownership with its strongest champions lies in the fact that users become partners. In the case of Maven, for example, many early investors also became teachers on the platform. As equity owners, they had the extra incentive to make the company successful.

While this is encouraging, we are only beginning to scratch the surface of the problem. Talent is equally distributed, opportunities are not. There is a lot more work that needs to be done, but the distributed ownership structure and the scholarship fund are the first tangible steps.

Second, raise money when you are fully immersed in building out your company. The ideal time is when you have a proven business model and are not desperate for funding. I had been building Network Capital as a side hustle for four years along with my job at Microsoft. While I could have raised funding at that time, I think it would have been suboptimal. When your community members back your company, they are essentially taking a bet on your hunger and capability to fulfil the mission. In order to do justice to their trust, you should be able to demonstrate your willingness to go above and beyond the call of duty. That usually happens when you are pursuing a focused mission.

I know that the idea of raising money when you don't necessarily need it is counter-intuitive, but I have found, especially when raising from the community, that funding at a time when you are in a position of strength helps drive investor confidence. I have been open with our community members about our metrics such as revenue, growth rates and monthly paying subscribers from the beginning. They knew where we were in our journey and understood what they were investing in. Knowing that Network Capital would continue to grow even without additional funding empowered them to make the decision.

Third, understand what you are building and what kind of investment will help you get to the next stage of growth. There are many sources of funding available these days. There are angel investors, VC funds, corporate funds, bank loans, etc. Funding is discussed incessantly in newspapers and social media, but there is a huge difference between raising funds and making a company successful. Funding is essentially a loan. Investors expect a return on their investment.

Founders need to find the investor–market fit, which is basically a mutual understanding of the timeline and expected rate of return. If there is a disconnect at this stage, companies are bound to fail. Suppose you are building a company that needs a large sum of money just to get the prototype ready, raising capital from an investor who expects an exponential return on their investment in a short time may not be the best idea. Just because everyone else is raising money in a certain way doesn't mean that you should follow their path. You must strive to find your investor–market fit.

Network Capital's real asset is its community. It has been built and shaped without spending a single dollar on sales and marketing. The love and support from our community have been our driving factor and primary growth channel. Now with 100 new patrons on board, I feel energized to co-create a more inclusive and accessible community. I don't have all the answers, but I do have 100 committed partners from around the world to lean on for help, one of whom lives in that tiny village in Lebanon where I was when I got that fateful call from Facebook.

CHAPTER 54

THE ACCESS ECONOMY

On 5 September, which is Teachers' day in India, I minted an NFT, which captured images and snapshots of teachers who had taught CBCs on Network Capital.

The simplest way to understand an NFT is that it is a unique digital art hosted on the blockchain. It is unique, and its value stems from the fact that it can't be replaced. Bitcoin, the most popular cryptocurrency, is fungible. Bitcoins can be traded for the same thing. There is no difference between any two Bitcoins. NFT, on the other hand, is non-fungible. If you trade one NFT for another, you'd have something completely different.

NFTs can be anything digital (music, art, image, tweet or article). Beeple aka Mike Winkelmann stunned the world when an NFT he created called 'Everydays—the First 5,000 Days' sold for $69 million at a Christie's online auction. The NFT was a collection of 5,000 images he had already posted online starting from 2007.[1]

While some may dismiss NFTs as a fad akin to the Tulip Mania in the Netherlands when a '*single*' tulip sold for this outrageous amount—'Two lasts of wheat, four lasts of rye, four fat oxen, eight fat swine, twelve fat sheep, two hogsheads of wine, four tuns of beer, two tons of butter, one thousand pounds of cheese, a complete bed, a suit of clothes, and a silver drinking cup'—it is worth exploring how value is determined in the digital world.

Status signalling is also part of the explanation. Just the way tulips were associated with the elites at the time, NFTs are linked to crypto enthusiasts and blockchain connoisseurs. Minting an NFT or purchasing something offbeat can also be about communicating a sense of style, a commitment to an offbeat community. There

1 https://www.theverge.com/2021/3/11/22325054/beeple-christies-nft-sale-cost-everydays-69-million

Passion Economy and the Side-Hustle Revolution

are clear similarities between fashion trends and NFTs. Wearing a stylish vintage jacket is not really about utility. It is self-expression and perhaps some signalling.

The palpable excitement around NFTs stems from two things. First is technology to create and sell digital art, more importantly, about access and patronage. Beauty lies in the eyes of the beholder. What makes the painting Mona Lisa unique is that it is the only one. There are millions of replicas but anyone who has been to the Louvre, waited for hours and managed to catch a glimpse of the original artwork knows the difference. Similarly, the value of an NFT can be explained by its uniqueness and assigned by the patron. I would be silly to compare the beauty of Mona Lisa with that of NFTs, but the basis on which both are valued is the same. At the very least, there are parallels.

NFTs also explain the emergence of the access economy. The willingness to pay for assets has been reducing. While this is most prevalent among millennials and Gen Zs who often prefer to subscribe for services instead of purchasing assets. Why buy a depreciating asset like a car when you can rent an Uber, Lyft or Ola! That is the prevailing sentiment. The one thing people are willing to pay for is deeper connect or greater access with people, organizations and communities.

One important service that Network Capital provides is meaningful access to top professionals. This is not just a one-off event but a regular feature in the content we create and the CBCs we run. Our community members value learning from and connecting with interesting people doing interesting things.

Of course, there is value in networking upwards, and I am sure that some community members pay for the tangible value towards their long-term career growth. That said, a large chunk of our community members consider access as an intangible asset. For them, it is about demonstrating patronage to the larger community and the foundation on which it is built.

One of our community members recently took the lifetime subscription to Network Capital which is priced at 25 times the cost of the monthly subscription. Then he enrolled his son in the

Network Capital School. Few months after, he spearheaded our efforts to launch the Product Management Fellowship. Finally, he invested in Network Capital. When the Network Capital NFT got launched, he made a serious offer to purchase it. He is a great example of a true patron.

With his actions, he has carved an indelible mark in the minds and hearts of our community members. As the founder of the community, I will always cherish his patronage and support.

Atelier Ventures founder Li Jin talks about 100 True Fans, building on top of Kevin Kelley's 1000 True Fans concept, where she explains that 100 patrons like the Network Capital community member referenced above can transform the way passion economy scales.

Li says,

> There is a substantive difference between monetizing through 1,000 True Fans (at $100 a year) and 100 True Fans (at $1,000 a year). Whereas a creator can earn $100 a year from a fan via patronage or donations, collecting $1,000 a year per fan requires a wholly different product. These fans expect to derive meaningful value and purpose from the product.
>
> This represents a move away from the traditional donation model—in which users pay to benefit the *creator*—to a *value* model, in which users are willing to pay more for something that benefits *themselves*. What was traditionally dubbed 'self-help' now exists under the umbrella of 'wellness.' People are willing to pay more for exclusive, ROI-positive services that are constructive in their lives, whether it's related to health, finances, education, or work. In the offline world, people are accustomed to hiring experts across verticals (think interior designers, organizational consultants, public speaking coaches, executive coaches, and SAT tutors) and are willing to pay premium prices for the promise of measurable improvement and results. Now that mindset is filtering into our digital lives, as well.

100 TRUE FANS AND DUNBAR NUMBER

'Dunbar's number' is the number of people with whom one can maintain stable social relationships.

By using the average human brain size and extrapolating from the results of primates, British anthropologist Robert Dunbar suggested that humans can maintain 150 stable relationships. He informally explained it as 'the number of people you would not feel embarrassed about joining uninvited for a drink if you happened to bump into them in a bar'.

Mega influencers and celebrities have millions of fans, but most of us do not. What we do have are 150 stable relationships. We can start the discovery of our 100 true fans from within our stable relationships. I started Network Capital by reaching out to my friends and mentors who knew me very well. To scale in terms of numbers wasn't my obsession. I wanted to scale intimacy. Scaling intimacy involves bridging access, but bridging access does not automatically scale intimacy. Those who understand this are likely to build their category of one in the passion economy space.

WHAT DO PEOPLE ACTUALLY PAY FOR?

NFTs can be thought of as overvalued images or unique digital creations placed on the blockchain which have intrinsic beauty in the eye of the beholder. A popular Beyoncé song 'Single Ladies' goes like:

> *Cause if you liked it then you should have put a ring on it*
> *If you liked it then you shoulda put a ring on it*
> *Don't be mad once you see that he want it*
> *If you liked it then you should put a ring on it.*

Recently, a hopeless romantic techie decided to riff on it. He said, 'I liked it so I put an NFT on it.'

What we don't know is how the object of his affection responded to the NFT. Maybe she found it funny, maybe silly or maybe to be the most creative expression of modern love.

Late Harvard Business School Professor Clayton Christenson came up with the 'jobs to be done framework' which broadly suggests that many companies focus on making their products better without understanding 'why' customers make the choices they do. Customers don't simply buy products or services. They 'hire' them to do a job. That job is not just utilitarian but also experiential. Those experiences have social and emotional aspects which may be even more important than the functional objectives.

The job to be done for the hopeless romantic minting NFTs was creating an experience for his girlfriend and getting deeper access to her. At least in terms of frameworks and mental models, he was thinking in the right direction.

Fundamentally, NFTs demonstrate the power of the access economy where people don't pay as much for things as they do for deeper access through unique digital experiences. Without getting into a value judgement, it surely is a sign of the changing times.

CHAPTER 55

CREATE CONSTRAINTS

What's something you would love to get stuck with?

Ghost is a platform which enables others to create newsletters. Its founder John O'Nolan lives on a boat and travels around the world. Today, Ghost makes more than $3 million in ARR. What's interesting is the fact that it is a non-profit organization, with specific constraints carved into its founding charter. For example, it will never be acquired, it will not hire more than 50 employees and its technology will live forever. Ghost will pass Bill Gates's platform test because now newsletter writers make substantially more than the platform on which they write.

You may wonder why a profitable, fast-growing software company is structured as a non-profit, open source technology platform. When you dive deep and explore the founding ideals of Ghost, you will realize that Nolan is a master of making constraints work for him. He is the first to admit that many of the constraints Ghost operates with are artificial. This non-profit venture can easily raise VC money, hire thousands of more employees, spend a substantial amount on branding and compete head on with the likes of Substack, Revue and Mailchimp.

The big question is whether it should compete with anyone. What would be the likely outcome of such competitive dynamics? Who would be the winners and losers in this game?

A non-profit organization like Ghost will never beat Substack playing Substack's game. Substack can outspend Ghost on almost every metric, but there are some areas where Ghost will have long-term strategic advantages. According to John, these advantages include product, longevity, business model and underlying narrative, and can be attributed to the power of constraints.

To be clear, this is not a newsletter about which is better, Substack or Ghost. Both are good platforms in their own way. We are interested in exploring something specific. Let's jump in.

Ghost is designed to last. Most venture-funded companies start with the end in mind—get acquired or go public. John structured his company as a non-profit because he saw himself running Ghost for the rest of his life. There is no exit or backup plan per se. This is a self-imposed constraint which forces him to be committed to the core problem instead of getting distracted by which competitor is raising how much.

It is important to know which problem you want to get stuck with just like it is important to know the people you want in your life forever.

You may remember liquid modernity and optionality referenced earlier in the book.

The world around is liquid. Lawyer Pete Davis explains that we can't rely on any job or role or idea or cause for long—and they can't rely on us to do so either. That is liquid modernity: the infinite browsing mode for everything in our lives.

We are paralysed by the thought of commitment. No one wants to be stuck behind a locked door, but nobody wants to live in a hallway either.

We get stuck behind a locked door when we make important choices without giving proper thought. Living in a hallway is a metaphor for keeping all options open but refusing to commit to any. The upside of living in a hallway is that you get to observe and evaluate everything. The downside is that you are an observer, not a participant; you are a spectator, not a player.

The constraint created by Ghost to not raise money from VCs and not ever getting bought or sold reinforces its founding principle. One can reasonably argue that these constraints might prevent it from reaching its full potential, but John says that this seemingly restrictive clause propels them to innovate harder on getting the product and underlying business model right.

Substack takes 10 per cent commission on each transaction, Revue takes 5 per cent, Ghost takes 0 per cent but charges a monthly subscription fee which enables it to make substantial revenue each year.

Facebook is also starting a newsletter service and has illustrious writers join its platform. Substack has been paying heavy upfront capital to well-known writers to come on board. Ghost cannot afford to do that, so it has no option but to play to its strengths and innovate on its core offering.

As of writing this section, Network Capital uses Substack, but the larger lessons offered by the way Ghost is being built are noteworthy, even as one thinks of building a career. Write down your core values, identify problems you like getting stuck with, play to your strengths and create your category of one. If you play the long game, you will leave a lasting impression and have measurable impact. You won't excel on all parameters, but you will on the ones that matter.

As a principle, we do not believe in competition. As Peter Thiel often says, it is for losers but even if you feel compelled to compete, avoid the mistake of competing with everyone on everything. Pick your battles carefully.

People who constantly look outside and compare end up exhausted and fatigued. You want to look within with a lot more intensity. The clarity that emerges from introspection followed by community engagement can be your true superpower.

CONCLUDING THOUGHTS

Carve out constraints in your life as they will propel you to discover your reason for being. Constraints could be artificial like in the case of Ghost or thought-through in case you have a full-time job and are working on a side hustle—and have just a few hours a day/

week to make progress on your side hustle. If you really want to do something and because of less than ideal situations (constraints) you are unable to carve out time, it just means that it isn't a priority. Wait to find something that really matters to you. When you do, time will figure itself out—it is elastic.

CHAPTER 56

LEARN TO CREATE
WIN-WIN OUTCOMES

Learn to create win-win outcomes at scale. Your goal is to make other people successful without burning out.

My mission in life is to help interesting people do interesting things. I measure my success on how I help others succeed. Through Network Capital, writing, speaking and in everything I do, I ask myself who will benefit from my endeavours the most. Once that is clear, I find myself energized and ready to go the extra mile. Sometimes seeing the result of your work becomes unclear if you are working in a large conglomerate or serving customers you can't really visualize. With more and more people working for themselves and embarking on the passion economy path, people are discovering novel ways to connect with who they are serving.

The key is to create win-win outcomes at scale. In any relationship, four outcomes are possible.

Win-lose: This is when you get the outcome you want but the other party feels that they have got the unfavourable outcome.

Lose-win: When you invest time and energy that led to a meaningful outcome for the other party but you feel under appreciated. If this happens repeatedly, you will find yourself drained of energy, burnt out and exploited.

Lose-lose: This is the worst of all worlds. Both you and your collaborator feel that they have lost by investing in the relationship.

Win-win: This is when you do things that help both you and the collaborator achieve meaningful outcomes. I have observed that creating win-win outcomes is more about empathy than skill. One needs to train oneself to look at problem from the lens of our collaborator. What would propel them to succeed? How can you create such synergistic relationships that leave you more inspired than drained?

As a creator or someone venturing into the passion economy, you need to enable these win-win outcomes to scale with the power of code, media and, most importantly, word of mouth. Stories scale. When you serve people in a way that serves and delights them, they are likely to talk about it with their friends. That's how you start building a brand for yourself as someone who makes others win.

Lenny Rachitsky, the Airbnb product manager turned newsletter writer, has an interesting introduction on his personal website: 'I write a newsletter, angel invest, run a job board, and generally just try to be helpful.'

To me, 'generally just try to be helpful' is the most interesting part of his introduction. It connotes that part of his identity is focused on serving others. It establishes his brand as a giver and signals to his readers, consumers of his job board and people raising investments that he is someone they can lean on for guidance.

As we discussed in the section on access economy, people don't pay as much for things as they do for deeper access through unique experiences. And who do people want access to? Do you think people want access to those who are obsessed with their individual goals with no regard to others? No, helpful givers who have the reputation for adding specific value to others are always in demand. People think that deeper access to them would be helpful to expand the pie for everyone involved.

Paul Erdős, probably the most loved, most networked and most talented mathematician, was known far more for being the creator of win-win outcomes at scale than any technical achievement (although he had many). The Fields Medal is the highest honour in maths. Erdős never won it, but several people he helped did. Erdős is best known for the 'Erdős Number'. It wasn't a theorem or a tool but a measure of how close you were to working with Paul Erdős. Research has shown that in many cases, mathematical prowess is proportional to how closely you worked with/were influenced by Erdős. Two Nobel Prize winners in physics have an Erdős Number of 2 and fourteen have an Erdős Number of 3. As Erik Barker puts it (drawing upon Adam Grant's research), Erdős made people great.

So what can you do to make people great, and how can you enable your customers and partners to flourish? Don't worry much about your talent, seniority or influence. Win-win outcomes come down to intent, changing focus from yourself to others.

The key is to not exhaust yourself. Balancing your goals with those of others is critical. I try to do my bit to make others great, but I know that I can only serve others if I take care of myself and remain energized by my core mission. I have specific time blocked on my calendar titled 'Help Others'. I conduct office hours, make helpful introductions and point people to the right sources in this slot. This leaves me motivated to work on my personal and organizational goals for the rest of the day. I have noticed that when I am less structured about this process, my overall efficacy drops. I am unable to help others effectively and unable to make progress on my goals.

Say you are a community builder. Your ultimate success will come from making your community members successful. By making them successful, you will automatically inch closer towards your goal, but it is important that you orient yourself that way. Now consider the reverse. Suppose you achieve great personal success and glory, but that does not mean that your community members will reach their goals. That is perhaps why so many celebrities and influencers who have tried to launch companies/communities fail.

The same principle is at play in almost every job today. Whether you are a teacher, a newsletter writer, a video creator or a coach, your success will be measured by who you serve and how. You may not be able to guarantee success, but people will remember whether you tried sincerely or not.

The following four steps will be useful to keep in mind.

1. **Start from those you are trying to serve:** Visualize your primary stakeholders. Think about their goals and objectives. Try and articulate what success looks like for them.

2. **Understand their unmet needs:** People you are trying to serve may be facing challenges they aren't able to overcome

themselves. They may be looking for a fresh perspective, someone to help fit the pieces of their jigsaw puzzle together.

3. **Figure out the specific value you can add to their lives:** This involves creating a fit between your skills and the core needs of people you are trying to serve. Suppose an athlete trying to prepare for a challenging race comes to you—a behavioural economist. You may not be equipped to give them advice on the right diet or training regimen, but you could very well offer techniques to use right nudges to overcome inevitable challenges which are likely to emerge. You may have ideas to make constraints work for the athlete based on interesting studies you have read/experiments you have conducted. You cannot be everything to everyone, but you surely can develop the art of adding deeper specific value to others at scale.

4. **Develop a strategy to make it happen:** A strategy is a lot about avoiding tempting traps and pitfalls. You need to figure out a way to help those you are trying to serve help themselves.

Relationships that last and partnerships that work are often where all parties involved grow together, succeed together. The key is to figure out efficient, synergetic ways to make it happen.

CHAPTER 57

BUILD THE RIGHT MINDSET

Stanford Professor Carol Dweck coined the term 'growth mindset' over 30 years ago when she became interested in how students process and perceive failure. She observed that some students rebounded, while other students were inconsolable by the slightest of setbacks. Her research suggests that when students believe that they can get better with deliberate practice, they understand that it correlates with achievement. Therefore, they put in extra effort, which leads to better results.

Thinking that we have one fixed self which is set in stone makes us believe that our intelligence, potential and capability cannot be altered. Such fatalistic thinking leads people to stop trying altogether. If things can't change, why bother, people with fixed mindsets seem to think.

After he became the CEO of Microsoft, Satya Nadella said that being a learn-it-all connotes a growth mindset, essential for both innovation and culture change. Scaling the growth mindset across the company was a key factor that led to Microsoft's cultural transformation aptly reflected in the company stock price increasing 10 times over the last 7 years.

Microsoft isn't predominantly a passion economy company, but the lesson from Satya's leadership is applicable for creators who must consider adopting the growth mindset and become learn-it-alls. Alternate careers, side hustles and passion economy are relatively new. There isn't much precedence. Nothing is set in stone; every aspect of this new space needs to be figured out. Growth mindset will help make sense of inevitable pitfalls and failures along the way. A new product not working doesn't mean you are inadequate. All it means is that you need to try harder and try differently. I adapted author Brene Brown's work on the difference between shame and regret to come up with this action point.

Regret is 'I did something bad.' Shame is 'I am something bad.' Regret can be healthy if we adopt a growth mindset, reflect on our actions and commit to making things better one day at a time. Shame, on the other hand, can lead us to resigning and accepting that we are beyond repair. Shame connotes a fixed mindset.

Most of us have lingering regrets which creep up in unexpected ways. It could be regret of action, inaction, indulgence and failure, among others. Sometimes these regrets lead us into the trap of shame. If and when that happens, we need to step back and check ourselves. I have a few regrets about some of our strategies at Network Capital, but I don't have any shame in the way I have gone about building it.

Radical tinkering and relentless experimentation are natural by-products of the growth mindset. That's the mindset of scientists and innovators. They aren't in love with their solutions; they love the problems they are solving and keep an objective view.

Being passionate or intrinsically curious about something augments your intuition. You are naturally driven to get into the weeds, explore more about the subject, but it can also lead you to ignore objectivity for intuition. I am a big believer in following the gut instinct as long as we complement it with objective truths. Getting fixated on a particular solution or strategy rarely ends well.

When Network Capital was just a small Facebook group, I would manually post and approve relevant content. I was guided by my intuition and people enjoyed the curation, but as we scaled, it occurred to me that it was a suboptimal approach. Even though things were working well, I realized that I had become the bottleneck. If I had adopted a fixed mindset and become reticent to change, we would never be able to build the culture of P2P sharing which by definition needs multiple people to be information, knowledge and network brokers.

Fixed mindset is the antithesis of rethinking. Without rethinking assumptions and recalibrating strategies, you won't be able to make the passion economy work for you.

CHAPTER 58

FOCUS ON YOUR SUPERPOWER AND OUTSOURCE EVERYTHING ELSE

Every passion economy builder has a superpower which they hope to monetize or create something of value. This superpower needs to be identified by introspection, experimentation and feedback from others.

Your superpower, whatever that might be—public speaking, writing, community building, shaping products, singing or dancing— is a massive reservoir of economic and social capital. It could also be at the intersection of two different skills or talents. You will figure that out once you conduct a range of micro-experiments which will reveal your strengths to you and to your community.

The challenge of building in the passion economy is that you typically need to excel at complex coordination. At any given point, you will have to work on a wide range of projects, figure out stuff with many unknown unknowns, coordinate logistics and put together a system that works. A lot of it is non-glamorous work.

Context switching refers to the process of juggling multiple projects and priorities. Passion economy builders, especially in the early days, need to learn to navigate this emotionally and physically exhausting process. That said, your goal should be to create systems and processes which help you scale yourself. You can't simply do that by working longer hours or sleeping less. I often feel that the hustle culture is glorified, and it is easy to be seduced by the illusion of hard work.

I have found that in the long run, it pays off to focus almost exclusively on your superpower and outsource everything else to other team mates. If you are working alone, you can consider getting volunteers on board or even paying for services to an external platforms and services.

Both time and energy are finite. You need to pay close attention to how you spend these precious resources. Say you are a newsletter curator and writing is your superpower; you should spend most of your time writing. Other activities such as marketing, social media evangelism and partnerships should be pursued in time which is left after you have completed your core job. An 80–20 split works well. Spend 80 per cent of your time and energy on your superpower and 20 per cent on other stuff you need to get done to keep things going.

Some creators spend four out of five working days on their core craft and reserve one day of the week on promotional activities. If you are unable to find this neat split, consider blocking out time for deep work every day where you focus exclusively on your superpower. You can also allocate time on your calendar for other stuff. As you can tell, I am a big fan of having stuff on the calendar. It makes things real for me and helps me plan my day.

The last thing you want to do is to stagnate in the proficiency level of your superpower. People pay you or enjoy going through your work because they find value in the output you produce. Everything else is secondary. It doesn't mean that other stuff doesn't matter—just that your time is best utilized on specific tasks, which moves the needle for you and your customers.

CHAPTER 59

BUILD A TRIBE OF MENTORS

Every creator needs a tribe of mentors. You shouldn't go around asking people to be your mentors. That happens to be one of the most inefficient ways to go about it. I find Facebook COO Sheryl Sandberg's approach helpful.

In her book *Lean In*, she writes, 'The strongest relationships spring out of a real and often earned connection felt by both sides.' Instead of telling professionals, "Get a mentor and you will excel',' she wrote, 'We need to tell them, "Excel and you will get a mentor."' This advice builds upon the concept of 'luck surface area' which is a product of doing great things and telling lots of people. As much as you need to find your mentors, your mentors need to find you as well. You can enhance the probability of that happening by working on your 'luck surface area'.

Healthy and long-lasting mentor–mentee relationships are syncretic. Both parties find value in the connection, enjoy learning from each other and find meaning in helping the other person grow. Building a tribe of mentors means finding a group of people with different areas of expertise invested in your success. You won't build this tribe in a day or a month or a year. It is an ongoing process.

Your tribe of mentors evolves with you. I have always treated relationships with mentors with a long-term lens. I do a good job of keeping in touch and always avoid the cardinal sin of mentorship—reaching out only when you need help and forgetting the person right after.

Whenever I find the opportunity, I attempt to add specific value to my mentors in my own small way. They often reciprocate with more generosity, kindness and specific feedback.

Over the years, I have been able to take difficult decisions by consulting with my tribe of mentors. Their presence in my life gives me confidence to pursue ambitious projects. Whenever I am stuck, I know I can reach out to them. I try and be specific and time-sensitive in my communication. This has proved to be helpful, and you should try it. Paraphrasing Tim Ferriss, mentorship punishes the vague wish and rewards the specific ask.

In a way, Network Capital is my attempt to help every person on the planet find their tribe of mentors. From the beginning, I have encouraged our community members to stop asking for mentors and ask specific questions instead. Since Network Capital is a group of more than 200,000 members, someone is always out there to help you. Your job is to find that person, engage with them meaningfully, add specific value to them and build a non-transactional relationship. Over time, that person might become your mentor. If you repeat this process with right intention, you will be able to build and nurture your tribe of mentors.

CHAPTER 60

BUILD A CHALLENGER NETWORK

A challenger network is designed to deliver uncomfortable truths to you. Feedback—both positive and negative—is necessary for progress. Often passion economy builders start alone or in small groups. It is easy to fall into the trap of listening to people we want to listen to, those who validate our views. While a tribe of mentors and cheerleaders is important, a challenger network is a useful complement to ensure we don't fall into an echo chamber.

Simply telling the uncomfortable truth isn't enough to include someone in our challenger network. We need to ensure that the underlying message reaches the intended audience effectively. CEO coach Kim Scott has developed a four-pronged behavioural awareness framework to guide important conversations. It is worth noting that these are behaviours, not personality types, which all of us fall into from time to time.

First is radical candour. It is a management philosophy: when a person cares for your growth and simultaneously presents a direct challenge. Scott learnt it first-hand from Facebook chief operating officer Sheryl Sandberg, who used to be her manager at Google. After a largely successful presentation, Sandberg privately told Scott that she needed a speaking coach to avoid awkward pauses.

To Scott, it seemed like a trivial point. She listened, but it was clear that she wasn't going to act on the feedback. Finally, Sandberg said, 'You know, Kim, I can tell I'm not really getting through to you. I'm going to have to be clearer here. When you say "um" every third word, it makes you sound stupid.'[1]

According to Scott, Sandberg's radical candour was the kindest thing she could have done for her professional growth.

1 https://review.firstround.com/radical-candor-the-surprising-secret-to-being-a-good-boss

There are four defining aspects of radical candour—it is humble, helpful, immediate and in-person (private if it's criticism and in public if praise).

In a high-trust environment, radical candour works like a charm, but it requires training. You first have to establish that you care for the person you are offering feedback to. Only after that can you expect to offer sharp critique and still manage to have a healthy relationship.

Second is obnoxious aggression. It is what happens when we challenge someone directly but don't establish that we care about them. This is commonly observed when someone with leverage and credibility publicly shames or mocks others to get the outcome they want. While the aggressor might feel powerful in the short term, it is a guaranteed way to not get the outcome they want in a longer time frame. In today's hyperconnected world, the way we treat people is public knowledge. We might have some leverage today, but nothing is permanent. As an obnoxious aggressor, one should keep in mind that we are making ourselves unemployable in the long term.

Third is manipulative sincerity, the hallmark of toxic culture. This is often an after-effect of obnoxious aggression and leads to a situation when we neither care nor challenge. Insincere praise, flattery and back-stabbing are commonly observed traits of manipulative sincerity.

Last is ruinous empathy. It is what happens when we want to spare someone's feelings in the short term and end up not telling them something they absolutely need to know. We care but fail to challenge. Ruinous empathy may feel safe but is ultimately damaging. Empathy is a great asset, but it can paralyse us if we prioritize relational comfort over what is good for the other person. Scott shares that 85 per cent of management mistakes are a direct result of ruinous empathy.

RADICAL CANDOUR AND CHALLENGER NETWORK

You need your challenger network to be radically candid with you. I chose my challenger network based on trust, comfort and time.

I trusted them blindly to offer the unvarnished truth to me under all circumstances. These were people I had known for a while, and they had seen me at the top of my game and at rock bottom.

We had a sense of comfort. I knew that they were telling me uncomfortable truths because they had enough context from the past and wished the best for my future.

Availability of time was another criterion I kept in mind. I wanted people in my challenger network to be able to spend 30 minutes with me every quarter.

Listening deeply was a skill I had to work upon as my challenger network matured. Initially, I would get defensive and start explaining why certain things had turned out the way they did. Instead of understanding where they were coming from, I would get into the respond and react mode. The result was that the time we spent turned out to be frustrating for me and annoying for them.

One afternoon, someone in my challenger network sat me down and made me realize that I was wasting our precious time with my defensive attitude. The irony was that I started getting defensive even while getting feedback on being defensive. After a few minutes, the irony was too much to handle and both of us started laughing. I learned my lesson that day and have done a good job of listening intently since then.

My challenger network helped me understand so many blind spots I had in my execution strategy, mindset, product road map and pricing. Being the leader of a massive global community is immensely satisfying. I get oodles of positive reinforcement, and I am ever so grateful for each one of them. That said, the uncomfortable truths from my challenger network have played an equally significant role in shaping me and Network Capital.

CHAPTER 61

DON'T FEEL PRESSURED
TO BE ON TOP OF EVERYTHING,
REMEMBER DONALD KNUTH

Don Knuth is a Professor Emeritus at Stanford University and recipient of the Turing Award (considered the Nobel Prize of computer science) who abandoned email in 1990. Among other books, he is the author of *The Art of Computer Programming* which concludes with a blurb from Bill Gates: 'You should definitely send me a résumé if you can read the whole thing.'

Knuth is a pioneer in 'literate programming', emphasizing the importance of writing code which is readable by humans as well as computers. He is a funky odd ball who pays people to find mistakes in his books, has a wager on whether Google co-founder Sergey Brin will finish his PhD and recently quipped: 'It started out that computer scientists were worried nobody was listening to us. Now I'm worried that too many people are listening.'

KNUTH VS EMAIL

Dr Knuth says that he has been a happy man ever since he abandoned his email, one that he had been using since 1975. In his typically witty voice, he says that it seems to him that 15 years of email is plenty for one lifetime.[1]

> Email is a wonderful thing for people whose role in life is to be on top of things. But not for me; my role is to be on the bottom of things. What I do takes long hours of studying

1 https://www-cs-faculty.stanford.edu/~knuth/email.html

and uninterruptible concentration. I try to learn certain areas of computer science exhaustively; then I try to digest that knowledge into a form that is accessible to people who don't have time for such study.

Being a pioneer in computer science and AI, he does need to communicate with thousands of people all over the world, including the likes of Gates. He does so via his books, snail mail (traditional post) and in batch mode, a technique you should strongly consider adopting.

What is batching?

It is what it sounds like. You respond to emails, pigeons, snaps and chats by bundling them. Instead of replying to emails and messages as they come (something modern workplaces incentivize and modern technology seduces you to), you reply to them in one/ few go/goes.

STAYING ON TOP VS GETTING TO THE BOTTOM OF THINGS?

Dr Knuth's lifelong project *The Art of Computer Programming* (one that Bill Gates commented on) will take another 25 years, he says. That is the one thing he wants to get done and has decided to dedicate almost all his waking hours to it. Because of its sheer complexity and depth, it needs (at least in his view) undisturbed, focused exploration for years on end.

That is how anyone gets to the bottom of things and finds treasures that escape those who feel compelled to be on top of things all the time.

Like everything in the world, staying on top and getting to the bottom of things have benefits and costs associated with them. Staying on top gives you control, connection and continual feedback. It comes at the cost of deep work and deliberate practice.

The question ultimately becomes:

Is benefit of staying on top of things > cost of staying on top of things?

No prize for guessing that the answer is 'it depends'.

The benefit can outweigh cost on certain days at certain stages in your career, but if staying on top of things becomes your default state, you are in for trouble. Your creativity will suffer and so will your productivity.

What should you do?

The good news is that you don't need to abandon your communication tools. Actually, you can't, even if you are a monk in the 21st century. That said, you can schedule daily digital detox and actually take a journey inward. In fact, this time of crisis is ideal for some personal reflection and inner exploration.

Such an endeavour will, of course, reveal to you what matters most to you and why (for those applying to business school will find short-term practical benefits of such reflection, as that happens to be an essay prompt). Start by asking: If there is one problem you could explore in the whole wide world, what might that be?

Not scheduling time for that is not called 'being busy'. It is called 'being lazy'—intellectually and otherwise.

Once you figure that out, you can take a leaf out of Dr Knuth's book and start getting to the bottom of your calling.

CHAPTER 62

BECOME BACKABLE

Remember that no one will believe in you until you believe in yourself

Four years before Barack Obama's Democratic National Convention (DNC) speech (the very speech that made him President), he ran for Congress and was defeated by a two-to-one margin. After the loss, the Obama family was $60,000 in debt. Barack Obama seriously considered quitting politics as a career.

Instead of giving up, he hit refresh. He started from scratch. It is hard to believe now, but back then Barack Obama was considered boring, stilted and professorial. His stump speech felt like a university lecture. Ted McClelland, a journalist who covered Obama during his congressional loss, said that his speeches were so dry that they 'sucked the life out of the room'.

So how did Obama transform?

Reflecting on his loss, Obama said, 'It taught me the importance of campaigning not based on a bunch of whitepapers and policy prescriptions but telling a story.'

Most great political speeches include three elements: the 'story of me', 'the story of you' and, most important, the 'story of us'.

Obama's professorial avatar was able to communicate the facts and figures, but it wasn't clear to the voters why he was saying what he was saying, where he was coming from, what his story was, how his story connected with them and, most importantly, it wasn't communicating why backing him will advance their collective stories forward.

Before his DNC speech, Obama was an unknown upstart who had lost an election badly. Those 17 minutes on stage transformed his life. By weaving in his story with the story of the voters and connecting it with the vision for America in a charged, passionate way, he paved his way to the presidency. Essentially, Obama became backable.

How might we become backable?

Suneel Gupta, a Harvard professor who was once the poster-child of failure (there was a full-fledged *The New York Times* article on failure with his photo next to it), recently wrote a fabulous book about becoming backable. He will be with us on 14 June sharing the behind the scenes details of his adventures and misadventures. Meanwhile, I am sharing seven key takeaways that each of us can leverage to futureproof our work life and become more backable.[1]

1. Convince yourself before convincing others. Backable people schedule incubation time to build up their ideas, think things through and then share them with those they need support from. Pitching ideas prematurely can make others think that we are unprepared.

   This doesn't mean you should not brainstorm ideas with your inner circle of friends and mentors. You absolutely should. In fact, such discussions lead to ideas maturing. Peter Thiel, the co-founder of PayPal and Palantir, and backer of start-ups including Facebook and Spotify, emphasizes the importance of such informal discussion with his tribe of peer mentors. He speaks with some of the smartest people he knows and continues to develop his thinking 'every day'.

   That said, there is a difference between brainstorming and pitching. When you need support—investment, partnership and publishing—make sure that you have first convinced yourself and prepared thoroughly.

   An important concept Gupta talks about is emotional runway. Intellectual interest is necessary but insufficient to succeed. Most ideas don't fail because of lack of capital or market forces but because the creator/entrepreneur runs out of steam. The emotional runway becomes zero.

---

1 https://www.networkcapital.tv/course/art-of-becoming-backable-with-suneel-gupta

2. Cast a central character. Let's take writing. Don't write a book for millions of people. Write for one person who you can visualize. If you can make that one person fall in love with your idea, hundreds will follow; those hundreds one day might become much larger. Having that one identifiable person is key to writing something compelling, something which has a story with insight and appeal. The same holds true for building something new or creating something that matters.

3. Find an earned secret. You can read about blockchain as much as you want, but unless you actually build or invest in it, you won't learn. Earned secrets emerge from deep engagement. Network Capital didn't start doing cohort-based fellowships because the market was large or because I invested in Maven. We spoke to thousands of people at length to figure out how they learn, what the current gaps in their learning methods are and then decided to launch a new fellowship every month.

4. Make it feel inevitable. Backable ideas are typically those which are already underway. The Airbnb founders had to convince investors that people would be happy to open their homes to strangers. Rather than explaining how the world should be, their pitch contained a slide with the massive uptick in the number of home-sharing listings on Craigslist and Couchsurfing.

   They made the investors realize that not backing them would mean missing out on a path-defining market trend.

5. Flip outsiders to insiders. Every idea needs its community, its tribe, to succeed. We need to transform people who could back us into co-creators of our vision. The most passionate backers are those who feel like they are part of your creative journey.

   As I wrote in my *Mint* article, most important career decisions happen when we are not in the room. Passive backers aren't of much use. We need advocates who are invested in our success, our ideas and our growth.

6. Practise in real contexts. You can't practise your pitch by simply going over your slide deck. Real feedback from real people is essential for progress. Jerry Seinfeld went back to the tiny club

he started at to see how his new jokes landed. It was a relatively low-stake playing field but one that proved to be critical to his job.

Backable people create opportunities to fine-tune their game. Embarrassment is okay; in fact, you want as much of it before the big arenas and high-stake platforms.

7. Ego is for losers. Let go of it. Your goal is to improve, not prove a point. Backable people nudge the spotlight from them towards their idea and the stakeholders they want to serve. This act of forgetting yourself is the first step towards letting go of your ego.

CHAPTER 63

KEEP THE JAPANESE PHILOSOPHY OF KINTSUGI IN MIND

The Japanese art of kintsugi (golden repair) is a method of repairing broken pottery which honours its unique, imperfect history by emphasizing its cracks.

The discovery of kintsugi was an accident. Legend has it that when the 15th-century *shogun* (hereditary military dictator) Ashikaga Yoshimasa broke his favourite tea bowl, he sent it to China for repairs and was disappointed that it came back stapled together looking particularly ugly. The local craftsmen came up with an ingenious solution: They filled the crack with a golden lacquer, making the bowl more unique and precious. This repair elevated the broken bowl back to its place as shogun's favourite and prompted a whole new art form which celebrates imperfections.

A life without cracks, falls and blemishes is an incomplete life. When we take risks, we can't be too worried about falling and failing. Cracks in our armour are inevitable, but most of us feel pressured to put forward sanitized, Instagrammable version of our lives. We carefully curate our image and go out of our way to hide our cracks, imperfections and weaknesses.

Kintsugi asks us to reconsider our approach. Far from running away from our shortcomings and mistakes, Kintsugi encourages us to wear them as badges of honour. To us on Network Capital, kintsugi has meant acceptance and kindness to our own selves.

MOST OF LIFE DOESN'T QUITE WORK OUT

Most things we will try in our lives won't work. That is a fact. The good news is that we don't need everything to work. Just a few high-impact projects, experiments and initiatives will suffice for a well-lived, successful, meaningful life. But to make these critical endeavours work, we need to reflect on our failures purposefully. We don't need to forget about them, distract ourselves or pretend they never happened.

BE CAREFUL NOT TO OVERINDULGE YOUR FAILURES

Kintsugi is not about becoming a victim to our circumstances or obsessing over our imperfections or fretting over failures. It is a reminder that striving for perfection is much more nuanced than hiding experiments that didn't work.

Fundamentally, kintsugi is about radical candour. We don't really believe in the Instagram lives of celebrities, do we? Intuitively, we know that they are putting on a show. The same holds true— to a certain extent—for our friends and for our own selves. If everyone knows that everyone else is putting on a show, what's the point? What if we consider being a bit more open about stuff that isn't working so well? What if we invite others to help us instead of trying to impress them with our perfection?

KINTSUGI RESUME

Resumes have become a bit of a joke. That one page listing our accomplishments is such an incomplete, inauthentic story. It is a massive lie/semi-truth entrusted by institutions for key professional decisions.

There are, of course, some people (usually very successful) who publish things like 'My Failure Resume', but those aren't really the ones submitted for job interviews. We think that real resumes should have a healthy mix of stuff which worked and stuff which backfired.

Adopting the kintsugi mindset will make resumes a lot more insightful for the recruiters, companies and candidates. A kintsugi resume will be more interested in reflections and learnings instead of humble bragging. It might eventually create a more reflective working environment which is safe, curiosity-inducing and kind.

Even cover letters should evolve into short, reflective essays, instead of mechanical regurgitation of facts and figures. We can tell far more about a person's capabilities from the way they reflect than we can from the way they convey suitability for a job they don't really know about.

Someone who can reflect intentionally about the past, accept failures and learn from them is likely to be a great asset. In today's fast-paced world, we can easily keep busy and occupied. We can even pretend that we haven't really failed, but deep down we know that it is a lie.

HOW CAN KINTSUGI HELP NAVIGATE YOUR CAREER?

Failures are inevitable. Embrace them, learn from them and wear them as a badge of honour.

Steve Jobs got fired from the company he started, Elon Musk almost went bankrupt twice, Satya Nadella got rejected from almost every engineering college he applied to as an undergrad, Ray Dalio was so broke after making horribly wrong predictions about the American economy that he had to borrow money from his dad to pay the rent and the list goes on.

What is common to all these illustrious examples is their kintsugi mindset. They accepted their failures, reflected on them and decided to work towards a better tomorrow. One might say that it was the way they negotiated with their failures that set them up for success.

The kintsugi mindset makes us anti-fragile. We strengthen through chaos and graduate with a memorable story.

Leonard Cohen famously said, 'There is a crack in everything, that's how the light gets in.' It is time to let the cracks reveal themselves and educate us through the process.

Personally, trying to adopt the Kintsugi mindset has been transformational. I have learned the importance of learning from setbacks keeping the larger picture in mind.

Running a large, global mentorship movement is a meaningful job but a tricky one. Issues of moral, social, political, business judgment need to be managed appropriately on a daily basis. This process is educational because there are so many aspects that one can get wrong on the first try but the goal isn't to become perfect from the start.

I strive for progress, not perfection, all thanks to the Kintsugi mindset. I keep Steve Jobs' iconic commencement speech at Stanford in mind. Knowing that dots connect backwards often in mystical and mysterious ways gives me strength to keep trying even on the hardest of days.

CHAPTER 64

SCHEDULE TIME FOR
LONG-TERM THINKING

Many times, passion economy operators struggle to differentiate the urgent from the important. There is so much to do just to keep the ship floating. That said, the ship won't float for long if we keep fighting fires and let the long term take care of itself.

It is important to spend time developing independent, first-principles-based perspectives on industries we operate in. For example, as an education entrepreneur and community builder, I must have intimate understanding of new trends in the sector, changing customer attitudes towards learning, new business models, evolving government policies and cutting-edge technologies such as AR, virtual reality (VR) and machine learning which are building the next wave of ed-tech products. I don't necessarily need to apply everything to my company, but being aware helps in visualizing the future.

Long-term thinking is not something that comes naturally to most of us. We routinely overestimate what we can do in 1 year and underestimate what we can do with consistent effort in 10 years. Building a long-term vision for yourself and the company/community you are building helps develop a mental road map of how you can get there. I often look at history for guidance. Mark Twain once said that history doesn't repeat itself, but it often rhymes. To project your future, you should also look at your past.

I have always been an introspective person. As a thirty year old, I tried remembering what I was like as a twenty-year-old. I allocated a whole day going through my past messages, inboxes and photographs. It was a profound experience in a way. I realized how different the reality of my thirty-year-old self was from my projection 10 years back. My goals had evolved, my world view had changed and I lived in a different country doing something radically different from what I thought I would end up doing.

Long-term plans rarely work out, but planning helps. As a twenty-year-old, I thought I would get good education, pursue an advanced academic degree and save enough money to risk it all and carve out a career in acting. Yes, at one point I seriously considered becoming a Bollywood actor. At thirty, I still pursued acting but as a hobby. Along the way I fell in love with community building and writing. That's basically what I do today. Even though I got many things wrong about my future, thinking about it and building a plan catapulted me forward.

Personal history is revealing, and so is the history of industries. The movie industry with streaming platforms looks radically different from what it was when people used CDs, cassettes and video recorders. Business models have changed, stardom has evolved, culture has changed and globalization is far more mainstreamed today than it has ever been in the past. That said, the music industry today and in the times to come can learn so much from the changes in the past.

In the middle of writing this book, I watched a movie in Hampstead Heath, a large park in London. It was a magical, open-air experience under a full moon. It was my first time watching a movie outside a cinema hall, and I discovered that before streaming came into being, people would often gather in parks and watch stuff together as a community.

Anyone who has researched the history of cinema would be able to recontextualize this experience in the post-pandemic world and create memorable experiences for people. It goes without saying that if done well, it could lead to a large community or a massive company. Perhaps its mission would be to create memorable offline cinematic experiences. Perhaps it would go on to create a community of cinema lovers, monetized via monthly subscriptions and teaching workshops.

Coming back to the central idea of this section, look to develop long-term perspectives for your own life and for the industry you are interested in by diving deeper into your personal history and that of your industry. Your long-term view cannot be the aggregation of everything you read about on social media and blogs. Carve out room for independent first-principles thinking and learn to have contrarian opinions based on facts.

CHAPTER 65

ALWAYS KEEP TALEB'S TWO CONCEPTS IN MIND: ANTI-FRAGILITY AND ERGODICITY

ANTI-FRAGILITY AND ERGODICITY: TWO CONCEPTS YOU MUST UNDERSTAND

Nassim Nicholas Taleb spent 21 years as a risk-taker (quantitative trader) before becoming a researcher in philosophical, mathematical and (mostly) practical problems with probability.[1] He predicted the 2008 financial crisis and alluded to the 2020 coronavirus outbreak way back in 2007 in his book *The Black Swan*. Take a look at the section below.

Taleb loves to quote David Hume: 'No amount of observations of white swans can allow the inference that all swans are white, but the observation of a single black swan is sufficient to refute that conclusion.'

He owes almost all of his personal wealth and fame to being a contrarian and predicting black swan events—random, unexpected occurrences sweeping the world.

Most of us revere people who are willing to risk failure—and have the gumption to bounce back from catastrophe—with courage. But Taleb's example shows that there is perhaps equal, if not more heroism, in taking the purposeful and painful steps to prepare for the unimaginable.

1 https://trendsfestival.com/en/speaker,prof.-nassim-nicholas-taleb,174.html

Passion Economy and the Side-Hustle Revolution

Not known for his restraint, sensitivity or political correctness, he tweeted in the middle of the coronavirus crisis, 'Those who panicked early don't have to panic today.' Knowing if one is vulnerable to the volatility of accelerated damage forms the core of Taleb's thought and has many applications in business and life, including our career.

While making long-term career plans, it is important to keep in mind that our forecasts are fragile and our strategies often do not take into account parameters which can create conditions akin to getting locked in on a highway with no exit.

There are two concepts that Taleb keeps coming back to, and it is important that you add it to your arsenal of mental models to make sense of the world around.

The first is anti-fragility (systems that strengthen through chaos).

We can think of history in many different ways. One way to think about it is to visualize it as a gloomy compendium of threats, pandemics and disasters—in other words, largely fragile and prone to implosion.

However, if we flip things around and look at the facts objectively, it becomes clear that we happen to be awe-inspiringly resilient.

The global system that we cohabit produces myriad benefits but also a few vulnerabilities. Shocks and backlashes are going to be key features of the 21st century. Resilience is not enough. Surviving one shock or one crisis does not mean that we will be ready for the next one.

We will need to make shocks and backlashes our teachers and learn from them. We will need to become stronger through chaos and crises. That is what Taleb calls anti-fragility.

More than 400 million people lost their jobs in 2020. These jobs are not coming back in the short term. Those who were fired, furloughed or let go will need to step back and figure out/build on their competitive strengths to create new jobs for themselves. In other words, they need to take concrete steps towards becoming anti-fragile.

So ask yourself, 'What am I doing to become more anti-fragile?' If the answer isn't clear to you, you should spend some time in the coming weeks thinking things through.

The next concept essential to making sense of life in the 21st century is ergodicity.

Following are some important pointers to keep in mind.

1. **Warren Buffet:** In order to succeed, you must first survive.
2. There is a huge difference between 100 people going to a casino and one person going to a casino 100 times.

   But
3. If 100 people flip a coin once or 1 person flips a coin 100 times, you get the same outcome.

Now let's define ergodicity.

Something is called ergodic if as time goes on, luck/random-ness plays less of a role in outcome. With this in mind, can you tell if the coinflip discussed in point 3 is ergodic?

Non-ergodic systems are defined when there is a possible ruin (that Warren Buffet talked about in point 1) in the future. We tend to think (and are taught to think) as though most systems are ergodic. However, pretty much every human system is non-ergodic.

A gambler walking into a casino is entering a non-ergodic system. He might get lucky a few times, but if he continues to play, he is bound to experience 'ruin', which means that you cease to survive and, as Buffet says, in order to succeed you must first survive.

Moral of the story: Don't take risks that will finish you out. Life is non-ergodic.

What is the ergodicity of your career strategy?

Ergodicity of your career strategy is critical to evaluating your worth in the job market. Following are the questions to ask yourself:

1. How ready are you to embrace a catastrophic disruption in your industry or the world at large?
2. Will you be obliterated or will your robustness increase if something really surprising happens? Will you become

anti-fragile? We hope you do and we are there for you to help you get there.

To sum up, keep in mind that

1. Resilience is not enough. You need to cultivate anti-fragility.
2. Life is non-ergodic.
3. But we are incorrectly taught to think of events as largely ergodic. That is the source of most judgement errors.

Never try to prove a point or convince others that you matter. If you are trying too hard to prove (instead of improving), you are getting distracted. More importantly, you are training yourself to become dogmatic. Rethink, tinker and test your hypothesis.

Remember that the pursuit of meaningful work is the ultimate pleasure and the ultimate reward. If you dislike the day-to-day aspects of your job, you are unlikely to feel much better at the end of the week/month/year/decade—unless you do something about it. There will be no mythical day when you will feel that you have 'arrived'.

Life deferment plan that sounds something like 'I will work hard, get fancy degrees, raise tons of money from VCs and exit making multiple millions of dollars so that I retire and chill by the beach' is destined to fail for most people. If you really feel like chilling by the beach, do it today. Don't delude yourself into thinking that torturing yourself today is preparation for a better tomorrow. Work shouldn't be done to seek insurance or impress others. The whole construct of passion economy is that people should be able to make a living doing what they love.

In conclusion, do what you love, get better at your craft, partner with people who resonate with your mission and enjoy the process. Success will likely be a by-product.

Measure progress based on how far you have come from your previous self.

The world today has this inexplicable way of making you feel like the ultimate winner and the ultimate loser at the same time. At any given instant, there are thousands of creators doing far better than you and thousands who would perhaps look up to you for inspiration. The same day Network Capital raised funding from Facebook, another company in an adjacent industry raised almost half a billion dollars. Funding from Facebook is cool, but half a billion dollars is a whole next level of operations.

Should I be happy that we raised capital from one of the most successful companies in the world or berate myself for being so much smaller than this other company that raised a heavy round of funding? I operate with the *mudita* mindset. Instead of being envious of other people and wishing my life were different, I find deep joy and inspiration in the success of others.

For me, it comes down to looking at my past self and objectively evaluating whether I have progressed or not. When the pandemic started, I had just decided to quit my job and start a new phase of my life as a full-time creator and entrepreneur. In the period between working on my company full time and publishing this book, I have had countless moments where I have asked myself if I am doing enough to fulfil my mission.

When you work for yourself and your community, as creators often do, you need to be your manager and performance development coach. Of course, having a tribe of mentors helps, but at many points you are bound to feel alone and distracted. In such moments, comparing and contrasting what you have done with others is a recipe for disaster. The only place to look at is within yourself. You need to ask yourself where you were last week, last month, last year and where you are today.

Progress is the ultimate reward for creators. Comparative progress can also be one of the metrics you look at once a while, but to build your category of one, you need to compete with yourself, not with others.

CHAPTER 66

LEARN, UNLEARN AND
RELEARN CONSTANTLY

The ability to reinvent is going to be the most important skill for creators in the times to come. Industries, business models and operating practices are evolving at a dizzying pace, so status quo is not really an option. At the same time, reinvention doesn't mean changing your identity inside out.

Microsoft CEO Satya Nadella's 'Hit Refresh' framework is the most practical framework for reinvention I have come across. As things change, we need to retain our core identity, remember things that made us successful but adapt to make ourselves relevant to the new context. Microsoft wouldn't be the trillion-dollar company it is today without hitting refresh under Nadella. Also, had it tried to mimic the model of any other company—say Facebook or Google—it would have failed to deliver on its mission.

Creators also need to 'hit refresh'. In India, for example, the Reserve Bank came up with a new regulation which made subscription-enabled businesses almost impossible to exist.[1] Then they relented and came up with a clause which made things pretty difficult but not impossible. For large companies and enterprises with bucket loads of cash, adapting is easier. For smaller players, it can make things particularly challenging. If you were a subscription-powered community or an online video creator thriving on monthly recurring donations, you would have had to rethink the way you operate your business.

Everything can be figured out. Thousands of creators in India repivoted their businesses and created hacks to make things

---

1 https://www.thehindu.com/business/effect-of-rbis-recurring-payment-rule-on-international-services/article37402242.ece

work. I was one such creator. My foundation was shaken when the announcement came out. I was not able to figure out the new direction of Network Capital for a long time. In the challenging time, love of the community I had nurtured for many years came to my rescue. Together, we moved to a new platform, put together an alternative payment gateway, linked to a new bank account in a different country and somehow made things functional again.

Then the Reserve Bank pushed its deadline forward, thereby creating a new phase of uncertainty. I am sure that they had their reason, but this challenging period toughened us up for the times to come. We knew that we had to design for such changes and we did. Looking back, this turned out to be a blessing in disguise. Moments of deep discomfort, if handled with the right mindset, can unleash a whole new spectrum of possibilities.

I have trained myself to relish hitting refresh. Curveballs come at me every week, but I get less flustered each time. The good news is that my company is not too big that I can afford being nonchalant or take refuge in the fact that we have enormous reserves of capital to save the day. It keeps me on my toes all the time. Occasionally, it is exhausting and I feel overwhelmed, but it propels me to look forward to the next day with a sense of adventure and possibility.

I often ask myself what gives me the legitimacy to write this book. I am not the top creator in the world, nor have I smashed tangible metrics out of the park. I have not discovered a new business model or made multiple millions in months and made flashy headlines. Perhaps my legitimacy comes from being able to hit refresh and survive to tell this story.

CHAPTER 67

BUILDING A PORTFOLIO
OF CAREERS

In their book *The 100-year Life: Living and Working in an Age of Longevity*, Lynda Gratton and Andrew Scott make three key points.

First, people have a real shot at living up to or more than 100 years.

Second, the longevity of companies will shrink.

Third, the whole concept of retirement and savings will change.

The traditional three-stage life—full-time education leading to full-time work leading to full-time retirement—will give way to something a great deal more fluid, flexible and multi-staged.

Keeping the 100-year life in mind, one of the most important skills of the 21st century will be the ability to reinvent oneself quickly and repeatedly. Even with the best technologies available for free, it can be very hard and lonely to do this alone. Instead, we should harness the power of communities, experiment till we figure out our superpower and then leverage that to carve out a meaningful career that gives us autonomy, mastery and purpose.

CAREER OR CAREERS?

One consequence of this 100-year life will be that people will have to build a portfolio of careers. We hosted Lightspeed Venture Partner Mercedes Bent on Network Capital. Among other things, she explained how she writes, learns about the gaming industry by playing video games and immerses herself in the crypto world by actually making investments. Five years back, she didn't even know how VC firms work; today, she is a partner at a major fund and is working on the side to figure out what she wants to do next—perhaps she will remain in the VC industry, perhaps she will write a book, perhaps she will create an alternate fund for the creator economy, perhaps she will become an adjunct professor at a business school. Who knows!

Despite her exceptionally impressive CV and long list of accomplishments, she is tinkering to figure out what her next career move will be. This unpredictability can be both adventurous and intimidating—adventurous because there is thrill in exploring the unknown, intimidating because no one really knows what the future will look like.

Uncertainty and anxiety go hand in hand, so if we want to make sense of our future selves, we should be prepared to build a portfolio of skills, networks and careers. The world is moving so fast that we have to learn to make sense of it as it evolves. The time for pre-planned strategies which are set in stone has long gone. We will need to learn to pivot our careers based on how economy, culture and society are evolving. Maybe, if we try hard enough, we can play a key role in shaping culture, but that is usually a function of many factors—again not always in our control. All we can do right now is to balance optionality and depth.

Depth matters because without really committing to something and exploring the hidden nuances of the fields we are interested in, excellence isn't possible. We can't expect to snack on industries and create a category of one. Optionality matters because something we go deep in may not be relevant to the market or our own preferences might change. We constantly underestimate the change we go through as people. Not factoring in optionality can be dangerous. So we are left in this limbo of trying to balance FOMO vs diving deep into something. Building a portfolio of careers empowers us to balance both.

A16Z: CONTENT COMPANY OR VC FUND

a16z, one of the most prominent VC funds, constantly says that it is a content company which monetizes via capital allocation. If you observe a16z carefully, you will observe that all its partners write, create podcasts, appear on prominent media outlets, tweet incessantly and do everything an ambitious and curious seventeen-year-old does today. Despite their stature and significant financial wherewithal, their (a16z employees and alumni) primary job can be understood as a combination of anthropology, psychology, content creation, relationship building and a dash of finance.

Now imagine if some of them decide to leave a16z and branch out. What might they do? Unbundling what they did could lead them into any of the above-mentioned careers or all of them. This unbundling or disaggregation is the power of building a portfolio of careers.

Li Jin, an a16z alumna, quit her job at the fund to start a small fund. She writes, creates YouTube videos, is involved in the NFT space and booked a one-way flight to Paris to explore new adventures.

What does this mean for you? How can you build a portfolio of careers?

1. **Figure out your superpowers:** Everyone is great at something, but everyone is not great at the same thing. Do not try to compete with others. Imagine if Lebron James was forced to solve calculus problems instead of playing basketball.

2. **Look for adjacencies:** Suppose you are a wonderful public speaker, look for industries where there is a premium for high-quality skills. You could explore podcasting, voiceover artistry, live commentating, emceeing, corporate coaching, motivational speaking, facilitating and teaching. The list is endless. You just need to start from your strengths and keep looking for areas where your strengths can create win-win outcomes for the stakeholders you wish to serve.

3. **Unbundle your work:** Instead of labelling your job as interesting or boring, do a deep dive to explore what you actually do. That means doing an analysis of the tasks you perform on daily, weekly and monthly bases. You will discover that within your one job, you are actually performing multiple micro-jobs. Say you are a sales professional, you are

pitching, building relationships, negotiating, writing, making presentations, counselling clients and managing teams, among other things. You could choose to be a salesperson who teaches negotiation on the side, become a coach who trains new sales professionals, start a CBC on building relationships and, again, the list goes on.

4. **Learn something new:** Building on your adjacencies and unbundling the work you actually do, there are new fields you can explore. For example, if you are a maths geek, you might find yourself drawn to international relations. Game theory is a useful tool to analyse how countries behave. Based on that knowledge, you might decide to become an investor who predicts markets based on macro geopolitical factors. The key is to keep an open mind and lead with curiosity. The ultimate adventure is in figuring things out, not knowing exactly how things will pan out.

Thomas Hobbes once said that life is solitary, poor, nasty, brutish and short. That isn't the life in the 21st century. We still have big challenges to solve for, but life today is community-driven, rich with abundance (on average), adventurous, unpredictable and long. If we want to thrive, we will need to reinvent ourselves multiple times and build a portfolio of curiosities, convictions and careers. Growth mindset and belief in the power of the possible will drive us forward. It won't be smooth, but no memorable adventure ever is.

'In the same way, sound isn't music, traffic isn't audience' (Jason Fried from Basecamp).

These days, it is easy to scroll through one's timeline and be entertained. Parts of the Internet seem dystopian, disturbing and downright silly. Everything seems to be about gaining fame by any means necessary. Many couples don't enjoy sitting next to the Eiffel Tower and observing the glimmering lights; they feel the urge to capture it on their social media stories and dance in front of it to win the game of likes. It is easy to confuse online shenanigans for the passion economy. Every dancing couple or prank video makes the algorithm, powering the platform stronger, but it doesn't necessarily add to the economic value of the participants.

In no way am I trying to convince you to try and be the next Charlie D'Amelio or Lil Nas X. Please do not try to become the something of somewhere. It won't be a defensible career strategy. In the war of fame and likes, the only winner is the platform. A small number of creators might make big bucks that way, but most of us won't, especially if we try and mimic them.

I love Basecamp founder Jason Fried's quote, 'In the same way sound isn't music, traffic isn't audience.' Most of us will not get millions of fans. We can spend our life trying to chase the mythical mirage of likes or spend the finite amount of time we have building real relationships with those we are trying to serve.

Every creator needs an audience, and traffic isn't audience. Doing something provocative for the heck of it is likely to backfire. Instead of trying to get fleeting traffic to our platform or performance, we need to develop a plan of action.

Some gimmicks work. Calm, the meditation app valued at multiple billion dollars, started with a static email collection page. Donothingfor2minutes.com was a catchy domain name, and Calm asked website visitors to not move their cursor for two minutes. There was a counter on the website which restarted if the visitor even touched their cursor. Donothingfor2minutes.com received over 2 million unique visits and led to the capture of 100,000+ email captures in 10 days.

Key to their success was flipping a problem on its head and make it into a fun game. Network Capital did something similar. It bought the domain name Idon'tknowwhatIwant todowithmylife.com and nudged people to join a live CBC taught by young professionals who had transformed their career confusion into a productive asset. We also got thousands of intrigued customers.

The difference between gimmicky moves like this one and others online is that of intent. We had a clear plan of action of why we were doing it and knew what outcome we wanted for the customer.

Simply creating viral videos or clickable content is not enough. In fact, in most cases, it gives negligible/zero ROI. Without knowing the deeper 'why', social media shenanigans are a waste of time and a race to the bottom.

CHAPTER 68

CO-CREATE THE JOURNEY

You don't need to have everything figured out. Building something meaningful in the passion economy means scaling trust and inviting your community members to co-create the next steps. For me, telling the truth and trusting people have worked well. From the beginning, I have been open and direct with Network Capital members. This doesn't just mean celebrating success and achievements. We often discuss failures and missteps. This helps scale trust and adds authenticity to every conversation.

Experience curation is an important element of the passion economy, but often people misunderstand what that really means. Curation isn't about toxic positivity. It comes down to staying true to your mission and figuring out ways for designing delightful user experiences.

★★★ These are the newsletters I sent to all community members the day we raised funding from Facebook.

> It is official! https://www.facebook.com/community/ accelerator/#utkarsh-amitabh
>
> I am happy to share that Facebook has invested in Network Capital as part of its community accelerator program that offers funding and strategic support to top communities around the world. We are one of the 130 communities selected from around the world (there are ~ 620 million Facebook communities globally) and look forward to helping students and young professionals from across different socioeconomic backgrounds build their category of one.
>
> This moment is special for us because we did this together. We have grown from being a small passion project I set up

while working at Microsoft to becoming one of the world's largest career intelligence communities without spending a single dollar on marketing or sales. Together we scaled trust and created an ecosystem of personalized mentoring from Patna to Paris, from Thiruvananthapuram to Tokyo, Lucknow to London, New Delhi to New York.

The central pillar of Network Capital is our community. All masterclasses, podcasts, cohort-based courses, online and offline meetups are designed and curated by our subscribers. They intimately understand the challenges faced by students and young professionals because they have been through similar dilemmas. We index on carving out a tribe of relatable mentors for all our subscribers.

Our flywheel is simple and efficient—people come to Network Capital for the community, learn from it and add specific value in ways they can. They enjoy the learning experience and tell their friends. While all of this is happening, we invite a few of our community members to become faculty, i.e, teach what they know best.

I truly believe that every single person has something to learn and something to share. All we need is a culture and community to enable it. Network Capital is that community. It is your community, one you have nurtured over the past five years, battled a gruelling pandemic with and come together in times of need to demonstrate to an increasingly polarized world that peer-to-peer kindness, peer-to-peer learning can be defining factors of the world we want to shape.

Network Capital is a movement, not just a company. It is a movement designed with the goal to help every person on the planet discover their superpower and carve a meaningful career around it. Together we are building Network Capital to last. While funding from Facebook is an important milestone, one that we cherish, we are always going to focus on learning outcomes and community trust.

I don't like to think of company success in terms of valuations and exits. I measure success only on one metric—did we help build a new generation of learners obsessed with carving their category of one? Yes or no.

With or without funding, that was going to be our destination. Thanks to your love and support, we thousands of monthly paying subscribers that allow us to have healthy revenues. We already offer huge scholarships to anyone who can't afford it, thanks to the generosity of some of our community members.

Now is the time to push the accelerator.

We plan to make Network Capital Schools need-blind as well.

Enter the Network Capital Talent Search examination. Please fill this form and the top 100 students will get to attend Network Capital School for free. Let's get cracking.

1. Make Network Capital Need-Blind: Talent is equally distributed, opportunities are not. With the funding from Facebook and support from our patrons, we plan to make Network Capital need blind. If you can't afford it, we will provide scholarships. Apply here.

2. Expand B2B Partnerships: Our mission is to help every person and every organization on the planet build their category of one. That is why, we are happy to share that a large number fast-growing tech companies and mission-driven social enterprises are now are B2B subscribers. This means that all employees will be offered a Network Capital subscription paid for by the company. Read more about our B2B offering.

3. Scale NITI Aayog Partnership: From the inception of the Mentor India Mission, we have served as a partner to NITI Aayog (Government of India). Today that propels mentoring 2.5 million school students. We want to do all we can to find the lost Einstiens who would benefit from our school offering but can't afford it.

4. Launch new cohort-based courses and scale existing ones: Recorded educational content in the form of MOOCs

(Massive Open Online Courses) have a completion rate of 3%. Network Capital's live cohort-based courses have a completion rate of 92%. Our next cohort of the community building fellowship starts on October 9. Enroll now.

5. Create strong offline communities and launch new subgroups: We love video conferencing tools but we also love creating powerful offline experiences for our community members. Pre-pandemic, Network Capital would have city meetups around the world. Now it is time to recreate some of that magic. Join us for the next one in your city.

There is a Latin motto '*Gradatim Ferociter*' which roughly translates to 'Step by Step, Ferociously'. With this mindset we can truly democratize mentorship and empower every person and every organization on the planet to build their category of one.

I am filled with gratitude to all Network Capital patrons, subscribers and community members. We are in this mission together and I cherish your support.

Global Challenges, Global Opportunities and Global Outlook: Network Capital's Global Design Principle

My immediate family comes from India, France, Lebanon, Belgium, United States, United Kingdom and Hong Kong. My memories from INSEAD, World Economic Forum, Microsoft, Wharton, Oxford were shaped by the most interesting people from 100+ countries. Over the last 7 years, I have traveled to 82 nations around the world—from smart villages in India to the WEF Annual Meeting in Davos, Switzerland. All these experiences have made me realize the importance of approaching global challenges and opportunities with a global outlook.

The big challenges in the world cannot be solved by any one country, one group of people. It needs radical collaboration across borders and boundaries. When I started Network Capital, my dream was to have students and young leaders from vastly different political, social, economic outlooks to learn with and from each other. Today I am happy to share that NC has local subgroups all across the globe. No matter where you are, you will find NC community members. By enabling peer-to-peer mentorship, we play a meaningful role in shaping meaningful careers and also sensitize our members towards different cultures and convictions.

Most people think that NC brings together likeminded, ambitious people to learn from each other. While that is true, the real joy of seeing NC in action is witnessing how people who have strongly differing political and economic views mentor each other, take cohort-based-courses together, participate in offline meetups, refer each other for jobs, provide thoughtful recommendations. A world where everyone is alike is a boring world. We must make room for diversity of all kinds to flourish. That is a key design principle of NC.

In a world where loud mouths are constantly highlighting our differences, building Network Capital made me realize how much all 7 billion people on Earth have in common. No matter where we come from, we want to find autonomy, mastery and purpose at work. We want to build meaningful careers.

Yes, people mostly come to NC for career advice and mentorship, but even when they achieve their short/medium term goals they stay on because they find deep connection with each other. That's the culture we have co-created every day since our inception.

With the Facebook funding announcement, I am of course glad we get capital and strategic support to grow. I look forward to collaborating with the 129 other impactful community builders and CEOs who also became part of the Facebook Accelerator. Most of them are a lot more experienced than me and I am eager to learn from them.

Our mission is to help every person and every organization on the planet build their category of one. This mission cannot be fulfilled alone. It gives me strength to have the support of all the NC members and the inspiring set of community leaders selected for the Facebook Community Accelerator. With the '*Gradatim Ferociter*' (step by step, ferociously), we can do this.

Through these newsletters, I just wanted our community members to celebrate the moment, take them along the journey we had been through together and reiterate our core values. Network Capital is a passion project turned into a technology platform. As companies/communities scale, they run the risk of overoptimizing for efficiency and underoptimizing for stories and human connection. That's why passion economy builders need to show rather than tell, lead by example rather than preach and co-create a shared vision rather than dictate the future strategy.

SECTION 5

PASSION ECONOMY CHALLENGES

CHAPTER 69

PLATFORM FATIGUE AND LANGUISHING

Houseparty, a social networking app which allowed up to eight people to video chat at once in a 'room', shut down in 2021. It had been around since 2016 and enabled tens of millions of people to connect in small groups. Back in July 2019, Houseparty was acquired by Epic Games for $35 million (maker of the popular online game Fortnite). Since then, the app was being used by Fortnite players to stream games with their friends.

Houseparty fans enjoyed floating between rooms, like at a real party, and discovered new use cases amid the pandemic as they struggled with COVID-19-induced loneliness. Why is it shutting down then?

METAVERSE: THE ANSWER TO MOST TECH QUESTIONS THESE DAYS

The team behind Houseparty is working on creating new ways to design social interactions in the metaverse, in line with the strategic direction taken by Epic Games. Since joining Epic, they have contributed to new features used by hundreds of millions of people in Fortnite and by developers around the world. According to Houseparty's official statement, the core team is unable to devote attention to non-gaming, non-metaverse use cases. Such pivots are common after acquisitions, and the shutting down of Houseparty, although disappointing for its fans, is not totally surprising.

Even if we forget the acquisition for a moment, it is uncertain how many networking apps like Houseparty will stand the test of time, make money and build a competitive moat around their offering.

ARE THERE PARALLELS BETWEEN HOUSEPARTY AND CLUBHOUSE?

Clubhouse, an audio-first app, launched with fanfare. There were long waiting lists, arms race for exclusive invites and big anticipation about the Android launch. Things worked well until they didn't. When was the last time you used Clubhouse?

Shaan Puri who sold his start-up to Twitch and now spends most of his time as a creator wrote a fascinating thread about the future of Clubhouse. In a witty style, he shares how Clubhouse is just the flavour of the season and is bound to fail, like countless others have. To be clear, Clubhouse isn't dead yet. It could very well revive or pivot into something different, but the hype has surely died down.

WHAT HAPPENED TO LUNCHCLUB?

In our Community Building Fellowship, we hosted Lunchclub.ai CEO Vlad.

In his masterclass, Vlad explains how he transitioned from the world of trading to building a networking tool which propels digital serendipity using sophisticated algorithms. His app saw massive uptick during the pandemic, just like Houseparty and Clubhouse. People craved for connection—Lunchclub offered curated 1:1 conversations—but over time, at least on Network Capital, started using it sparingly. What happened?

Even on Network Capital, we introduced 'Serendipity Thursdays' to help our subscribers connect with others in a relaxed setting with no explicit agenda. It is doing well, but the numbers have been flickering. Those who join say that they enjoy the experience, others either don't know about it or have a lot on their minds to focus on building new connections.

The more established platforms such as Facebook, Instagram, TikTok, LinkedIn and Twitter also witnessed surprising usage patterns and had to introduce a wide range of new services to keep people engaged. Twitter acquired Revue to help newsletter writers connect with their social networks, Facebook launched rooms to compete with other videoconferencing tools, LinkedIn hired a community head and TikTok launched a creator fund. Almost all large technology platforms did well in terms of growth and revenue, but the digital overload did take a toll on a large percentage of users online.

SO WHAT HAPPENED TO THE NETWORKING ECOSYSTEM?

It languished. Bestselling author Adam Grant explains in his *The New York Times* opinion piece and recently published TED Talk:

> Languishing is a sense of stagnation and emptiness. It feels as if you're muddling through your days, looking at your life through a foggy windshield. And it might be the dominant emotion of 2021.
>
> Languishing is the neglected middle child of mental health. It's the void between depression and flourishing—the absence of well-being. You don't have symptoms of mental illness, but you're not the picture of mental health either. You're not functioning at full capacity. Languishing dulls your motivation, disrupts your ability to focus, and triples the odds that you'll cut back on work. It appears to be more common than major depression—and in some ways it may be a bigger risk factor for mental illness.

NETWORKING AND LANGUISHING

Effective networking and languishing cannot go hand in hand. The whole premise of networking is adding specific value to others and creating win–win outcomes. How can one add value to others when one is out of energy?

Showing up for Zoom calls and meetings doesn't mean anything if we aren't immersed. It has become a chicken and egg problem.

Zoom calls tend to be a bit too structured, leaving little room for serendipity; then new apps such as Houseparty and Lunchclub which are designed for serendipity end up unintentionally adding to the Zoom doom. For most of us, building meaningful relationships during the pandemic wasn't easy.

That said, some people have managed to strengthen their network quotient (NQ). I spoke to 19 such professionals—creators, entrepreneurs, policy professionals, activists and artists—who gave us insights into techniques for effective networking in the largely online world.

1. **Use media to scale:** People who created content and built a community around it found it easier to scale themselves. Networking for them became more about their digital product than themselves. One such person is Alex Danco, who we have discussed earlier. He built his brand and strengthened his network based on the power of ideas through essays, podcasts and philosophical seminars. Oh, by the way, his day job is at Shopify.

    A podcaster and product strategist, Eric Jorgensen created a book compiling all original content created by Angel List founder Naval Ravikant. The book turned out to be a solid networking tool for Eric who would largely be unknown today had he not worked on compiling Naval's reading.

    Cold emails work sometimes, but they are exhausting. Creating and engaging with content is a more efficient and creative networking strategy.

    As your leverage media to scale, make sure to pick the platform which works best for you. If you are terribly shy of the camera, YouTube or TikTok may not be the platforms you choose. Pick something that you would do for the pleasure of the pursuit. George Bernard Shaw once said, 'I write for the same reason a cow gives milk.' Don't force yourself to pick something just because you think you should. Such attempts are often unsustainable.

2. **Conserve your energy:** You can't possibly connect with everyone who seems interesting. Instead of the 'spray and pray' tactic, pick the people you believe you can add most value to and work to figure out those who you can learn most from. Showing up for a meeting exhausted and distracted is a lot worse than not showing up at all.

   It helps to know whether you are an extrovert, an ambivert or an introvert. Design your networking to suit your personality type. Adobe has designed a fascinating creative assessment.

3. **Design your network for the long term:** The most effective networkers are those whose relationships last. These people can pick up the phone and call anyone. Others are always delighted to hear from them. Their secret sauce is playing long-term games with long-term people.

   They pick carefully and stick diligently. What does this mean? Basically, they are intentional about who they add to their inner circle but once they do, they stick with them through thick and thin.

   One of my mentors was mentored by former McKinsey CEO Rajat Gupta who had to spend some time in jail for charges on insider trading. That mentor stuck with Rajat even when most others abandoned him. He even went and met him in prison, just to say hello and check on him.

   I understand that this is a tricky terrain and I do not want to pass moral judgement. I just want to comment on the extent to which some people go to maintain relationships that matter. There will be times when your relationships will have to endure the most arduous of tests. If that relationship is worth it, sticking to it makes sense.

   The floundering of some tech platforms is less about products and more about the times we live in. We are languishing, and it is okay to say it out loud once a while.

   It has been a hard couple of years. Don't let the social media influencers confuse you into believing that all is well. Don't let productivity porn confuse into hustling for the sake of it or sending half-baked 'networking' messages like this one.

Give yourself the mental space and time to design your network to make it work for you. Hopefully, these techniques will help you build your NQ.

CHAPTER 70

PUBLIC POLICY, GOVERNMENTS AND PASSION ECONOMY

I learned about Savitri and Sanatan Mahto, a brother–sister duo who achieved serious fame on TikTok, from a report published by online journal *Rest of World*. They live in a tiny hamlet called Nipania in the state of Jharkhand, miles away from the faintest of signs of urbanization. Going to a restaurant means walking 15 miles on a long, meandering dirt road.

They started using TikTok in 2018 and amassed 2.7 million followers who were charmed by their singing and dancing on local tunes. The Mahtos could have been making over $2,000 every month from advertising revenues alone, 15 times their monthly income from farming.

TikTok was banned in India in June 2020 as a response to geopolitical tension arising from the Chinese attack on Indian borders in the Northeast. At that time, over 200 million Indians were using the short-form app and many creators like the Mahtos in tier 3 towns and villagers were using the app to create substantial income. Overnight, they lost their most lucrative channel of monetization.

Soon Instagram Reels and a range of other local clones sprung up, but they didn't quite match the TikTok experience. According to the *Rest of World* report, rural creators couldn't relate much to the urban and aspirational feel of Instagram and the local clones didn't have comparable reach.

I am not saying that India's decision to ban TikTok was wrong or right. Geopolitical relationships are managed at the governmental level, and I am sure that there are nuances that merit deeper scrutiny. My purpose of writing this chapter is to explain that government decisions and public policy can have a huge impact on how the passion economy evolves and matures.

Even though there will be many more creators like Mahtos creating new income streams online, most governments around the world have not seriously considered the passion economy as a source of employment. Elected representatives around the world would struggle to define a creator and talk about the framework required to provide a fillip to this new evolving digital landscape. Truth of the matter is that passion economy cannot be an after-thought.

In the post-pandemic world, there is urgent need to create scalable systems and processes which empower creators to build their ventures on the cloud. The market isn't just restricted to where the creators live. The entire Internet is their oyster.

Creator collaboration across borders can redefine global culture in the times to come. Imagine the spectrum of possibilities if the local creators like the Mahtos collaborate with their counterparts in Europe, North America and Africa! The Internet does offer permissionless leverage to some extent, but policy frameworks are required to scale such partnerships. Things like income tax, local digital regulations and intellectual property rights need to be harmonized and adapted. The larger goal must be to bring down the cost of collaboration so that creators are able to focus on their craft.

Governments also need to understand the challenges of creators today. During the pandemic, the American government created a $15 billion package to help cultural venues. This was a welcome step but happened six months after a bunch of countries had created programmes and schemes to help their creators.

French President Emmanuel Macron was one of the first world leaders to act to help freelance workers in the arts. The French unemployment system might have critics, but it has always recognized the challenges faced by performing artists, including but not limited to seasonality of work. To counter the spectre of the pandemic, France removed the clause which requires a certain minimum requirement of hours of work. France also set up an insurance scheme for TV, theatre and film shoots.

Britain followed France's footsteps and announced a cultural bailout package worth about $2.1 billion. This corpus saved hundreds and thousands of performing art spaces, theatres, comedy clubs and music venues from closure. Major institutions such as the National Theatre and Royal Shakespeare Company were also given long-term loans which helped keep the creators afloat.

Germany announced a $1.2 billion fund to get cultural life reinvigorated after the pandemic. Its finance ministry developed plans to pay bonus to organizers of smaller cultural events. Austria came up with a similar event insurance policy.

New Zealand, a country with population roughly equalling that of South Delhi, decided to offer $268 million to support creators (especially musicians) over four years. South Korea's government stepped up to provide almost $280 million to support cultural institutions.

These measures by different governments have some precedents. Just after the Great Depression, the New Deal was announced in America and included concrete measures to overcome unemployment and create a new normal for work. One such measure was Federal Project Number One, which devoted more than $500 million in today's terms to create employment for artists, musicians, designers, actors and writers. Among other things, the programme wanted to make arts accessible to the broader society. Some of America's most celebrated artists, including Jackson Pollock, Willem de Kooning, Lee Krasner and Mark Rothko, joined the movement which yielded over 100,000 works which define American culture even today.

- **Video:** While a handful of creators have made substantial money, the vast majority of earners on Twitch have made less than $120 this year so far, per the report.

- **Newsletters:** The top 10 publications on Substack collectively make more than $20 million a year in subscription revenue, while less popular newsletters typically make tens of thousands annually.

- **Podcasts:** The top 1 per cent of podcast earners make the vast majority of podcast ad revenue, although efforts to broaden podcast revenue through new creator programmes at Apple and Spotify will hopefully help more creators get paid.

Investor Li Jin and Stanford student Lila Shroff put forward an interesting idea of universal creator income (UCI) in their newsletter. Their analysis suggests that someone with a familial income of $100,000 is twice as likely to become a creator than someone from a family with $50,000 income. And those from households with an annual income of $1 million are '*10 times*' more likely to become artists and creators than those from families with a $100,000 income. Clearly, income influences career choices.

UCI tries to imagine a more democratic creative world. Why should only wealthy people become artists and creators? Could governments and public and private companies create a corpus which would provide a basic income to creators so that they devote time on honing their craft instead of worrying about ways to make ends meet. TikTok launched a creator fund which will start with $200 million to help support ambitious creators in the United States who want to build careers in digital content creation.

Jin and Shroff add that successful implementation of UCI would bring improvements in creator stress and mental health, and create a more equitable path for a more diverse array of creators to be able to pursue content creation as a career.

Personally, I would like to see governments around the world work with corporates and start-ups to create 'fast grants'. In April 2020, Stripe co-founder Patrick Collison, economics professor and blogger Tyler Cowen and Berkeley Assistant Professor Patrick Hsu raised around $50 million of funding from a bunch of investors and started giving out fast grants to aid emergency science funding during the pandemic.

Within a week, they got 4,000 serious applications, with virtually no spam. Without wasting too much time on getting the process perfected, they started to distribute millions of dollars of grants and, over the course of 2020, they made over 260 grants.

The first round of grants were given out within two days. Later rounds of grants, which needed additional scrutiny of earlier results, were given out within 14 days.

Collison, Cowen and Hsu write,

> Fast Grants pursued low-hanging fruit and picked the most obvious bets. What was unusual about it was not any cleverness in coming up with smart things to fund, but just finding a mechanism for actually doing so. To us, this suggests that there are probably too few smart administrators in mainstream institutions trusted with flexible budgets that can be rapidly allocated without triggering significant red tape or committee-driven consensus.

Even though the context is different, Fast Grants can transform the passion economy by offering capital to artists without random red tape and process bottlenecks. There are some funds which offer support to creators, but their application and review process is often way too complicated and time-consuming. What if things were radically simplified and time-bound?

Instead of identifying the superstars and giving them mega prizes, these Fast Grants could focus on creating a new cadre of artists across socio-economic backgrounds. Excellence must be rewarded, but there are already several avenues for the creators who have carved out a niche for themselves and established their name.

The fledgling creators need most support, and they are the ones who are less likely to crack the regular routes of funding available today. In the pandemic research grant created by Collison, Cowen and Hsu, most of the $50 million corpus came from individuals, not organizations. I see this trend replicating in the creator Fast Grants as well.

Organizations have their own goals and agendas. Aligning them with the overall societal goal can take time. Individuals are likely to make swift decisions if they know that their funds will be used well and towards a cause they care about.

I will happily invest a chunk of my money if there were such a creator Fast Grant fund. I conducted a survey among the subscribers of Network Capital. Seventy-five per cent respondents said that they would want to financially support the artists in their city if they knew their collective capital was being deployed. They did not demand any ROI. The cause was powerful enough for them. I suspect that this is a broader trend.

As an experiment, governments should create such a fund, hire a top-notch team and see how much capital it can crowdsource from citizens. UCI must be enabled through repeated tinkering and experimentation. We won't know until we try. Not doing anything because the process isn't foolproof seems to backfire hard.

A robust society needs its creators to thrive and reimagine the status quo. We would waste their collective potential by waiting for the perfect system to emerge. I would like to see early-stage creators pursue their craft knowing that there are funds available to support their dreams. Without this inbuilt insurance, many creators would only partake of safe projects. How do we empower them to take risks and create art which pushes the society forward?

CHAPTER 71

THE CHALLENGES OF BEING YOUR OWN BOSS

Being your own boss is incredibly liberating but also incredibly lonely. You need to manage your output, productivity, creativity, expenses, contractors and the list goes on. There will be bad days, of course. You need to figure out ways to keep yourself motivated and energized. The key is to not expect an 'Instagrammable' life each day. Like everybody else, you will be dealing with the trials and tribulations of daily life. Not having a manager might give you more autonomy, but that also means that you need to take greater ownership of your work. You will have to train yourself to own your failures, learn from them and bounce back on days where things are going berserk.

Further, FOMO is real. Passion economy adventures have a high gestation period. It takes a very long time to get things going. All of us will not get to millions of followers and true fans overnight. The truth is that no one does, but social media makes us compare the drudgery of our daily lives with the perfectly curated, edited and refined lives of megastars. The real challenge then is to keep our heads down and do the work—bit by bit, play by play—ignoring our all so natural impulse to compare and contrast ourselves with others. Today, one of the best ways to torture ourselves and get terribly distracted is to play the envy and comparison game with others. I wrote my first *Harvard Business Review* article 'Category of One' because I was pained by the suffering of millennials and Gen Z who were wasting their lives with the FOMO and fear of better option (FOBO).

Funding used to be a massive issue, although things are quickly changing. Traditional funding avenues like VC, angel investors, banks and institutional investors are yet to build a thesis on the creator economy space. This means that in most parts of the world, creators need to figure out profitable businesses from the start. Contrast that hyperscale VC-powered businesses which remain unprofitable even after initial public offering (IPO). For example, DoorDash in the United States, Zomato in India and scores of other unicorns bleed millions of dollars in losses every month. This is something creators cannot afford. Even one bad month can be disastrous for them, especially in the beginning. COVID-19 tested the resilience of creators. While the online ones did well, those who were building physical goods or operating things such as cafes and restaurants struggled.

Passion economy tends to favour superstars, ones with massive following. Maths geeks will associate this with the power law. A tiny minority of creators get almost all financial benefits. For example, most musicians don't make much money on Spotify—a musician makes $0.00437 per stream, meaning an artist needs ~3,500,000 streams just to earn the minimum wage of $15,000 per year. Unless you're Drake or Beyoncé, it's tough to make a living on streaming revenue.

One study found that reaching the top 3.5 per cent of YouTube channels—which means about 1 million views each month—only gets you $12,000–$16,000 a year.[1] That's right around the federal poverty line. About 97 per cent of YouTube creators aren't making minimum wage from YouTube. One popular YouTuber, Shelby Church, wrote a blog post about how getting 3,907,000 views on a video only made her $1,276.

If you try to be the single point of contact for every activity, you will also end up becoming the single point of failure. You don't want to be in a situation where if you take time off or need to attend to an emergency, your entire business falls apart. Making your business anti-fragile is every entrepreneur, every hustler, every creator's ultimate aspiration because shocks and crises will be the defining elements of the 21st century.

1 https://www.washingtonpost.com/news/the-switch/wp/2018/03/02/why-almost-no-one-is-making-a-living-on-youtube/

Another issue that early-stage creators have to grapple with is balancing short and long terms. British economist John Maynard Keynes once said, 'In the long run we are all dead.' While this is true, obsessing over short term and not formulating a long-term vision and implementation plan can be lethal. It is easy to get caught up fixing the urgent and ignoring the important.

The creators who only stick to long-term vision setting will struggle to deal with the less sexy, operation-heavy tasks of the day. Basically, the point I am getting at is that finding the sweet spot between daily tasks vs insights which will make the business thrive over the long run isn't straightforward. There aren't too many playbooks available.

Then there are challenges with respect to hiring top talent. Heavily funded start-ups and larger companies have the financial wherewithal to attract the best professionals to help them get to their vision. At early stages, creators don't have anything apart from their portfolio and an ambitious vision riddled with myriad unknown unknowns.

To build something that lasts, we need to recognize that individual effort won't suffice. Delegation, setting up processes, team building will be essential elements. It is common to see creators burn out because they feel that they need to do everything themselves.

Unfortunately, things like taking time out to rejuvenate are still not common among creators. They run the risk of exhausting themselves out of the game. Hustle porn on the Internet such as 'sleep is for the weak' does disservice to everyone, especially those early-stage dreamers anchoring their ship alone.

I love the saying: 'Play long-term games with long-term people.' Creators need to internalize this to ensure that they are keeping their long-term well-being in mind as they march ahead.

Let this section of the book not deter you from embarking on your journey. It is important to know the challenges in advance so that you can prepare and design your future, career and lifestyle to be in the arena on days when things get tough.

You have/are about to embark upon the adventure of a lifetime, an experiment that might give you the autonomy, mastery and purpose to fulfil your vision on your terms. Some bottlenecks might be catalysts for your growth. You should welcome them.

In my own adventures in the passion economy, constraints and bottlenecks have been my best friends. They have fuelled my hunger to serve my community members in innovative ways. For the longest time, all I had was a passion project I worked on after my day job at Microsoft—no funding, no employees, no resources and an educational loan of $200,000. By learning to operate with an infinite mindset with negligible resources, I prepared myself for the adventures of tomorrow. I would like to emphasize that there are thousands of equally or more talented people who will embark upon their adventures in the passion economy. I hope that some of my experiences and adventures nudge them to launch now. It doesn't need to start as a big bang. It can be a micro-step, one that opens up new possibilities towards carving out a new kind of career and a more intentional relationship with work. Challenges will be recurring part of the adventure; perhaps the challenges will ignite that relentless spirit of discovery. I don't know how Columbus felt when he discovered America, but I hope there are millions of Columbuses in the 21st century unpeeling the layers of the passion economy and creating a new normal for what we call work. The outcomes need to be measured by the scale but by the spirit. Adventure of pursuits are means and ends in themselves. When the pursuit, marked by infinite challenges, becomes the ultimate reward, you know you have discovered something worth cherishing. In my own small way, I found my ultimate adventure. Taking baby steps towards the mission gives me meaning in ways that I can't quite capture. One secret thrill close to my heart is hearing future stories—not of conquest but of pursuit—looking up to something, looking forward to something and finding something worthy of chase. None of it screams stability or conquest or proving a point to someone. In a way, it is what makes us who we are.

Summing this section up, all challenges that make passion economy ventures challenging to run are what make them exhilarating. You chose this path for greater autonomy, mastery and purpose for building something you truly care about. Looking beyond the daily rigmarole of a daily job creates a wide range of possibilities and adventures, but no adventure is truly worth it without the element of surprise. I love this question: What would it look like if it were easy? For creators and passion economy proponents that would entail creating a video or a newsletter on a breezy summer afternoon after which fans, brands and revenue would follow suit without any hustle. It might even happen once or twice but without the hustle, there would be no feedback and no incentive to get better, try new things and figure out whatever it takes to make your dream come true.

If it were easy, it would be boring, not unlike a conventional 9–5 job you left behind. There would be no thrill in chasing the impossible. You didn't venture in this space just for the prize at the end of the road. The road less travelled is the prize in and of itself. Unless you truly see it that way, maintaining momentum will be hard. The process and the pursuit will be riddled with misadventures. So what?

Think of any story you heard growing up. If you still remember it, it is most likely because the path to the goal was non-obvious. You remember the path, not the prize. But in today's culture obsessed with accolades and appreciation and recognition, it might be tempting to believe that the whole purpose is the end result.

I am not saying that the final outcome is meaningless, but it is worth remembering that we embarked upon this journey because it promised novelty, surprises and unexpected avenues of growth— both personal and professional.

You won't be the same person again. If you go through with it and give your dream the time and resilience it deserves to come to fruition, your transformation will be momentous. You will toughen up and become more empathetic in all likelihood. Toughen up because you will need it to survive and live to see another day, and become empathetic because you won't take others' struggles for granted.

You only realize what it takes when you try. You can't learn this vicariously or by reading books like this one. The whole reason I wrote this book was to give you more clarity on the path ahead. All I have to offer is my set of experiences and reflections. I am no big shot. I have not 'arrived'. There are miles to go before I get to a position of reasonable stability. As I write this, my whole life hangs on a tricky thread. I have hope towards what lies at the end of the tunnel and lots of diligence to complement it, but I often ask myself: Why am I doing this? I could easily be working in a large company doing a job which was both meaningful and financially rewarding but I would have always regretted not trying.

Even if you are risk-averse, you should take heart from the fact that all of us will have many careers. For whatever reason, if something does not work out, we can rebuild our life. The good news is that we won't have to build from scratch. The lessons from our hustle will hold us in good stead. You learn so much from giving something your all. It is irrational, but this is one irrationality that actually pays off.

I would just like to caution you against treating your passion project or creative pursuit as something you try knowing that failure will be the inevitable outcome. If you approach it with that mindset, each day will be inching closer towards an inevitable doom.

Optimism and pessimism are both self-fulfilling prophesies. If you believe that either of them is strong enough, they will come true. There have been so many days when I could feel my dream turn its back on me. Rejections, failures—micro and macro— and gut-wrenching feedback are part and parcel of the adventure that I and millions of others signed up for in the middle of the pandemic.

What would it look like if things were easy? The honest answer is that I don't fully know. What I do know is that because it isn't easy, I am learning more than I have ever done in all my academic and professional pursuits.

SECTION 6

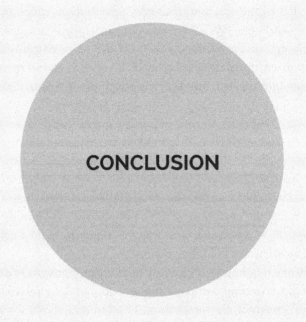

CONCLUSION

American poet Maya Angelou said,

> I have great respect for the past. If you don't know where you've come from, you don't know where you're going. I have respect for the past, but I'm a person of the moment. I'm here, and I do my best to be completely centered at the place I'm at, then I go forward to the next place.

Keynes' 1930 essay is important even for the passion economy. The most important thing is that he forecasted something 100 years ahead of time. Now is the time to do something similar for the next 100 years. What would be the economic and social opportunities for our grandchildren?

To understand where the passion economy is going, one has to look at the history of the Internet and contextualize the different phases of evolution. The first phase or Web 1.0 was about democratizing information, the second about P2P exchange and trust leaps which led to the creation of iconic gig economy conglomerates, and the third one—Web 3.0—is about participants having real skin in the game in the platforms they choose to participate in. This decentralized, distributed, co-created and co-owned Internet offers a glimpse into the tech utopia of a relatively more egalitarian online world.

Web 3.0 brings to bare important questions about socialism, Marxism and capitalism. I attempted to explain how this new Internet might be able to make both Karl Marx and Adam Smith happy in ways. That said, this book isn't a social science critique or an ethnographic analysis or an activist's manifesto. It is a book which traces the evolution of work through the eyes of millennials and Gen Zs and advances practical techniques to build a category of one in whatever field they choose.

While building your category of one is monumentally difficult in the gig economy world, passion economy pays a premium for personal creativity and innovation. The Internet allows for niches to scale. No matter what you are interested in, you can mind a minimum viable audience to monetize. You are no longer restricted by geography. With the help of Web 2.0 and Web 3.0 tools, you can write newsletters, create videos, play videogames, pursue offbeat art and music projects in your living room, and sell to the world at large.

As we discussed, to build your category of one, you don't need to reach millions of people tomorrow. Finding 1,000 true fans, figuring out unique ways to delight them and building a community will set you up well. I don't mean to make it sound easy. My goal is to help you realize that it is practical and possible.

Venturing into the passion economy or building your side hustle won't be easy, but it could turn out to be the single most meaningful career decision you ever take.

When Network Capital raised funding and strategic support from Facebook, one of earliest community members commented saying, 'Congratulations. You make it look so easy and effortless.' I remember smiling. At the time, I was sitting in a small village in Lebanon with no electricity and flickering Internet. There was a candle next to me. As I typed up my reply to him, my laptop ran out of charge and shut down.

Building Network Capital into a global career experimentation and advancement platform wasn't easy. The road to whatever little success we have had so far has been sprinkled with myriad existential challenges and practical roadblocks. This book hasn't been written as a victory lap. I am a tinkerer who has barely scratched the surface. The pursuit, a challenging one, is the ultimate pleasure. A straightforward pursuit where everything is clear and figured out is a solved problem. No one needs to build it out, especially if the creator wants to build something that lasts, that stands the test of time.

Paraphrasing Amazon founder Jeff Bezos's advice, focus on things that won't change while you observe and participate in the changing landscape of the digital world. Too many creators burn out trying to keep up with what's hot. Pause to rejuvenate and reflect, and offer your community something it needs but hasn't yet figured out how to get. That's the essence of functional creativity that will blossom in the passion economy era.

I chose career exploration as my area of focus because how people choose their line of work fascinates me. I have been trying to understand this ever since I was a little boy toying between ambitions to become an actor and curiosity about technology. It so happens that people will always want to build meaningful careers. In the past, they didn't have the tools, support system and relatable mentors to do something they loved. That's changing, and I am thrilled to be playing a small part in the passion economy and the side-hustle revolution.

Of course, it is a large market and a huge business opportunity, but my real driving force is helping shape a world where pursuit, passion, productivity and creativity can converge. This book is a micro-step in that direction.

Through the various sections of the book, I hope you found a tribe of mentors, a set of mental models and a collection of case studies which you can apply to your work life. The passion economy world is flat in a way. Today, you can reach out to whoever you want to. You just need to spend time figuring out what you want and how you can add specific value to others. One of my favourite quotes from the book *Tribe of Mentors* is 'Life punishes the vague wish but rewards the specific ask.'

To complete this book, I reached out to hundreds of creators, investors, authors, coders, techies and top CEOs. It helped that Network Capital is large, and I was able to find mutual connections in many cases. That said, almost everyone I sent a cold email to responded to my questions. Some even came onboard as faculty members for our CBCs. All of this happened online. COVID-19 ensured that in-person meetings were not possible, and while it was challenging all along, I felt that the digital serendipity propelled me to explore uncharted territories of the passion economy and creator space.

All said, this is an incomplete book. The passion economy space is evolving with frantic pace and history is being written in front of our eyes. It is often said that history is written and edited by the victors. My hope is that the Web 3.0 world will change that by subverting the power structures and transforming the observers into co-creators and equity owners. Together, we shall shape the history, moral geography and future of work.